Layered Design for Ruby on Rails Applications

Discover practical design patterns for maintainable web applications

Vladimir Dementyev

BIRMINGHAM—MUMBAI

Layered Design for Ruby on Rails Applications

Group Product Manager: Rohit Rajkumar

Publishing Product Manager: Himani Dewan

Book Project Manager: Sonam Pandey

Content Development Editor: Abhishek Jadhav

Technical Editor: Simran Udasi

Copy Editor: Safis Editing

Proofreader: Safis Editing

Indexer: Rekha Nair

Production Designer: Joshua Misquitta

DevRel Marketing Coordinator: Nivedita Pandey

First published: September 2023

Production reference: 2280823

Packt Publishing Ltd

Grosvenor House

11 St Paul's Square

Birmingham

B3 1RB, UK.

ISBN 978-1-80181-378-5

www.packtpub.com

To trains, train riders, and little train lovers.

– Vladimir Dementyev

Contributors

About the author

Vladimir Dementyev is a principal backend engineer at Evil Martians, a product development consultancy from Earth, focusing on building maintainable web applications and developers' productivity. He is the creator of popular open source tools, such as AnyCable and TestProf, and a contributor to many other open source projects, including Ruby on Rails and Ruby itself. Vladimir plays an active role in the Ruby community through his code contributions and by speaking at conferences and sharing his passion for coding via articles and blog posts. For his contributions to the Ruby ecosystem, Vladimir was awarded the Fukuoka Ruby Award in 2021 and the Ruby Hero Russia Award in 2017.

I would like to thank my family, who support my extracurriculars, such as writing a book; the humans from Mars, and especially Phobos, for shaping my vision of how to write code; the Saint-P Ruby community for heated though well-argumented discussions; the MetroNorth and Amtrak trains for non-distracting writing environments; and the Peekskill Coffee House for the coffee and crepes that fueled Chapters 4, 8, and 12.

About the reviewer

Mahabub Islam is a seasoned software developer with a strong focus on Ruby on Rails and JavaScript. With six years of experience in the industry, he has honed his expertise in building robust and scalable web applications. Mahabub's passion for clean code and efficient design led him to explore various design patterns and best practices, making him the perfect reviewer for the book *Rails Design Patterns and Best Practices*.

His in-depth knowledge of the framework, coupled with his experience in building complex applications, allows him to provide valuable insights and practical advice to developers seeking to optimize their Rails projects.

Table of Contents

3

More Adapters, Less Implementations   41

4

Rails Anti-Patterns?   57

Part 2: Extracting Layers from Models

8

Pulling Out the Representation Layer   149

Part 3: Essential Layers for Rails Applications

9

Authorization Models and Layers   169

10

Crafting the Notifications Layer   193

11

Better Abstractions for HTML Views   213

12

Configuration as a First-Class Application Citizen   231

Preface

Ruby on Rails is a powerful and influential open source framework specifically designed to facilitate the rapid development of web applications. As a full stack framework, Rails provides developers with the tools necessary for frontend and backend web development, allowing for the seamless integration of HTML, CSS, JavaScript, and server-side scripting.

At the heart of Rails is the adoption of the **Model-View-Controller** (**MVC**) architectural pattern. This pattern divides an application into three interconnected parts: the Model, which pertains to the application's data and business logic; the View, responsible for the output of the information; and the Controller, which manages the flow of data between the Model and the View.

Alongside MVC, another central pillar of Rails is the convention-over-configuration principle. This philosophy manifests in many predefined settings and defaults within the Rails framework, significantly reducing the number of decisions a developer has to make.

Sticking to MVC-based framework components and leveraging conventions is **The Rails Way**. It aims to streamline the development process, allowing developers to focus on crafting product features rather than getting burdened by the complexities of taming the framework and its components.

However, as with most things, this initial simplicity can be a double-edged sword. It can sometimes spiral into an intricate labyrinth of complexities, potentially transforming a neatly organized code base into a difficult-to-manage, convoluted mess. This book seeks to equip you with strategies and techniques to help you control your Rails application's complexity while ensuring maintainability.

We start by exploring the framework's capabilities and principles, allowing you to utilize Rails' power fully. Then, we start the layering process by gradually extracting and introducing new abstraction layers in a way that plays nicely with The Rails Way. Thus, the ideas expressed in this book could be considered **The Extended Rails Way**, the patterns and approaches that can help you enjoy the framework and increase Ruby developers' happiness at scale.

As you conclude this journey, you'll emerge as a proficient specialist in code design, possessing an in-depth understanding of the Rails framework's principles.

Who this book is for

This book is for Rails application developers struggling to cope with the ever-increasing complexity of their projects and looking for ways to keep code maintainable and approachable.

This book is a perfect fit for developers who have just launched their first Rails MVP and those who have already encountered difficulties moving forward with a majestic monolith.

The reader will need to have an understanding of core Rails principles (described in the official guides) and have some experience with building web applications using the framework.

What this book covers

Chapter 1, Rails as a Web Application Framework, provides a high-level overview of the framework and its core components specific to it being a tool for building web applciations

Chapter 2, Active Models and Records, focuses on the Rails model layer and how to better leverage its building blocks, such as Active Record and Active Model, to extract responsibilities and prevent God objects.

Chapter 3, More Adapters, Less Implementations, focuses on the design patterns used by Active Job and Active Storage.

Chapter 4, Rails Anti-Patterns?, discusses Rails' controversial features, such as callbacks, concerns, and globals.

Chapter 5, When Rails Abstractions Are Not Enough, focuses on the Service Object phenomenon in Rails and introduces layered architecture principles.

Chapter 6, Data Layer Abstractions, focuses on extracting data manipulation logic (querying and writing) from models.

Chapter 7, Handling User Input outside of Models, provides an overview of abstraction layers to move user input handling out of models, such as form and filter objects.

Chapter 8, Pulling Out the Representation Layer, focuses on abstractions used to prepare model objects for displaying in the UI, for example, presenters and serializers.

Chapter 9, Authorization Models and Layers, focuses on authorization aspects and the corresponding abstractions.

Chapter 10, Crafting the Notifications Layer, focuses on extracting an abstraction layer to handle logic related to user notifications (email, SMS, and so on.).

Chapter 11, Better Abstractions for HTML Views, discusses abstractions to maintain HTML templates in Rails applications.

Chapter 12, Configuration as a First-Class Application Citizen, discusses the problem of configuring web applications.

Chapter 13, Cross-Layers and Off-Layers, focuses on Rails application infrastructure aspects, such as logging and monitoring, and provides examples of abstraction-driven service extraction.

To get the most out of this book

This book assumes intermediate knowledge of the Ruby programming language and experience in writing web applications with the Ruby on Rails framework. If you haven't had prior experience with Ruby on Rails, please familiarize yourself with the official guides (`https://guides.rubyonrails.org`) first.

Software/hardware covered in the book	Operating system requirements
Ruby on Rails 7.1 (many examples will work with earlier versions)	Any OS that runs Ruby
Ruby 3.2 (many examples will work with earlier versions)	Any OS that runs Ruby

If you are using the digital version of this book, we advise you to type the code yourself or access the code from the book's GitHub repository (a link is available in the next section). Doing so will help you avoid any potential errors related to the copying and pasting of code.

Download the example code files

You can download the example code files for this book from GitHub at `https://github.com/PacktPublishing/Layered-Design-for-Ruby-on-Rails-Applications/tree/main`. If there's an update to the code, it will be updated in the GitHub repository.

The answers to the Questions in the book can be found at `https://github.com/PacktPublishing/Layered-Design-for-Ruby-on-Rails-Applications/blob/main/Answers%20to%20Questions.docx` and the solutions to the Exercises can be found at `https://github.com/PacktPublishing/Layered-Design-for-Ruby-on-Rails-Applications/blob/main/Solutions%20to%20Exercises.docx`

Conventions used

There are a number of text conventions used throughout this book.

`Code in text`: Indicates code words in text, database table names, folder names, filenames, file extensions, pathnames, dummy URLs, user input, and Twitter handles. Here is an example: "All we need to make this code work as we want is to add a couple of `has_many` declarations to our models."

A block of code is set as follows:

```
class User < ApplicationRecord
  has_many :posts, -> { order(id: :desc) }
end
class Post < ApplicationRecord
  has_many :comments, -> { order(id: :desc) }
end
```

When we wish to draw your attention to a particular part of a code block, the relevant lines or items are set in bold:

```
Rails.application.routes.draw do
  # The same as: resources :posts, only: %i[index]
  get "/posts", to: PostsController.action(:index)
end
```

Any command-line input or output is written as follows:

```
$ git log --format=oneline -- app/models/user.rb | wc -l
```

> **Tips or important notes**
> Appear like this.

Get in touch

Feedback from our readers is always welcome.

General feedback: If you have questions about any aspect of this book, email us at customercare@packtpub.com and mention the book title in the subject of your message.

Errata: Although we have taken every care to ensure the accuracy of our content, mistakes do happen. If you have found a mistake in this book, we would be grateful if you would report this to us. Please visit www.packtpub.com/support/errata and fill in the form.

Piracy: If you come across any illegal copies of our works in any form on the internet, we would be grateful if you would provide us with the location address or website name. Please contact us at copyright@packt.com with a link to the material.

If you are interested in becoming an author: If there is a topic that you have expertise in and you are interested in either writing or contributing to a book, please visit authors.packtpub.com.

Share your thoughts

Once you've read *Layered Design for Ruby on Rails Applications*, we'd love to hear your thoughts! Scan the QR code below to go straight to the Amazon review page for this book and share your feedback.

`https://www.amazon.in/review/create-review/error?asin=1801813787`

Your review is important to us and the tech community and will help us make sure we're delivering excellent quality content.

Download a free PDF copy of this book

Thanks for purchasing this book!

Do you like to read on the go but are unable to carry your print books everywhere?

Is your eBook purchase not compatible with the device of your choice?

Don't worry, now with every Packt book you get a DRM-free PDF version of that book at no cost.

Read anywhere, any place, on any device. Search, copy, and paste code from your favorite technical books directly into your application.

The perks don't stop there, you can get exclusive access to discounts, newsletters, and great free content in your inbox daily

Follow these simple steps to get the benefits:

1. Scan the QR code or visit the link below

https://packt.link/free-ebook/9781801813785

2. Submit your proof of purchase
3. That's it! We'll send your free PDF and other benefits to your email directly

Part 1: Exploring Rails and Its Abstractions

This part is dedicated to the framework, Ruby on Rails, itself. You will learn about design patterns, the architecture decisions behind Rails, and the concepts and conventions powering the framework. You will also learn about Ruby on Rails' controversies and limitations, which we will try to resolve in the following parts.

This part has the following chapters:

- *Chapter 1, Rails as a Web Application Framework*

- *Chapter 2, Active Models and Records*

- *Chapter 3, More Adapters, Less Implementations*

- *Chapter 4, Rails Anti-Patterns?*

- *Chapter 5, When Rails Abstractions Are Not Enough*

1
Rails as a Web Application Framework

Ruby on Rails is one of the most popular tools to build web applications, which is a huge class of software. In this chapter, we will talk about what makes this class different from other programs. First, we will learn about the HTTP request-response model and how it can naturally lead to a layered architecture. We will see which layers and HTTP components Ruby on Rails includes out of the box. Then, we will discuss the off-request processing layer, background jobs, and the persistence layer (databases).

In this chapter, we will cover the following topics:

- The journey of a click through Rails abstraction layers
- Beyond requests – background and scheduled tasks
- The heart of a web application – the database

By the end of this chapter, you'll have a better understanding of the core web application principles and how they affect Rails application design. You will learn about the main Rails components and how they build up the basic abstraction layers of the application.

These fundamental ideas will help you to identify and extract abstractions that better fit natural web application flows, thus leading to less conceptual overhead and a better developer experience.

Technical requirements

In this chapter and all chapters of this book, the code given in code blocks is designed to be executed on Ruby 3.2 and, where applicable, using Rails 7. Many of the code examples will work on earlier versions of the aforementioned software.

You will find the code files on GitHub at `https://github.com/PacktPublishing/Layered-Design-for-Ruby-on-Rails-Applications/tree/main/Chapter01`.

The journey of a click through Rails abstraction layers

The primary goal of any web application is to serve web requests, where *web* implies communicating over the internet and *request* refers to data that must be processed and acknowledged by a server.

A simple task such as clicking on a link and opening a web page in a browser, which we perform hundreds of times every day, consists of dozens of steps, from resolving the IP address of a target service to displaying the response to the user.

In the modern world, every request passes through multiple intermediate servers (proxies, load balancers, **content delivery networks** (**CDNs**), and so on). For this chapter, the following simplified diagram will be enough to visualize the journey of a click in the context of a Rails app.

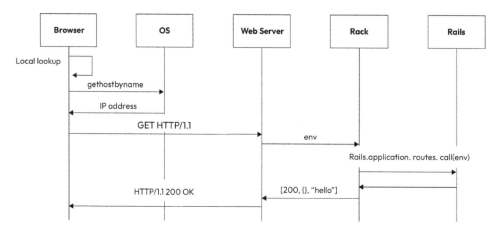

Figure 1.1 – A simplified diagram of a journey of the click (the Rails version)

The Rails part of this journey starts in a so-called *web server* – for example, Puma (`https://github.com/puma/puma`). It takes care of handling connections, transforming HTTP requests into a Ruby-friendly format, calling our Rails application, and sending the result back over the HTTP connection.

> **Communication models**
>
> Web applications can use other communication models, and not only the request-response one. Streaming and asynchronous (for example, WebSocket) models are not rare guests in modern Rails applications, especially after the addition of Hotwire (`https://hotwired.dev/`) to the stack. However, they usually play a secondary role, and most applications are still designed with the request-response model in mind. That's why we only consider this model in this book.

Next, we will take a deeper look at the right part of the diagram in *Figure 1.1*. Getting to know the basics of request processing in Rails will help us to think in abstraction layers when designing our application. But first, we need to explain why layered architecture makes sense to web applications at all.

From web requests to abstraction layers

The life cycle of a web application consists of the bootstrap phase (configuration and initialization) and the serving phase. The bootstrap phase includes loading the application code, and initializing and configuring the framework components – that is, everything we need to do before accepting the first web request – before we enter the serving phase.

In the serving phase, the application acts as an executor, performing many independent **units of work** – handling web requests. *Independent* here means that every request is self-contained, and the way we process it (from a code point of view) doesn't depend on previous or concurrent requests. This means that requests do not share a lot of state. In Ruby terms, when processing a request, we create many disposable objects, whose lifetimes are bound by the request's lifetime.

How does this affect our application design? Since requests are independent, the serving phase could be seen as a conveyor-belt assembly line – we put request data (raw material) on the belt, pass it through multiple workstations, and get the response box at the end.

A natural reflection of this idea in application design would be the extraction of **abstraction layers** (workstations) and chaining them together to build a processing line. This process could also be called **layering**. Just like how assembly lines increase production efficiency in real life, architecture patterns improve software quality. In this book, we will discuss the layered architecture pattern, which is generic enough to fit many applications, especially Ruby on Rails ones.

What are the properties of a good abstraction layer? We will try to find the answer to this question throughout the book using examples; however, we can list some basic properties right away:

- An abstraction should have a *single responsibility*. However, the responsibilities themselves can be broad but should not overlap (thus, following the *separation of concerns* principle).

- Layers should be *loosely coupled* and have no circular or reverse dependencies. If we draw the request processing flow from top to bottom, the inter-layer connectors should never go up, and we should try to minimize the number of connections between layers. A physical assembly line is an example of perfect layering – every workstation (layer) has, at most, one workstation above and, at most, one below.

- Abstractions *should not leak their internals*. The main idea of extracting an abstraction is to separate an interface from the implementation. Extracting a common interface can be a challenging task by itself, but it always pays off in the long term.

- It should be possible to *test abstractions in isolation*. This item is usually a result of all the preceding, but it makes sense to pay attention to it explicitly, since thinking about *testability* can help us to come up with a better interface.

From a developer's perspective, a good abstraction layer provides a clear interface to solve a common problem and is easy to refactor, debug, and test. A clear interface can be translated as one with the least possible conceptual overhead or just one that is simple.

Designing simple abstractions is a difficult task; that's why you may hear that introducing abstractions makes working with the code base more complicated. The goal of this book is to teach you how to avoid this pitfall and learn how to design good abstractions.

How many abstraction layers are nice to have? The short answer is, *it depends*.

Let's continue our assembly line analogy. The number of workstations grows as the assembly process becomes more sophisticated. We can also split existing stages into multiple new ones to make the process more efficient, and to assemble faster. Similarly, the number of abstraction layers increases with the evolution of a project's business logic and the code base growth.

In real life, the efficiency metric is speed; in software development, it is also speed – the speed of shipping new features. This metric depends on many factors, many of which are not related to how we write our code. From the code perspective, the main factor is maintainability – how easy it is to add new features and introduce changes to the existing ones (including fixing bugs).

Applying software design patterns and extracting abstraction layers are the two main tools to keep maintainability high. Does it mean the more abstractions we have the more maintainable our code is?

Surely not. No one builds a car assembly line consisting of thousands of workstations by the number of individual nuts and screws, right? So, should we software engineers avoid introducing new abstractions just for the sake of introducing new abstractions? Of course not!

Overengineering is not a made-up problem; it does exist. Adding a new abstraction should be evaluated. We will learn some techniques when we start discussing particular abstraction layers later in this book. Now, let's move on to Rails and see what the framework offers us out of the box in terms of abstraction layers.

A basic Rails application comes with just three abstractions – controllers, models, and views. (You are invited to decide whether they fit our definition of *good* or not by yourself.) Such a small number allows us to start building things faster and focus on a product, instead of spending time to please the framework (as it would be if had a dozen different layers). This is the *Rails way*.

In this book, we will learn how to extend the Rails way – how to gradually introduce new abstraction layers without losing the focus on product development. First, we need to learn more about the Rails way itself. Let's take a look at some of the components that make up this approach with regard to web requests.

Rack

The component responsible for *HTTP-to-Ruby* (and vice versa) translation is called **Rack** (`https://github.com/rack/rack`). More precisely, it's an interface describing two fundamental abstractions – *request* and *response*.

Rack is the contract between a web server (for example, Puma or Unicorn) and a Ruby application. It can be described using the following source:

```
request_env = { "HTTP_HOST" => "www.example.com", …}
response = application.call(request_env)
status, headers, body_iterator = *response
```

Let's examine each line of the preceding code:

- The first one defines an HTTP request represented as a Hash. This **Hash** is called the request environment and contains HTTP headers and Rack-specific fields (such as `rack.input` to access the request body). This API and naming convention came from the old days of CGI web servers, which passed request data via environment variables.

> **Common Gateway Interface**
> **Common Gateway Interface** (**CGI**) is the first attempt to standardize the communication interface between web servers and applications. A CGI-compliant program must read request headers from `env` variables and the request body from `STDIN` and write the response to `STDOUT`. A CGI web server runs a new instance of the program for every request – an unaffordable luxury for today's Rails applications. The FastCGI (`https://fastcgi-archives.github.io/`) protocol was developed to resolve this situation.

- The second line calls a Rack-compatible application, which is anything that responds to `#call`. That's the only required method.

- The final line describes the structure of the return value. It is an array, consisting of three elements – a status code (integer), HTTP response headers (Hash), and an enumerable body (that is, anything that responds to `#each` and yields string values). Why is body not just a string? Using enumerables allows us to implement streaming responses, which could help us reduce memory allocation.

The simplest possible Rack application is just a Lambda returning a predefined response tuple. You can run it using the `rackup` command like this (note that the `rackup` gem must be installed):

```
$ rackup -s webrick --builder 'run ->(env) { [200, {}, ["Hello,
Rack!"]] }'
[2022-07-25 11:15:44] INFO  WEBrick 1.7.0
[2022-07-25 11:15:44] INFO  WEBrick::HTTPServer#start: pid=85016
port=9292
```

Try to open a browser at `http://localhost:9292` – you will see `"Hello, Rack!"` on a blank screen.

Rails on Rack

Where is the Rack's #call method in a Rails application? Look at the config.ru file at the root of your Rails project. It's a Rack configuration file, which describes how to run a Rack-compatible application (.ru stands for *rack-up*). You will see something like this:

```
require_relative "config/environment"
run Rails.application
```

Rails.application is a singleton instance of the Rails application, its web entry-point.

Now that we know where the Rails part of the click journey begins, let's try to learn more about it.

The best way to see the amount of work a Rails app does while performing a unit of work is to trace all Ruby method calls during a single request-response cycle. For that, we can use the trace_location gem.

> **What a gem – trace_location**
>
> The trace_location (https://github.com/yhirano55/trace_location) gem is a curious developer's little helper. Its main purpose is to learn what's happening behind the scenes of simple APIs provided by libraries and frameworks. You will be surprised how complex the internals of the things you take for granted (say, user.save in Active Record) can be.
>
> Designing simple APIs that solve complex problems shows true mastery of software development. Under the hood, this gem uses Ruby's **TracePoint API** (https://rubyapi.org/3.2/o/tracepoint) – a powerful runtime introspection tool.

The fastest way to emulate web request handling is to open a Rails console (rails c) and run the following snippet:

```
request =
  Rack::MockRequest.env_for('http://localhost:3000')
TraceLocation.trace(format: :log) do
  Rails.application.call(request)
end
```

Look at the generated log file. Even for a new Rails application, the output would contain thousands of lines – serving a GET request in Rails is not a trivial task.

So, the number of Ruby methods invoked during an HTTP request is huge. What about the number of created Ruby objects? We can measure it using the built-in Ruby tools. In a Rails console, type the following:

```
was_alloc = GC.stat[:total_allocated_objects]
Rails.application.call(request)
```

```
new_alloc = GC.stat[:total_allocated_objects]
puts "Total allocations: #{new_alloc - was_alloc}"
```

For an action rendering nothing (head :ok), I get about 3,000 objects when running the preceding snippet. We can think of this number as a lower bound for Rails applications.

What do these numbers mean for us? The goal of this book is to demonstrate how we can leverage abstraction layers to keep our code base in a healthy state. At the same time, we shouldn't forget about potential performance implications. Adding an abstraction layer results in adding more method calls and object allocations, but this overhead is negligible compared to what we already have. In Rails, *abstractions do not make code slower* (humans do).

Let's run our tracer again and only include #call methods this time:

```
TraceLocation.trace(format: :log, methods: [:call]) do
  Rails.application.call(request)
end
```

This time, we only have a few hundred lines logged:

```
[Tracing events] C: Call, R: Return
C /usr/local/lib/ruby/gems/3.1.0/gems/railties-7.0.3.1/lib/rails/
engine.rb:528 [Rails::Engine#call]
  C /usr/local/lib/ruby/gems/3.1.0/gems/actionpack-7.0.3.1/
  lib/action_dispatch/middleware/host_authorization.rb:130
  [ActionDispatch::HostAuthorization#call]
    C /usr/local/lib/ruby/gems/3.1.0/gems/rack-2.2.4/lib/rack/
  sendfile.rb:109 [Rack::Sendfile#call]
      C /usr/local/lib/ruby/gems/3.1.0/gems/actionpack-7.0.3.1/lib/
  action_dispatch/middleware/static.rb:22 [ActionDispatch::Static#call]
        // more lines here
      R /usr/local/lib/ruby/gems/3.1.0/gems/actionpack-7.0.3.1/lib/
  action_dispatch/middleware/static.rb:24 [ActionDispatch::Static#call]
    R /usr/local/lib/ruby/gems/3.1.0/gems/rack-2.2.4/lib/rack/
  sendfile.rb:140 [Rack::Sendfile#call]
  R /usr/local/lib/ruby/gems/3.1.0/gems/actionpack-7.0.3.1/
  lib/action_dispatch/middleware/host_authorization.rb:131
  [ActionDispatch::HostAuthorization#call]
R /usr/local/lib/ruby/gems/3.1.0/gems/railties-7.0.3.1/lib/rails/
engine.rb:531 [Rails::Engine#call]
```

Each method is put twice in the log – first, when we enter it, and the second time when we return from it. Note that the #call methods are nested into each other; this is another important feature of Rack in action — **middleware**.

> **Pattern – middleware**
>
> **Middleware** is a component that wraps a core unit (function) execution and can inspect and modify input and output data without changing its interface. Middleware is usually chained, so each one invokes the next one, and only the last one in the chain executes the core logic. The chaining aims to keep middleware small and single-purpose. A typical use case for middleware is adding logging, instrumentation, or authentication (which short-circuits the chain execution). The pattern is popular in the Ruby community, and aside from Rack, it is used by Sidekiq, Faraday, AnyCable, and so on. In the non-Ruby world, the most popular example would be Express.js.

The following diagram shows how a middleware stack wraps the core functionality by intercepting inputs and enhancing outputs:

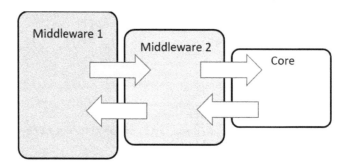

Figure 1.2 – The middleware pattern diagram

Rack is a modular framework, which allows you to extend basic request-handling functionality by injecting middleware. Middleware intercepts HTTP requests to perform some additional, usually utilitarian, logic – enhancing a Rack env object, adding additional response headers (for example, X-Runtime or CORS-related), logging the request execution, performing security checks, and so on.

Rails includes more than 20 middlewares by default. You can see the middleware stack by running the bin/rails middleware command:

```
$ bin/rails middleware
use ActionDispatch::HostAuthorization
use Rack::Sendfile
use ActionDispatch::Static
use ActionDispatch::Executor
use ActionDispatch::ServerTiming
use Rack::Runtime
... more ...
use Rack::Head
use Rack::ConditionalGet
use Rack::ETag
```

```
use Rack::TempfileReaper
run MyProject::Application.routes
```

Rails gives you full control of the middleware chain – you can add, remove, or rearrange middleware. The middleware stack can be called the **HTTP pre-/post-processing layer**. It should treat the application as a black box and know nothing about its business logic. A Rack middleware stack should not enhance the application web interface but act as a mediator between the outer world and the Rails application.

Rails routing

At the end of the preceding middleware list, there is a `run` command with `Application.routes` passed. The `routes` object (an instance of the `ActionDispatch::Routing::RouteSet` class) is a Rack application that uses the `routes.rb` file to match the request to a particular resolver – a controller-action pair or yet another Rack application.

Here is an example of the routing config with both controllers and applications:

```
Rails.application.routes.draw do
  # Define a resource backed by PostsController
  resources :posts, only: %i[show]

  # redirect() generates a Redirect Rack app instance
  get "docs/:article",
      to: redirect("/wiki/%{article}")

  # You can pass a lambda, too
  get "/_health", to: -> _env {
    [200, { "content-type" => "text/html" }, ["I'm alive"]]
  }

  # Proxy all matching requests to a Rack app
  mount ActionCable.server, at: "/cable"
end
```

This is the routing layer of a Rails application. All the preceding Rack resolvers can be implemented as Rack middleware; why did we put them into the routing layer? Redirects are a part of the application functionality, as well as WebSockets (Action Cable).

However, the health check endpoint can be seen as a property of a Rack app, and if it doesn't use the application's internal state to generate a response (as in our example), it can be moved to the middleware layer.

Similar to choosing between Rack and routes, we can have a routes versus controllers debate. With regards to the preceding example, we can ask, why not use controllers for redirects?

C for controller

Controllers comprise the next layer through which a web request passes. This is the first abstraction layer on our way. A controller is a concept that generalizes and standardizes the way we process inbound requests. In theory, controllers can be used not only for HTTP requests but also for any kind of request (since the controller is just a code abstraction).

In practice, however, that's very unlikely – implementation-wise, controllers are highly coupled with HTTP/Rack. There is even an API to turn a controller's action into a Rack app:

```
Rails.application.routes.draw do
  # The same as: resources :posts, only: %i[index]
  get "/posts", to: PostsController.action(:index)
end
```

> **MVC**
>
> **Model–view–controller** is one of the oldest architectural patterns, which was developed in the 1970s for GUI applications development. The pattern implies that a system consists of three components – Model, View, and Controller. Controller handles user actions and operates on Model; Model, in turn, updates View, which results in a UI update for the user. Although Rails is usually called an MVC framework, its data flow differs from the original one – Controller is responsible for updating View, and View can easily access and even modify Model.

The controller layer's responsibility is to translate web requests into business actions or operations and trigger UI updates. This is an example of single responsibility, which consists of many smaller responsibilities – an actor (a user or an API client) authentication and authorization, requesting parameters validation, and so on. The same is true for every inbound abstraction layer, such as Action Cable channels or Action Mailbox mailboxes.

Coming back to the routing example and the redirects question, we can now answer it – since there is no business action behind the redirection logic, putting it into a controller is an abstraction misuse.

We will talk about controllers in detail in the following chapters.

Now, we have an idea of a click's journey through a Rails application. However, not everything in Rails happens within a request-response cycle; our click has likely triggered some actions to be executed in the background.

Beyond requests – background and scheduled tasks

Although the primary goal of web applications is to handle HTTP requests, that's not the only job most Rails applications do. A lot of things happen in the background.

The need for background jobs

One of the vital characteristics of web applications is throughput. This can be defined as the number of requests that can be served in a period of time – usually, a second or a minute (**requests per second (RPS)** or **requests per minute (RPM)**), respectively).

Ruby web applications usually have a limited number of web workers to serve requests, and each worker is only capable of processing one request at a time. A worker is backed by a Ruby thread or a system process. Due to the **Global Virtual Machine Lock (GVL)**, adding more threads doesn't help us to increase the throughput. Usually, the number of threads is as low as three to five.

> **Choosing the right number of threads**
>
> Since Ruby 3.2, it's been possible to measure the exact time a Ruby thread spends waiting for I/O using, for example, the GVLTools library (`https://github.com/Shopify/gvltools`). Knowing the exact time, you can choose the number of threads that fits your application the best.

Scaling with processes requires a proportional amount of RAM. We need to look for other solutions.

> **Beyond processes and threads – fibers**
>
> Ruby has the solution to this concurrency problem – fibers (`https://rubyapi.org/3.2/o/fiber`). We can describe it as a lighter alternative to a thread, which can be used for cooperative concurrency – a concurrency model in which the context switch is controlled by the user, not the VM. Since Ruby 3, fibers can automatically yield execution on I/O operations (networking, filesystem access, and so on), which makes them fit the web application use case well. Unfortunately, Rails itself is not fiber-ready yet, so we cannot fully use web servers that leverage this technology, such as Falcon (`https://github.com/socketry/falcon`).

For many years, Rails applications relied on the following idea – to minimize a request time (and, thus, increase throughput), we should offload as much work as possible to background execution. Libraries, such as Sidekiq and Delayed Job, brought this idea to life and popularized it, and later, with the release of Rails 4, Active Job made this approach official.

> **What a gem – sidekiq**
>
> Sidekiq (`https://github.com/mperham/sidekiq`) is one of the most popular Ruby gems and the number one background processing engine. It relies on the idea that background tasks are usually I/O heavy, and thus, we can efficiently scale processing by using Ruby threads. Sidekiq uses Redis as a queueing backend for jobs, which reduces the infrastructure overhead and positively impacts performance.

What is a background job? It is a task that's executed outside of the request-response loop.

A typical example of such a task would be sending an email. To send an email, we must perform a network request (SMTP or HTTP), but we don't need to wait for it to be completed to send a response back to the user. How can we break out of the synchronous request-handling operation in Ruby? We could use threads, which might look like this:

```ruby
class PasswordResetController < ApplicationController
  def create
    user = User.find_by!(email: params[:email])
    Thread.new do
      UserMailer.with(user:).reset_password.deliver_now
    end
  end
end
```

This simple solution has a lot of rough edges – we do not control the number of threads, we do not handle potential exceptions, and we have no strategy on what to do if there are failures. Therefore, background job abstraction (Active Job, in particular) arose – to provide a general solution to common problems with asynchronous tasks.

Next, let's talk about the fundamental concepts of background processing in Rails.

Jobs as units of work

The background job layer is built on top of job and queue abstractions.

Job is a task definition that includes the actual business logic and describes the processing-related properties, such as retrying logic and execution priority. The latter justifies the need for a separate abstraction, Job; pure Ruby objects are not enough.

Queues are natural for background jobs in web applications, since we usually want our offloaded tasks to be executed on a *first in, first out* basis. Background processing engines can use any data structure and/or storage mechanism to keep and execute tasks; we only need them to comply with the queue interface.

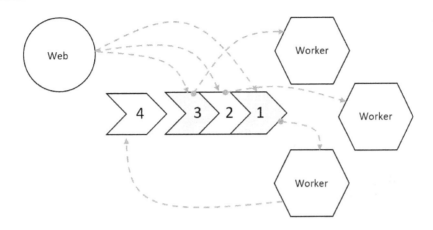

Figure 1.3 – A high-level overview of the background tasks queue architecture

Background jobs are meant to be independent and can be executed concurrently (although we can enqueue jobs within jobs forming background workflows). Thus, similar to web requests, background jobs are also *units of work*.

Each unit of work in a Rails application can be associated with an **execution context**. Execution context is an environment (state) associated with a particular execution frame, which has a clearly defined beginning and end. For web requests, an environment is defined by an HTTP request and its properties (for example, user session). Background jobs do not have such natural environments but can define one. Thus, another utilitarian responsibility of a background job is to define an execution context for the corresponding business operation.

Thus, the background jobs layer can be seen as the internal inbound layer. Unlike external inbound layers (for example, controllers), we do not deal with user input here, and hence, no authentication, authorization, or validation is required. Otherwise, from a software design point of view, jobs can be treated the same way as controllers.

Most background jobs are initiated within web requests or other jobs. However, there is another potential trigger – time.

Scheduled jobs

Scheduled jobs are a special class of background jobs that are triggered by a clock, not as a result of a user action or another job execution. Besides that, there is no difference between scheduled jobs and regular background jobs.

However, since Rails doesn't provide a solution to define a jobs schedule out of the box, it's easy to escape from the abstraction and come up with a unique (that is, *more difficult to maintain*) solution.

For example, many gems, such as **whenever** (`https://github.com/javan/whenever`) or **rufus-scheduler** (`https://github.com/jmettraux/rufus-scheduler`), allow you to run arbitrary Ruby code or system commands on schedule, not only enqueuing background jobs.

Such custom jobs lack all the benefits of being executed by a background jobs engine – failure handling, logging, instrumentation, and so on. They also introduce additional conceptual complexity. Scheduled jobs belong to the same abstraction layer as regular background jobs and, thus, should be a part of the layer, not its own abstraction (or a lack of it).

We have covered the basics of Rails inbound layers, those responsible for triggering units of work essential for all web applications. Irrespective of the kind of request that initiates the work, in most situations such work in a web application would be associated with data reading and writing.

The heart of a web application – the database

A typical web application can be seen as an interface for data. Whether it's a blogging platform, an e-commerce service, or a project-management tool, most user interactions are coupled with reading or storing some information. Of course, there are data-less web applications – for example, proxy services – but you're unlikely to choose Ruby on Rails to implement them.

Data is likely to be the most valuable part of your product or service. Just imagine you accidentally dropped your production database and all the backups – could you carry on? The database is also usually the most heavily loaded component of your application. The overall performance of your application depends on how you use the database and keep it in a healthy state.

Thus, while designing our application, we should keep in mind possible performance degradations related to the database.

The trade-off between abstractions and database performance

One of the main purposes of abstractions is to hide away the implementation details. In theory, a user should not know what's happening under the hood of a certain API method. Consider the following example:

```
class User
  def self.create(name:)
    DB.exec "INSERT INTO users (name) values (%)", name
  end
end
names = %w[lacey josh]
names.each { User.create(name: _1) }
```

The `User` class is our abstraction to work with a database. We added a convenient interface to insert new records into a database table, which is assumed to be used throughout the application.

However, this abstraction could be over-used, thus introducing additional load to our database – whenever we want to create N users, we execute N queries. If we didn't use the abstraction, we would write a single `"INSERT INTO..."` statement – a much more performant way of achieving the same result.

This is just a basic example that demonstrates the following – *hiding implementation details is not equal to not taking implementation specifics and limitations into account*. Abstractions and APIs should be designed so as to make it harder to shoot yourself in the foot when using them.

One common technique, which leads to non-optimal database interactions, is using **domain-specific languages** (**DSLs**) to define query-building rules. DSLs are powerful tools, but with great power comes great responsibility.

Let's look at a more realistic example using the **CanCanCan** (`https://github.com/CanCanCommunity/cancancan`) library. This library allows you to define authorization rules (*abilities*) using fancy DSL. The DSL defines a ruleset, which could be used to scope database records. Here is an example:

```
can :read, Article do |article|
  article.published_at <= Time.now
end
```

The rule states that only the already published articles can be accessed by users. This rule is used every time we call `Article.all.accessible_by(user)` (for example, when we want to show a user a list of articles on a home page). How do you think the scoping would be handled in this case?

If we wrote `#accessible_by` by hand, we would probably perform a single query to return the desired records – `"SELECT * FROM articles WHERE published_at < now()"`. What will our library do? It will fetch and then filter all the records using the `rule` block.

The result is the same, but it would require much more system resources (memory to load a lot of records and additional CPU cycles to run the block many times). Luckily, *CanCanCan* allows you to add a hint on how to transform the block into a query condition:

```
can :read, Article, "published_at < now()" do |article|
  article.published_at <= Time.now
end
```

This is an example of a **leaky abstraction**, an abstraction that exposes implementation details to its users. In the preceding snippet, our DSL-based configuration file contains the parts of the underlying database query. In this case, this is a necessary evil. And it can also be seen as an indicator that we chose the wrong level of abstraction to solve the problem, and now we have to patch it.

When designing abstractions, we should think of potential performance implications beforehand to avoid leaky abstractions in the future.

Database-level abstractions

Abstractions need not be defined in the application code only; we can also benefit from using abstractions in the database.

The main motivation for considering this approach could be the application performance. Another possible reason is consistency – the database is the primary source of truth, and databases (relational) are usually good at enforcing consistency; thus, moving some logic to the database layer can minimize the risk of data becoming inconsistent.

Even though you can move all your business logic into a database by defining custom functions and procedures, that's not the way web (and especially Rails) applications are built. It could be an ideal way if the only thing we cared about was performance, but we chose web frameworks for productivity.

Nevertheless, some functionality can be implemented at the database level and bring us performance and productivity benefits. Let's consider particular examples.

One common task that can be handled at the database layer is keeping track of record changes (for audit purposes). We can implement this in our Ruby code by adding hooks everywhere we create, update, or delete records, or go the Rails way and define model-level callbacks (as PaperTrail (`https://github.com/paper-trail-gem/paper_trail`) does).

Alternatively, we can leverage database features, such as triggers, and make our database responsible for creating audit records (as Logidze does). The latter approach has the benefits of being more performant and reducing the code base complexity. It is worth considering when audit records are not first-class citizens of your business logic (that is, not involved in other processes beyond auditing).

> **What a gem – logidze**
>
> Logidze (`https://github.com/palkan/logidze`) is a combination of a database extension (via PostgreSQL functions) and a Ruby API to track individual record changes incrementally. It can be used as a general auditing tool and a time-travel machine (to quickly access older versions of a record).

Another potential use case for giving the database a bit more responsibility is soft deletion. Soft deletion is an approach where a record is marked as deleted (and made invisible for users) instead of removing it from the database whenever a logical delete operation should occur. This technique can be used to provide undo/restore functionality or for auditing purposes.

Besides performance considerations, we may want to add database abstractions for the sake of consistency. For example, in PostgreSQL, we can create domain types and composite types. Unlike general constraints, custom types are reusable and carry additional semantics. You can use the `pg_trunk` (`https://github.com/nepalez/pg_trunk`) gem to manage custom types from Rails (as well as other PostgreSQL-specific features).

In general, enhancing database logic with custom abstractions is viable if the purpose of the abstraction is to act as *data middleware* – that is, treat data in isolation from the application business logic. Technically, such isolation means that abstraction should be set up once and never changed. I use the term *middleware* here to underline the conceptual similarity with Rack middlewares.

Summary

In this chapter, you learned about the primary features and components of web applications. You learned about the abstraction layers present in Rails applications and how they correspond to the web nature of Rails and its MVC philosophy. You learned about the unit of work and execution context concepts and their relationship with the inbound abstraction layers.

You also learned about the potential trade-offs between abstractions and application performance and, in particular, the database. This chapter demonstrated the fundamental ideas behind the layered software architecture, which we will refer to a lot throughout the book.

In the next chapter, you'll dig deeper into the *M* part of the MVC architecture and learn about the design ideas that make Active Record the most significant part of the Ruby on Rails framework.

Questions

1. Do Rails core abstractions (controllers, models, and views) satisfy our requirements for good abstraction layers?
2. How many abstraction layers should a Rails application have?
3. Does the number of abstraction layers affect a Rails application's performance?
4. Which problem do we solve by moving execution to background jobs?
5. What is a leaky abstraction?

Exercises

We learned that handling a web request involves thousands of method calls and allocated Ruby objects. What if skip the Rack middleware and pass the request to the router directly (`Rails.application.routes.call(request)`)? What about skipping the router and calling a controller action right away (for example, `PostsController.action(:index).call(request)`)? Using `trace_location` and `GC.stats`, conduct some experiments and analyze the results. What are the overheads of the Rack middleware and the router?

Further reading

Polished Ruby Programming (*Section 3, Ruby Web Programming Principles*): `https://www.packtpub.com/product/polished-ruby-programming/9781801072724`

## 2

Active Models and Records

In this chapter, we will dig deeper into the model layer of web applications and how it is implemented in Rails. The model layer, in a broad sense, is where the actual business logic of the application lives. If the database is the heart of a web application, the model is its life-blood system. Thus, it requires your careful attention.

We will learn about the components Rails provides to build the model layer. First, we'll take a quick look at a basic **Active Record** model and examine its responsibilities, from persistence to whatever you can imagine. Then, we'll discuss the role of **Active Model** and how it could be useful on its own. Finally, we'll talk about the phenomenon of God objects and how it relates to Active Record.

We will cover the following topics:

- Active Record overview: persistence and beyond
- Active Model: the hidden gem behind Active Record
- Seeking God objects

This chapter aims to familiarize you with the model layer of Ruby on Rails applications and teach you about its powers and potential pitfalls. This will prepare you for future work on reducing Active Record's responsibility in Rails applications and making the model layer healthy and maintainable.

Technical requirements

In this chapter and all chapters of this book, the code given in code blocks is designed to be executed on Ruby 3.2 and Rails 7. Many code examples will work on earlier versions of the software.

You will find the code files on GitHub at `https://github.com/PacktPublishing/Layered-Design-for-Ruby-on-Rails-Applications/tree/main/Chapter02`.

Active Record overview – persistence and beyond

Ruby on Rails as a framework consists of multiple components or sub-frameworks, each playing a role in various web application processes (for example, serving HTTP requests or executing background tasks). Components include Action Pack, Action Cable, Action View, Active Job, and more—the list changes as Rails matures; some sub-frameworks are being retired (such as Action Web Service), while others are joining the family.

Among the moving parts, there are constants, and in Rails, such constants are Action Pack and Active Record. Action Pack is responsible for the HTTP layer (rack and controllers), which was discussed in *Chapter 1, Rails as a Web Application Framework*. Active Record's responsibility is for the model layer, which we will cover in this chapter.

> **Action or Active?**
>
> How do maintainers decide which prefix to use for a new component: Action or Active? The rule is not set in stone, but a pattern is noticeable: anything related to user interactions has the Action prefix (this likely comes from the fact that controllers have *actions*). On the other hand, model-related libraries use Active (probably because of Active Record—the first of the kind). Finally, there is a library that glues both parts of the *rail* together—Railties.

In the MVC pattern, the model manages data and business logic. How many responsibilities does this statement hide? Is a single abstraction, such as a model backed by Active Record in Rails, capable of handling all of them? Let's try to answer these questions by dissecting the Active Record functionality from the bottom (a database) to the top (business logic).

Object-relational mapping

The primary responsibility of the Active Record library is to provide access to the application data stored in a relational database.

There are two general ways to code communication between an application and a SQL database:

- Writing plain SQL queries and using raw result data (for example, arrays and hashes in the case of Ruby)
- Using the **object-relational mapping (ORM)** technique

Although sometimes we can benefit from writing SQL by hand, in most cases having an abstraction to work with a database is more productive. Thus, we will focus only on the second way of coding communication between an application and a SQL database—ORM.

> **ORM**
>
> ORM implies the use of object-oriented language to communicate with the data store. For example, a database is queried via ORM API methods; the results are objects, not primitives (arrays, hashes, scalars). Similarly, writing to a database is done by creating or updating an object. An ORM implementation performs all the required low-level operations, such as building SQL queries, under the hood.

ORM is an abstract abstraction. It's employed by other abstractions, providing actual interfaces. There are two major ORM abstractions: Data Mapper and Active Record. Let's explore these two in a bit more detail.

Rails' Active Record is apparently an implementation of the Active Record pattern. With this pattern, objects not only represent database records but also encapsulate read and write operations. In other words, every model knows how to retrieve data and how to insert or update it (that's why it's called Active).

Consider a simple example:

```
class Book < ApplicationRecord
end
# Inserting data into the database
Book.create!(title: "The Ruby on Rails book")
# Retrieving data via model finder methods
book = Book.find_by(title: "The Ruby on Rails book")
# Modifying data
book.update!(category: "programming")
# Deleting data
book.destroy!
```

As you can see, we need only a single class to operate on a particular database table and the corresponding business logic entity. Furthermore, adding Ruby to the equation makes the code extremely readable— it's almost plain English. These features make Active Record one of the pillars of Ruby on Rails' productivity. But what makes you productive in the beginning will hurt you as you grow—let's talk about the cons of the Active Record pattern.

The main criticism of the Active Record pattern is based on the fact that it violates the separation of concerns principle by being both a persistence object and a business model object (or domain object). Hence, domain objects are highly coupled with the database schema (or vice versa). This high coupling comes with a lot of consequences:

- The introduction of database schema changes becomes more complicated since models affected by them could be used across the code base
- Testing is barely possible without creating real database records
- Hiding actual database operations could lead to performance degradations when developers forget which object methods can perform a query call

This list is incomplete; Active Record is not a perfect pattern, but it's still the default in Rails. Why? The answer is simple: having all-in-one objects outweighs the drawbacks associated with productivity and conceptual overhead (more precisely, the lack of it). In addition, it's great for quick prototyping and bringing ideas to life, which is more important in the early days of a product than having a clean architecture.

Nevertheless, the tradeoffs we just described do not disappear after a successful product launch. You will have to deal with them eventually—we will talk about *how* in the second part of this book.

What about the Data Mapper pattern? Does it have the same problems, and if not, why is it not used by Rails? The following diagram shows the architectural difference between the patterns:

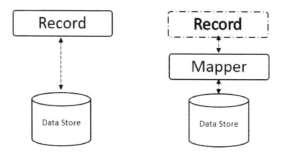

Figure 2.1 – Active Record (left) and Data Mapper (right) architectures

The main difference between Active Record and Data Mapper is that the latter separates models from persistence. In other words, objects do not know how to persist themselves. Models are just (or could be) plain Ruby classes, with no strings attached. As a result, separate entities (mappers, repositories, relations) are used to put objects into and retrieve them from a data store.

For example, the pseudo-code using the Data Mapper pattern could look like this:

```
class Book < Struct.new(:title, :category)
end
# BookRepository is our mapper implementation
id = BookRepository.insert(title: "Rails and ORM",
    category: "programming")
book = BookRepository.find(id)
book.title #=> "Rails and ORM"
```

As you can see, the overhead of enforcing the model-persistence separation is not that big: just one additional Ruby class. However, this is only true for simple use cases such as in the preceding examples. The biggest challenge when using data mappers is dealing with associations.

Associations are naturally coupled with the persistence layer (a database schema) and thus cannot be defined in the models and usually go to the mappers. Consider a typical Active Record usage example—showing the top-three latest comments for the latest user's post:

```
user.posts.last.comments.limit(3)
```

All we need to make this code work as we want is to add a couple of has_many declarations to our models:

```
class User < ApplicationRecord
  has_many :posts, -> { order(id: :desc) }
end
class Post < ApplicationRecord
  has_many :comments, -> { order(id: :desc) }
end
```

To achieve the same with a Data Mapper-backed framework, for example, the Hanami Model (https://hanamirb.org, v1.3), we need to write the following code:

```
class PostRepository < Hanami::Repository
  associations do
    has_many :comments
  end

  def latest_for_user(user_id)
    posts.where(user_id:).order { id.desc }.limit(1).one
  end
end

class CommentRepository < Hanami::Repository
  def latest_for_post(post_id, count:)
    comments.where(post_id:)
            .order { id.desc }
            .limit(count).to_a
  end
end

latest_post = PostRepository.new.latest_for_user(user_id)
latest_comments = CommentRepository.new.latest_for_post
  (latest_post.id, count: 3)
```

Basically, we rewrote everything that Active Record does for us under the hood, from scratch. On the one hand, we had to write more (boring) code. On the other hand, we now have full control of our queries and must think about our database communication APIs. And thinking never hurts.

> **What a gem – rom-rb**
> **Ruby Object Mapper** (`https://rom-rb.org`), or **ROM**, is the most popular library implementing the Data Mapper pattern. It allows us to describe objects (called *structs*) and mappers (called *relations*) in a storage-agnostic way, thus, being a real data mapper, not just a SQL mapper. This level of abstraction gives us a distinctive feature of the library: an ability to combine mappers backed by different storage implementations. The other thing about ROM is that it relies on *changesets* for write operations without using the actual objects and their state tracking. That makes ROM deviate from the classic definition of the Data Mapper pattern.

We will touch on the Data Mapper pattern and its concepts later in the book. Now let's continue talking about Rails Active Record and go one step up from the persistence layer to the actual model layer.

From mapping to the model

The application state, or model, doesn't only deal with a persistence schema. Moreover, the database schema is just a reflection of the application model (and in the case of Data Mapper, it could be called a faint reflection, just an approximation of the application model). The model also describes transition and consistency rules.

Transition rules define how and when it's possible to modify the state. Consistency rules define the restrictions on the possible states. Here are two examples:

- **Transition**: A post cannot be turned into a draft after it has been published

- **Consistency**: A post can be created only if it has a non-empty title

The key difference here is that consistency rules are static: we want our state to satisfy consistency rules at any given time. Transition rules only make sense in the dynamics of the application lifetime.

In Rails, we can define both transition and consistency model rules within Active Record models via validations. The following code snippet implements the rules from the preceding example:

```ruby
class Post < ApplicationRecord
  validate :prevent_drafting_published,
    if: -> { published? && will_save_change_to_draft? }

  validates :title, presence: true

  def prevent_drafting_published
    errors.add(:base, "Switching back to draft is not
      allowed for published posts")
  end
end
```

From the code perspective, the difference between transition and consistency rules is reflected in the necessity to use conditions for the former ones: the validation is only applied if there is a change in the record's state. (The `#will_save_change_to_draft?` method returns `true` if the subsequent call to `#save` updates the `draft` attribute.)

Rails provides a powerful validations API (or **domain-specific language (DSL)**); you can use it (and many do) to define all the rules in Active Record models. Again, this is great from the conceptual overhead perspective: whenever you need to implement a rule, you pick the right model and add a validation. That's it. Now let's talk about the tradeoffs of Rails validations.

First and foremost, validations contribute to the model's class bloat, especially complex ones using custom methods (such as `#prevent_drafting_published` in the example). This way, we turn our model into a **validator** (or *self-validator*), thus mixing responsibilities: a model may declare required validations but not implement them.

So, for example, when we use the built-in `presence: true` validation, we rely on the `PresenceValidator` provided by Rails. Similarly, we can extract custom validations into *validation objects*, as seen in the following code (and we don't even need to go beyond the Rails Way for that):

```
class Post::DraftValidator < ActiveModel::Validator
  def validate(post)
    return unless post.published?
    return unless post.will_save_change_to_draft?

    post.errors.add(:base, "Switching back to draft is not
      allowed for published posts")
  end
end

class Post < ApplicationRecord
  validates_with DraftValidator
end
```

Validator objects may perform multiple validations related to each other. For example, all the rules related to a post-publishing process could be combined within `PublishingValidator`:

```
class Post::PublishingValidator < ActiveModel::Validator
  def validate(post)
    return unless post.published?

    validate_publish_date(post)
    validate_author(post)
    # … more validations related to post publishing
  end
end
```

Each validate_x method performs its checks and populates the #errors set if necessary:

```ruby
def validate_publish_date(post)
  unless post.publish_date.present?
    return post.errors.add(:publish_date, :blank)
  end

  # Assuming we only publish posts on Tuesdays
  if post.publish_date.wday != 1
    post.errors.add(:publish_date, :not_tuesday)
  end
end

def validate_author(post)
  post.errors.add(:author, :blank) unless post.author
end
```

In both the DraftValidator and PublishingValidator examples, we have extracted the implementation into separate classes, but they stayed coupled with the model via the state checks (such as post.published?). Although we performed pure code refactoring, our model's behavior hasn't changed.

This leads us to the second tradeoff of keeping validations in the model class: such validations are *context-free*; they are applied every time we call #save (or #update) independently of the *execution context*. For example, a record could be updated or created in response to a user action or during internal process execution.

Must we apply the same validations in both cases? Unlikely. Validations are usually redundant for internal operations since we have better control over data. And user-driven updates could also affect different model attribute subsets, so we don't need to re-validate everything.

Active Record has a built-in mechanism to define validation contexts—the on option. We usually use it to define on: :create or on: :update validations. These two are built-in contexts, but you can define your own named contexts. Let's, for instance, introduce the publish context to our model:

```ruby
class Post < ApplicationRecord
  validates_with PublishingValidator, on: :publish
  def publish
    self.status = :published
    save!(context: :publish)
  end
end
```

That would allow us to drop the `post.published?` check from the validator and, thus, make it less dependent on the model.

This technique helps us stay as close to the Rails Way as possible while keeping a decent level of maintainability in our models. However, as the number of contexts grows, tracking them all within a single model class becomes more difficult. We will discuss the abstractions that could be used to deal with the growing model layer complexity regarding validations and rules in *Chapter 7, Handling User Input outside of Models*, and *Chapter 8, Pulling Out the Representation Layer*.

So far, we've been mainly considering transition and context-sensitive consistency rules. What about context-free consistency rules, such as `validates :title` and `presence: true`? We may think of such rules as *invariants*, which should never be violated; hence, keeping them in the model is the best option. Here, we should note that for database-backed models, actual consistency enforcement happens in the database via **constraints**. Thus, invariant rules should be backed by the corresponding constraints.

What a gem – database_validations / database_consistency

The `database_validations` (`https://github.com/toptal/database_validations`) gem adds uniqueness and association presence validators, which ensure that the corresponding constraints (foreign keys or unique indexes) are present in the database. The `database_consistency` (`https://github.com/djezzzl/database_consistency`) tool compares validations with database constraints and reports when an inconsistency is detected.

The opposite is not always true; not every constraint should be ported to the application model as a validation. Why? We add validations to handle potential state violations gracefully and react to them (for example, provide feedback to users). If a bug in the program could only trigger a constraint failure, it's better to rely on exceptions. Validations are for humans; constraints are for machines.

Rules, or validations, describe how an application state can be modified. Every modification can be seen as an event. Events allow us to chain operation sequences representing the application business processes. For example, in a hypothetical library application, we could have the following chain: when a new user is registered, create a personal bookshelf for them, issue a library card, and send a welcome email. What is a typical Rails Way to implement this in the application code? To use Active Record callbacks.

Active Record callbacks (and Rails callbacks in general) are a vast topic, which we will discuss in *Chapter 4, Rails Anti-Patterns?*. However, for this chapter, we note that Active Record also carries the responsibility of an event dispatcher.

Let's move from the application state to the other layers, which could be mixed into Active Record models.

From model to anything

A typical Active Record class in a Rails application contains many more things than just validations, callbacks, and scopes (we will cover the latter in *Chapter 6, Data Layer Abstractions*). Trying to fit all the functionality into the default Rails project layout, a developer tends to turn models into bags of methods.

We can find pretty much anything in Active Record models:

- Presentation helpers, such as the famous `User#full_name`

- Other mappers, for example, `Post#to_elasticsearch_data`

- Calculators and number crunchers, say, `Subscription#effective_payment_for_today`

- All kinds of notifications: `Campaign#send_promo_sms`, `Meeting#notify_one_hour_before`

- External API calls: `Facility#lookup_geolocation!`

To sum up, Active Record is the all-in-one solution to describe the application state as well as to access the underlying data storage. It's a great example of conceptual compression: just a single object instead of a combination of mappers, repositories, validators, event dispatchers, presenters, and so on.

So far, we have been using only the term *Active Record* in this chapter. However, some features and APIs (for example, validations) are not Active Record's own; they're inherited from Active Model, the core framework for Rails models.

Active Model – the hidden gem behind Active Record

Active Model has been extracted from Active Record in Rails 3.0 (released in 2010). The primary goal of this extraction was to untie Active Record from Action Pack, to make controllers and views uncoupled from the persistence layer: the database. Thus, Active Model became a building block for the M in Rails MVC, covering both persistent and non-persistent models.

Let's take a closer look at this Rails component and learn how it could be helpful beyond Active Record.

Active Model as an interface

Although usually invisible to developers, Active Model contributes a lot to Rails' productivity. Many Rails helpers, such as `#redirect_to`, `#link_to`, and so on, rely on the Active Model interface. In Ruby, when we say *interface*, we imply **duck typing**.

> **If it quacks like a duck, then it must be a duck**
>
> **Duck typing** is a technique of writing code based on the assumption that an object responds to a given method without checking the object type. Thus, duck types could be seen as implicit interfaces. However, when using Ruby type signatures, duck types usually correspond to interface types.

To demonstrate the Active Model duck type in action, let's consider a simplified version of the #link_to helper:

```
def link_to(name, record)
  parts = [""]
  if record.persisted?
    parts << record.model_name.singular_route_key
    parts << record.to_param
  else
    parts << record.model_name.route_key
  end
  content_tag("a", name, {href: parts.join("/")})
end
```

In the preceding code snippet, the highlighted methods represent the Active Model interface (part of it). Any Ruby object could be used as a record if it satisfies the interface—see this, for example:

```
class Book
  attr_reader :id
  def initialize(id) = @id = id
  def persisted? = true
  def to_param = id.to_s
  def model_name
    ActiveModel::Name.new(self.class)
  end
end
```

Then, we can use a Book object with view helpers like this:

```
link_to("Object", Book.new(2023)) #=> "/books/2023"
```

Of course, it's not necessary to implement all methods yourself to define Active Model-compatible Ruby classes. Rails gives you a specific module called ActiveModel::API to attach the Active Model behavior to any object:

```
class Book
  include ActiveModel::API
```

```
    include ActiveModel::Attributes

    attribute :id

    def persisted? = true
  end

  link_to("Object", Book.new(id: 2023)) #=> "/books/2023"
```

We also include the `ActiveModel::Attributes` module, which provides the `.attribute` method to declare the model attributes in an Active Record fashion. Attributes can be used to provide default values and perform type coercions. We will consider these features in further chapters.

If you decide to go with a custom interface implementation without using `ActiveModel::API`, you can enforce Active Model compatibility by adding a set of conformance tests via the `ActiveModel::Lint` module:

```
  class BookTest < ActiveSupport::TestCase
    include ActiveModel::Lint::Tests

    def setup() = @model = Book.new
  end
```

As you can see, the Active Model API provides a lot of naming methods (via `#model_name`). This is a consequence of the *convention over configuration* principle, the core principle of the Ruby on Rails framework.

> **Convention over configuration**
>
> **Convention over configuration** (CoC) is a design paradigm that assumes relying on object names and project file structure to automatically (or implicitly) infer as much functionality as possible to reduce the developer's burden, so they can focus only on what matters for their specific project instead of spending time on connecting framework pieces together. A great example of CoC is Active Record: all you need is to name a class according to the name of the database table (`books` => `Book`), and you can use it right away without any additional configuration.

Adhering to the Active Model interface or using its API directly makes it easier to follow Rails conventions (and, thus, be closer to the Rails Way). Let's consider an example: implementing a book collection virtual model for a library application.

Assuming that our library consists of only two collections, `ruby` and `other`, we could have the following implementation:

```
  class Category
    include ActiveModel::API
```

```
  ALL = %w[ruby other].freeze
  def self.all = ALL.map { new(category: _1) }
  alias_method :id, :category
  def persisted? = true
  def books = Book.where(category:)
end
```

We can now use this model in our controllers:

```
# books_controller.rb
class BooksController < ApplicationController
  def index
    @categories = Category.all
  end
end
```

We can also use it in our view templates:

```
# books/index.html.erb
<!-- Uses the categories/_category partial
<%= render @categories %>

# categories/_category.html.erb
<li>
  <!-- Prints /categories/ruby and /categories/other -->
  <%= link_to category.name, category %>
</li>
```

As you can see, we use our category model like a typical, Active Record-backed, Rails model. We don't need to introduce new concepts or helpers, and we don't have to write a lot of boilerplate code (such as specifying partials and link URLs explicitly). Another benefit of this approach is that going from a virtual model to a persistent one wouldn't require changing the existing code that uses it. Thus, Active Model can be used as a refactoring primitive for the model layer.

Let's see how we can use Active Model to refactor Active Record classes.

Active Model as an Active Record satellite

Active Model can be used to tame an Active Record class's complexity by introducing sidecar objects backed by the same persistence data. Let's consider two examples: modeling unstructured data and extracting domain objects from database rows.

The popularity of the PostgreSQL database (https://www.postgresql.org) among Rails developers led to the common usage of Active Record stores: attributes containing arbitrary hashes or arrays, backed by JSONB or HSTORE columns in the database. Using NoSQL (or document-oriented) features brings a lot of flexibility: we can rely on a single column in a database, whereas previously we would need to either add new columns or use intermediate tables (like in the *Entity-Attribute-Value* approach).

Stores are especially useful for read-only data. For example, let's consider storing a user's mailing address as a JSON-encoded string:

```ruby
class User < ApplicationRecord
  store :address, coder: JSON
end
user = User.create!(address: {country: 'USA',
  city: 'Bronx', street: '231st', zip: 10463})
user.address #=> {"country"=>"USA", "city"=>"Bronx",
  "street"=>"231st", "zip"=>10463}
```

The value of the address attribute is just a hash. We can't use it with Action Pack helpers; we can't extend it with custom logic. Wrapping it into an Active Model object could bring these benefits:

```ruby
class User::Address
  include ActiveModel::API
  include ActiveModel::Attributes
  attribute :country
  attribute :city
  attribute :street
  attribute :zip
end

class User < ApplicationRecord
  store :address, coder: JSON
  def address() = @address ||= Address.new(super)
end
user = User.create!(address: {country: 'USA', city:
  'Bronx', street: '231st', zip: 10463})
user.address #=> #<User::Address:…>
```

We can go further and add validations to our Address model, and thus, keep all the logic related to a user's address in a dedicated model:

```ruby
class User::Address
  # …
  validates :country, :zip, presence: true
end
class User < ApplicationRecord
```

```
  validate do |record|
    next if address.valid?
    record.errors.add(:address, "is invalid")
  end
end

user = User.create(address: {})
user.valid? #=> false
user.errors.full_messages #=> ["Address is invalid"]
```

Wrapping a `store` attribute into a model requires some additional work. Luckily, there is a library to make it as easy as possible—Store Model.

> **What a gem – store_model**
>
> Store Model (`https://github.com/DmitryTsepelev/store_model`) allows you to attach a model to a store and takes care of integrating it into the host record life cycle (validations and so on). This gem also supports *union types* for stores, that is, using a custom wrapper model depending on the underlying raw data characteristics.

What if we kept our address data in multiple columns instead of putting it into a JSON store? Let's assume our user model has `address_country`, `address_city`, `address_street`, and `address_zip` attributes. Then, we can use the Active Record built-in `.composed_of` method to define an `Address` domain object on top of these attributes:

```
class User < ApplicationRecord
  composed_of :address,
    class_name: "User::Address",
    mapping: [%w(address_country), %w(address_city),
      %w(address_street), %w(address_zip)],
    constructor: proc { |country, city, street, zip|
      Address.new({country:,city:,street:,zip:})
    }
end
```

Here's an example of `composed_of` in action:

```
user = User.create!(address_country: "UK", address_city:
  "Birmingham", address_street: "Livery st", address_zip:
    "B32PB")
user.address.zip #=> "B32PB"
```

We defined a custom constructor to use our `Address` class with Active Model attributes. It's not necessary to use Active Model-backed objects with `.composed_of`; you can define a pure Ruby class or `Struct`:

```
Address = Struct.new(:country, :city, :street, :zip)
```

The question arises of how to choose between a pure Ruby object and Active Model. The answer lies somewhere between performance and user experience.

Active Model versus Struct – performance implications

Enhancing objects with Active Model features comes at a price, which becomes noticeable when you initialize tons of such objects during a single unit of work execution. Both CPU (time) and memory are affected.

Let's perform a benchmark test to compare Active Model objects with similar Ruby `Struct` instances:

Class backed by Active Model API

```
class ActiveUser
  include ActiveModel::API

  attr_accessor :a, :b, :c, :d, :e
end
```

Class backed by Active Model attributes

```
class ActiveAttributesUser
  include ActiveModel::API
  include ActiveModel::Attributes

  %i[a b c d e].each { attribute _1 }
end
```

Plain Ruby Struct

```
StructUser = Struct.new(:a, :b, :c, :d, :e, keyword_init: true)
```

To measure the performance difference, we will use the `benchmark-ips` (`https://github.com/evanphx/benchmark-ips`) gem:

```
Benchmark.ips do |x|
  x.report('struct') { StructUser.new(a: 1, b: 2, c: 3, d:
    4, e: 5) }
```

```
    x.report('active model api') { ActiveUser.new(a: 1, b: 2,
      c: 3, d: 4, e: 5) }
    x.report('w/attributes') { ActiveAttributesUser.new(a: 1,
      b: 2, c: 3, d: 4, e: 5) }
    x.compare!
  end
```

To measure the memory footprint, we will use the `benchmark-memory` (`https://github.com/michaelherold/benchmark-memory`) gem:

```
Benchmark.memory do |x|
    x.report('struct') { StructUser.new(a: 1, b: 2, c: 3, d:
      4, e: 5) }
    x.report('active model api') { ActiveUser.new(a: 1, b: 2,
      c: 3, d: 4, e: 5) }
    x.report('w/attributes') { ActiveAttributesUser.new(a: 1,
      b: 2, c: 3, d: 4, e: 5) }
    x.compare!
  end
```

When running this benchmark on Ruby 3.1.2 and Rails 7.0.3, we can see the following results:

```
Comparison:
            struct:  2015985.4 i/s
  active model api:   580159.3 i/s - 3.47x  (± 0.00) slower
      w/attributes:   164878.1 i/s - 12.23x (± 0.00) slower

Comparison:
            struct:      248 allocated
  active model api:      448 allocated - 1.81x more
      w/attributes:     1376 allocated - 5.55x more
```

As you can see, adding Active Model attributes makes building such objects much slower and performs more allocations, thus putting additional stress on the Ruby garbage collector, again slowing down the overall execution. In most cases, we do not create hundreds or thousands of Active Model objects simultaneously so this overhead would be negligible.

However, there is a particular scenario when you may shoot yourself in the foot by overusing Active Model: dealing with large collections. For example, if we had an API endpoint returning thousands of users and their address information (from the previous example), switching from Active Model to `Struct` could reduce the request time.

In summary, performance could be a concern on rare occasions, but in most cases, we can afford a bit of overhead. What about user experience?

Active Model for an Active Record-like experience

So far, we have considered Active Model interface features mostly in the context of Action Pack and Action View helpers or as a mechanism to define non-persistent models. However, Active Model is more than that.

Active Model is a fundamental element of providing an Active Record-like experience. It could be used to provide a familiar interface to any data sources, from NoSQL databases (see Mongoid: `https://github.com/mongodb/mongoid`) to REST APIs (see Active Resource: `https://github.com/rails/activeresource`).

Why is it important to quack like Active Record? Because all Rails developers know Active Record, and leveraging well-known patterns is helpful from the principle of least astonishment point of view, one of the vital software development principles.

> **What a gem – frozen_record**
>
> FrozenRecord (`https://github.com/byroot/frozen_record`) allows you to turn static data stored in a filesystem in any format (for example, YAML, JSON) into a queryable virtual database and access it via Active Record-like models.

Throughout the book, we will use Active Model extensively as a building block for new abstraction layers. Our goal is to refactor our application to improve its health (or maintainability). In a typical Rails monolith, the unhealthiest layer is the model layer. So, let's talk about how we can detect models which require emergency refactoring.

Seeking God objects

Active Record is the largest part of Rails; its code base contains twice as many files (over 1,000) and lines of code (over 100,000) as the second largest, which is Action Pack. With that amount of machinery under the hood, it provides dozens of APIs for developers to use in their applications. As a result, models inherited from Active Record tend to carry many responsibilities, which we were trying to enumerate in the previous sections of this chapter. Such over-responsible Ruby classes are usually referred to as God objects.

From the code perspective, a lot of responsibility means a lot of lines of source code. The number of lines itself can't be considered an indicator of unhealthy code. We need better metrics to identify good candidates for refactoring in our code base. The combination of churn and complexity has been proven to be such indicators.

Churn describes how often a given file has been modified. A high change rate could indicate a code design flaw: either we're adding new responsibilities or trying to eliminate the shortcomings of the initial implementation. Let's see how we can obtain the churn factor.

Today, every project uses a version control system; thus, we can calculate a given file's churn as the total number of commits where the file has been affected. With Git, the following command returns the churn factor for the User model:

```
$ git log --format=oneline -- app/models/user.rb | wc -l
408
```

We can go further and use the power of Unix commands to get the top-10 files according to churn:

```
find app/models -name "*.rb" | while read file; do echo $file `git log
--format=oneline -- $file | wc -l`; done | sort -k 2 -nr | head
```

Depending on the project age, you might want to limit the commit date range (by using the `--since` option).

With regard to complexity, there is no single algorithm for code complexity to calculate the corresponding metrics. In Ruby, a tool called **Flog** (`https://github.com/seattlerb/flog`) is the de facto instrument to calculate source code complexity.

This is how we can get the overall complexity for a single file:

```
$ flog -s app/models/user.rb
  274.3: flog total
    8.1: flog/method average
```

I will leave you to devise a Unix one-liner to get the top-N most complex source files in the project.

Armed with these two metrics, churn and complexity, we can now define the rule of thumb for identifying Ruby classes that deserve the most refactoring attention. Usually, the `churn * complexity` product is used as a cumulative metric. Still, for simplicity, we can say that the intersection of the top-10 lists for churn and complexity is the starting set.

What a gem – attractor

Attractor (`https://github.com/julianrubisch/attractor`) is a code complexity calculation and visualization tool. It calculates both churn and complexity (using Flog) for you and provides an interactive web interface to analyze the collected data. It supports Ruby and JavaScript, thus being a complete solution for Rails web applications.

In Ruby on Rails projects, the most complex class, according to the cumulative value, would likely be one of your core models: user, account, project, or similar. These are typical God object names.

There is no one-size-fits-all solution to return such objects from heaven to earth, but the strategy described in this book (extracting abstraction layers) will help you keep your objects' feet on the ground.

Summary

In this chapter, you've taken a deeper look at Rails applications' model and persistence layers. You've learned about two fundamental object-relational mapping patterns, Active Record and Data Mapper, their pros and cons, and why Active Record better fits the Ruby on Rails paradigm. You've learned about the Active Record framework and its areas of responsibility.

You've learned about the Active Model interface and library and how it can be used to build Active Record-like models and to extract domain models from Active Record. You also learned about the God object problem and its relationship with code churn and complexity characteristics.

In the next chapter, we will branch out of the MVC path and talk about supporting Rails sub-frameworks, such as Active Job and Active Storage, and learn about their architectural ideas.

Questions

1. What is the principal difference between the Active Record and Data Mapper patterns?

2. When should we use model validations and when should we use database constraints?

3. What is duck typing, and how is it utilized by Rails?

4. In which cases are pure Ruby objects (such as `Struct` instances) preferable to Active Model enhanced classes?

5. What is churn, and how does it relate to code complexity?

Exercises

Prepare a Unix one-liner to show top-N complex Ruby files using Flog. Can you combine it with our churn *calculator* to show top-N files by `churn * complexity`?

Further reading

- *Patterns of Enterprise Application Architecture* (where the Active Record and Data Mapper patterns were originally introduced by Martin Fowler): `https://martinfowler.com/books/eaa.html`

- *Polished Ruby Programming* (*Chapter 15, The Database Is the Key*): `https://www.packtpub.com/product/polished-ruby-programming/9781801072724`

3

More Adapters, Less Implementations

In this chapter, we take a tour of the satellite frameworks of Ruby on Rails, such as **Active Job** and **Active Storage**, and learn about their design patterns and techniques. We will start by talking about the adapter pattern and how it relates to the flexibility, extensibility, and testability of code. We will also discuss the technique of object serialization in the context of Active Job. Finally, when talking about Active Storage, we will compare the adapter pattern with the plugin-based architecture.

We will cover the following topics:

- Active Job as a universal queue interface

- Active Storage and its adapters and plugins

- Adapters and wrappers at your service

This chapter aims to familiarize the reader with design techniques that could help to separate the application code from specific third-party implementations and make application code extensible and testable.

Technical requirements

In this chapter, and all chapters of this book, the code given in code blocks is designed to be executed on Ruby 3.2 and Rails 7. Many of the code examples will work on earlier versions of the previously mentioned software. You will find the code files on GitHub at `https://github.com/PacktPublishing/Layered-Design-for-Ruby-on-Rails-Applications/tree/main/Chapter03`.

Active Job as a universal queue interface

In *Chapter 1*, *Rails as a Web Application Framework*, we talked about the background jobs layer and its importance for Rails applications. Before Rails 4.2, we only had implementation-specific mechanisms to build this layer: Sidekiq workers, delayed method calls (via the `delayed_job` gem), and so on.

The more implementations, the more code styles and patterns are in use; hence, the higher the learning curve for a new developer joining a Rails project. Rails' *omakase* was incomplete—no item from the *Background processing* category was on the menu.

> **What is omakase?**
>
> **Omakase** is a Japanese term used to describe a meal consisting of dishes selected by the chef. *Rails is omakase* means that the framework maintainers have chosen the building blocks for your application, and they play together nicely.

To solve these problems, the Active Job framework was introduced in Rails 4.2. What is Active Job? Let's consider a minimal example—a background job to send an analytics event to some third-party service:

```
class TrackAnalyticsJob < ApplicationJob
  queue_as :low_priority

  def perform(user, event)
    Analytics::Tracker.push_event(
      {user: {name: user.name, id: user.id}, event:}}
    )
  end
end
TrackAnalyticsJob.perform_later(user, "signed_in")
```

Active Job provides an abstract interface to enqueue and process background units of work. Such a unit of work is represented as an instance of a job class with a single entry-point method—#perform. The job class also provides methods for enqueuing jobs—.perform_later, .perform_at, and so on.

Finally, job classes declare the execution rules: which named queue to use by default, when to retry, and when to discard the job. For example, we can configure our job class to retry on HTTP API errors and discard the job if a user is not recognized by the analytics service:

```
class TrackAnalyticsJob < ApplicationJob
  queue_as :low_priority
  retry_on Analytics::APIError, wait: 3.seconds
  discard_on Analytics::UserNotFound
  # ...
end
```

To summarize, an Active Job class is a Ruby class with a standardized public API and abstract queueing rules.

Let's see how we go from abstract queues to actual implementations.

Adapterizing queues

There are plenty of background processing options for Rails applications: Sidekiq, which we already mentioned, Resque, GoodJob, and Sneakers to name a few. They serve the same purpose but have completely different implementations. However, when using Active Job, choosing a backend is achieved by specifying a single configuration parameter:

```
config.active_job.queue_adapter = :sidekiq
# or
config.active_job.queue_adatper = :good_job
```

> **What a gem – good_job**
>
> GoodJob (`https://github.com/bensheldon/good_job`) is a multi-threaded Active Job backend using PostgreSQL as the underlying jobs storage and distribution engine. It supports recurrent jobs, provides a built-in real-time monitoring dashboard, and can be run within a Rails server process to reduce deployment complexity (and costs).

How can Active Job work with incompatible backends and provide a unified interface at the same time? By using the **adapter pattern**.

Figure 3.1 – Adapter pattern diagram

As you see from the preceding figure, an adapter object knows about both the host (or client) application and the implementation, while the other two have no direct connections. Let's see how the adapter pattern is employed by Active Job.

> **Pattern – adapter**
>
> **Adapter** is an object that converts an existing interface into another interface expected by the *client* (an object using the adapter). Thus, an adapter allows incompatible objects to be used together. The adapter itself usually doesn't provide any additional functionality beyond being a translator. The pattern can be easily found in the physical world: power socket adapters, USB plugs for cars, and plumbing pipe fittings.

The interface *expected* by Active Job consists of just two methods and can be described using the following Ruby type signature:

```
interface ActiveJobAdapter
  def enqueue: (ActiveJob::Base job) -> void
  def enqueue_at: (ActiveJob::Base job, Time ts) -> void
end
```

Then, the simplest possible adapter can be defined as follows:

```
class NoOpAdapter
  def enqueue(*) = nil
  def enqueue_at(*) = nil
end
```

You can attach it to Active Job to disable background jobs completely (since our adapter does nothing):

```
config.active_job.queue_adapter = NoOpAdapter.new
```

Even such a simple adapter demonstrates the benefits of using adapters: you only need to change a single place in your code base to switch between adapters. The application code stays abstract, which brings lesser coupling and, thus, improves maintainability and reusability.

Although the no-op adapter might look impractical, there could be a situation when you want to turn off the functionality completely (for example, in test or sandbox environments). Speaking of tests, adapters positively impact the *testing experience*.

For example, when using the Active Job test adapter, there are the following benefits:

- We can avoid using actual queue backends in tests, thus avoiding additional setup and overhead (especially when a queue is backed by a database)
- We can still ensure the correctness of the system under test by verifying the interface contract

To achieve the latter, the Active Job test adapter tracks all enqueued jobs and provides convenient helpers to use in tests:

```
class UserTest < ActiveSupport::TestCase
  include ActiveJob::TestHelper

  test "analytics job scheduling" do
    assert_enqueued_with(
      job: TrackAnalyticsJob,
      args: [@user, "signed_in"]) do
      @user.track_event("signed_in")
    end
  end
end
```

We don't need to test that a job has been pushed to a specific queue implementation; that's not the responsibility of the application code but the adapter. Still, we need to test the fact that the correct job has been enqueued, and the test adapter is enough for that. To sum up, adapters improve the maintainability and testability of code.

In the preceding test example, we can see that we pass an instance of the User class as an argument (@user). In production, background processing usually happens in a separate Ruby process (a dedicated *background worker*). How is it possible to *move* Ruby classes across isolated environments? To answer that, we need to look at another prominent feature of Active Job—**argument serialization**.

Serializing all things

In addition to providing a common jobs interface, Active Job also implicitly assumes that queueing backends may process jobs in separate application processes or even physical machines. So why do we need to take the *application topology* into account?

A **job** (unit of work) could be described as a pair of the job's class name and the list of arguments. A class name is just a string, while arguments can be of any nature. And we need a way to represent the arguments in a format that can be sent over the wire.

One approach could be to avoid using complex Ruby objects as job arguments. For example, if we used plain Sidekiq, without Active Job, we would rewrite our class from the previous example as follows:

```
class TrackAnalyticsWorker
  include Sidekiq::Worker
  def perform(user_id, event)
    user = User.find(user_id)
    Analytics::Tracker.push_event(
      {user: {name: user.name, id: user.id}, event:}}
    )
  end
end
TrackAnalyticsWorker.perform_async(user.id, "signed_in")
```

We replaced user with user_id and added an additional step to our #perform method: retrieving a user from the database using the User.find(user_id) identifier.

The difference may not look like a significant one. However, it becomes noticeable when you try to write the corresponding test case:

Unit-testing an Active Job class

```
test "analytics active job" do
  event_checker = lambda do |event|
    assert(event => {user: {name: "Vova"}, event: "test"})
```

```
    end
    user = User.new(name: "Vova")
    Analytics::Tracker.stub :push_event, event_checker do
      TrackAnalyticsJob.perform_now(user, "test")
    end
  end
```

Unit-testing a Sidekiq worker class

```
test "analytics Sidekiq worker" do
  event_checker = # similar
  user = User.create!(name: "Vova") # !!!
  Analytics::Tracker.stub :push_event, event_checker do
    TrackAnalyticsWorker.new.perform(user.id, "test")
  end
end
```

Testing Active Job classes relying on Active Record objects can be accomplished without hitting a database, while for pure Sidekiq workers, we need to have a database involved in testing (let me leave the case of stubbing User.find for a different book).

So, how does Active Job handle passing complex objects as arguments? The answer is by using **serialization**.

Serialization is the process of transforming an object into a format that could be moved to a different *execution environment* and reconstructed later. The object performing (de)serialization is called a **serializer**:

In the Ruby world, popular serialization formats are JSON and YAML. There is also the Ruby Marshal standard library, which allows the conversion of any Ruby objects into byte streams and vice versa.

However, Active Job uses custom serialization. Why so? Although the actual reasons are unknown to the author, we can assume that one of them is handling Active Record objects. Since the Active Record object is highly coupled with the persistence layer, we must use this layer to restore it from any format because the state of the object might have changed after the serialization.

To solve this problem, the GlobalID identification mechanism has been introduced (via the corresponding library). GlobalID allows representing Ruby classes as **uniform resource locators** (yes, **URLs**). Take the following example:

```
user = User.find(1)
user.to_global_id #=> gid://app/User/1
```

Here, app is the locator namespace. Each namespace has its deserialization implementation (*locator*). Then goes the model name (User) and the model ID (1). The default locator for Active Record is defined as follows:

```
GlobalID::Locator.use :app do |gid|
  gid.model_name.constantize.find(gid.model_id)
end
```

To restore a record from a GlobalID, you should use the GlobalID::Locator. locate(gid) method.

GlobalID URLs may also contain query params. This makes it possible to use GlobalID for arbitrary Ruby objects with just a few lines of code. First, we register our custom locator:

```
GlobalID::Locator.use :pogo do |gid|
  gid.model_name.constantize.new(**gid.params)
end
```

Then, we make our Ruby class globally identifiable:

```
class Category < Struct.new(:name, keyword_init: true)
  include GlobalID::Identification
  alias_method :id, :name
  def to_global_id(options = {})
    super({name:}.merge!(options).merge!(app: "pogo"))
  end
end
```

This is how you can use GlobalID::Locator to restore an object from its identifier:

```
original = Category.new(name: "ruby")
located = GlobalID::Locator.locate(original.to_global_id)
located == original #=> true
```

Now that we know about GlobalID, we may deduce how Active Job serialization works. Whenever an argument supports GlobalID identification, transform it via the #to_global_id method when enqueuing a job. Before calling the #perform method, restore all the serialized arguments using the GlobalID::Locator.locate method. Thus, for an Active Record object, Active Job calls .find for us implicitly.

GlobalID is not the only way to serialize complex job arguments. You can also define a custom serializer for your class:

```
module ActiveJob::Serializers
  class CategorySerializer < ObjectSerializer
    def serialize(cat) = super("name" => cat.name)
```

```
    def deserialize(h) = Category.new(name: h["name"])
    private def klass = Category
  end
end


# in your application.rb
config.active_job.custom_serializers <<
  ActiveJob::Serializers::CategorySerializer
```

The following diagram demonstrates the role and place of serializers in Active Job:

Figure 3.2 – Payload serialization in Active Job

Implicit serialization can simplify your job classes and reduce their responsibility (they no longer need to convert the arguments to the actual objects). However, like every implicit functionality, it could lead to confusion. It would help if you never forgot that the objects enqueued and the objects received by a job instance are not the same Ruby objects.

The objects passed to #perform are fresh, reconstructed versions, unless you instantiate job class instances explicitly in your code for some reason (and thus, break the idea of Active Job being an execution context boundary).

Let's move to Active Job's sibling, Active Storage, and see what these two libraries have in common and what other patterns Active Storage relies on.

Active Storage and its adapters and plugins

Active Storage is a relatively new addition to Ruby on Rails (added in 5.2). This library aims to satisfy your needs regarding file uploads.

With Active Storage, enhancing a model with a file-backed attribute is as simple as adding a single line of code:

```
class Post < ApplicationRecord
  has_one_attached :image
end
```

Then, you can attach a file to a record by simply passing it along with other attributes:

```
# Now you can create a post with an image
image = File.open("example.png")
```

```
post = Post.create!(title: "Test")
post.image.attach(io: image, filename: "example.png")
# Use a variant of the image somewhere in a template
<%= image_tag post.image.variant(resize: "400x300") %>
```

From an architectural point of view, Active Storage can be divided into four components:

- Uploading and serving files (controllers, helpers, and client libraries)
- Active Record integration (`has_one_attached` and other macros, the Attachment model)
- Storage integration (services)
- Processing utilities (analyzers and transformers)

The first two components provide most of the public API we use in applications. This API is abstract; it has no assumptions regarding how and where we store and process files (the latter two components). To draw an architectural line between these two groups, Active Storage uses the adapter and the **plugin** patterns.

The adapter pattern is used for Active Storage *services*: objects responsible for communicating with the underlying storage implementations (filesystem, cloud providers, and so on). On the other hand, being an adapter, a service object provides a known Active Storage interface (`#download`, `#upload`, `#exists?`, and so on). This makes it possible to use different storage backends in different environments freely:

Development: use local hard disk

```
# config/storage/development.yml
primary:
  service: disk
  # …
```

Production: use Google Cloud Storage

```
# config/storage/production.yml
primary:
  service: GSC
  # …
```

Note that in the preceding example, I use the same service name but different backends for different environments instead of keeping a single `storage.yml` file with all definitions and setting `config.active_storage.service` for each environment (the approach widely spread among Rails developers).

This way, we avoid leaking storage information to the application in case we have different backends configured for different models. For example, compare the following two versions of the same class:

Using implementation-specific service name

```
class User < ApplicationRecord
  # With storage.yml, service names refer to implementation
  has_one_attached :avatar, service: :s3
end
```

Using application-specific (abstract) service name

```
class User < ApplicationRecord
  # With per-environment configs, we use abstract names
  has_one_attached :avatar, service: :small_images_storage
end
```

The benefits of the adapterized storage are roughly the same as in Active Job and its queueing backends: flexibility, extensibility, and testability. By testability, here I mean making it possible to write integration tests involving file manipulations without needing to configure external storage—using the local filesystem is enough.

What about file processing? That's where the plugin-based architecture comes onto the stage.

Adapters versus plugins

As we already mentioned, Active Storage allows you to transform uploaded files: generate image variants and extract previews and metadata from many file formats. To transform images, the ImageProcessing (https://github.com/janko/image_processing) gem is used, and Rails allows you to choose between ImageMagick and libvips to do the actual work (adapters, again). Previewers and analyzers (metadata extractors) are designed differently—they are plugins.

> Pattern – plugin
>
> **Plugin** is a standalone, independent component that could be used to enhance the core system with additional capabilities or custom processing logic. In a plugin-based architecture, the core system provides the extension points for plugins to hook into (and plugins must implement a common interface expected by the core system).

Let's look at the default previewers and analyzers included in Rails 7:

Default Active Storage previewers

```
config.active_storage.previewers = [ActiveStorage::
  Previewer::PopplerPDFPreviewer, ActiveStorage::
    Previewer::MuPDFPreviewer, ActiveStorage::
      Previewer::VideoPreviewer]
```

Default Active Storage analyzers

```
config.active_storage.analyzers = [ActiveStorage::
  Analyzer::ImageAnalyzer::Vips, ActiveStorage
    ::Analyzer::ImageAnalyzer::ImageMagick, ActiveStorage::
      Analyzer::VideoAnalyzer, ActiveStorage::
        Analyzer::AudioAnalyzer]
```

The class names indicate that each previewer/analyzer relies on a particular tool, and thus, we might call them **adapters**. Why do we call them plugins, then? The key difference between adapters and plugins is that *plugins provide additional functionality*, not just an expected interface.

For example, an Active Storage analyzer can return any hash as metadata; that is, we can use an analyzer to retrieve data specific to our application, not just to comply with the framework.

However, Active Storage's plugin system is limited: even though we have lists of plugins, only a single previewer/analyzer can be applied to a file. The chosen one is selected by using the **activation callback** (.accept?). Take the following example:

```
module ActiveStorage
  class Analyzer::AudioAnalyzer < Analyzer
    def self.accept?(blob)
      blob.audio?
    end
  end
end
```

This activation callback is an important technique when using plugins since it makes plugins self-contained. Thus, we can add and remove them from the registry without changing anything else in our system.

To overcome the singleton limitation, we can use inheritance as a workaround. Let's consider the following use case—retrieving ID3 tags from MP3 files in addition to general metadata:

```
class CustomAudioAnalyzer < ActiveStorage::
  Analyzer::AudioAnalyzer
```

```ruby
  def metadata
    super.merge(id3_data)
  end

  private def id3_data
    tag = download_blob_to_tempfile do |file|
      ID3Tag.read(File.open(file.path))
    end
    {title: tag.title, artist: tag.artist}
  end
end
```

This example also demonstrates the usage of analyzers to solve an application-specific task, thus advocating for calling them plugins rather than adapters.

Continuing the comparison, we can say that plugins have the same advantages as adapters. For example, we can use different plugins in a test environment. This is how we can speed up tests by stubbing preview generation:

```ruby
class DummyVideoPreviewer < ActiveStorage::Previewer
  def self.accept?(...) = true
  def preview(**options)
    io = File.open(Rails.root.join "spec" / "files" /
      "1.png")
    yield io:, filename: "#{blob.filename.base}.png",
      content_type: "image/png", metadata: {"dummy" =>
        true}, **options
  end
end
# config/environments/test.rb
config.active_storage.previewers = [DummyVideoPreviewer]
```

Now that we have learned about how Rails uses adapters and plugins, let's see how we can apply the same techniques to our application code.

Adapters and wrappers at your service

Ruby on Rails is a universal web framework, and the usage of adapters and plugins could be easily justified. But do we need the same level of flexibility and extensibility in applications built with Rails? The answer is, as always, it depends. So let me share some particular use cases when using separation patterns is especially helpful.

Modern applications are not isolated pieces of software. Usually, we rely on dozens of third-party services to outsource some functionality. For example, we send emails and other notifications, perform data analysis, collect analytics, and so on. In most cases, there are a variety of third-party providers to choose from.

We can start injecting the provider directly into our application code without using any pattern. Let's consider, for example, adding a URL-shortening feature.

Assuming we chose *bit.ly* and the corresponding gem (`https://github.com/philnash/bitly`) as the implementation, we might define a singleton API client and use it directly in the application code:

```
# config/application.rb
config.bitly_client = Bitly::API::Client.new(
  token: Rails.credentials.bitly_api_token
)
# any/where.rb
short_url = Rails.application.config
    .bitly_client.shorten(long_url: url).link
```

Congratulations! We just implanted a third-party service into our application domain, thus increasing the maintenance cost (consisting of the costs of refactoring, testing, and debugging).

The simplest fix would be to introduce a `Shortener` domain object, and use it as a **wrapper** over a `Bitly` client:

```
class Shortener
  class << self
    delegate :shorten, to: :instance
    def instance = @instance ||= new
  end
  def initialize(token: Rails.credentials.bitly_api_token)
    @client = Bitly::API::Client.new(token:)
  end
  def shorten(long_url)
    @client.shorten(long_url:).link
  end
end
```

Here is an example usage of the `Shortener` object:

```
Shortener.shorten("https://rubyonrails.org")
```

The wrapper pattern could be seen as a degenerate case of the adapter pattern. With a wrapper object, we have both an application-level interface and the implementation encapsulation. However, to switch between implementations, we need to rewrite the wrapper code. Thus, a wrapper is an application-level *gateway* to implementation, as depicted in the following diagram:

Figure 3.3 – Wrapper pattern diagram

Using a wrapper, we localized all the code depending on a third-party vendor to a single class. This allows us to introduce changes and fixes much easier (for example, add exception handling, instrumentation, and logging). What about testability? Wrappers are usually much easier to deal with in tests than implementations. In our shortener example, performing actual API calls in tests is not desirable; so, we can use *stubs*:

```
test "with shortener" do
  Shortener.stub :shorten, "http://exml.test" do
    result = some_method_using_shortener
    assert result.include?("http://exml.test")
  end
end
```

We can go further and introduce *real adapters*. For example, we may want to disable URL shortening in some environments (such as staging). This can be achieved by adding a conditional check to the #shorten method, but such modification would violate the single responsibility principle.

We can do better and adapterize our shortener:

```
class Shortener
  class << self
    attr_writer :backend
    delegate :shorten, to: :backend
    def backend
      @backend ||= BitlyBackend.new
    end
  end
  class BitlyBackend
   # …
  end
  class NoOpBackend
    def shorten(url) = url
  end
end
```

Now we can use a custom implementation in different environments, as in the following example:

```
# config/environments/staging.rb
Shortener.backend = Shortener::NoOpBackend.new
```

A question may arise: aren't we overengineering here? No, we aren't. As soon as we face the requirement of using different implementations in different environments (even non-production ones), using adapters is justified. Otherwise, wrappers are good enough.

In this chapter, we, for the first time, went through the process of refactoring for maintainability. Step by step, we improved the quality of our code by utilizing design patterns. Note that we introduced breaking changes only in the first step. This is an important principle of *gradual refactoring*: localizing the code under refactoring first and subsequently improving its quality in isolation. We will follow this principle in the rest of the book.

Summary

In this chapter, you got familiar with Rails components such as Active Job and Active Storage and the architectural patterns used by them. You've learned how adapters help us to decouple application code from particular functionality providers. You've learned about how plugins allow us to extend the application functionality without interfering with other code.

You've learned about important characteristics of code, such as flexibility, extensibility, and testability, and how to improve them using the aforementioned patterns. You also learned about the process of gradual refactoring and its key principles.

In the next chapter, we will finish exploring the classic Rails way by looking at its controversial patterns and techniques, such as callbacks and global state objects.

Questions

1. What is serialization, and how does Active Job benefit from using it?
2. What is the difference between an adapter and a plugin?
3. What is the difference between a wrapper and an adapter?
4. What is the key principle of gradual refactoring?

Exercises

Without looking into the Rails source code, try to build an inline Active Job adapter (which performs jobs right after they have been enqueued). Then, think about how to implement an `#enqueue_at` functionality with pure Ruby.

Further reading

- *Gem Check. Writing better Ruby gems checklist*: `https://gemcheck.evilmartians.io/`
- *Polished Ruby Programming, Jeremy Evans* (*Chapter 8, Designing for Extensibility*): `https://www.packtpub.com/product/polished-ruby-programming/9781801072724`

## 4

Rails Anti-Patterns?

In this chapter, we will touch on the hot topic of the Rails way controversy. Being almost a 20-year framework, Ruby on Rails has gotten its portion of criticism (it's doubtful that software used by millions would get only positive feedback). We select the most debated Rails features and discuss how to make friends (not foes) with them. We will start by discussing **Action Controller** and **Active Record** callbacks. Then, we will move on to **Rails concerns**. Finally, we look at different examples of using global state in Rails applications.

We will cover the following topics:

- Callbacks, callbacks everywhere
- Concerning Rails concerns
- On global and current states

This chapter teaches you how to use these debated techniques mindfully and what alternatives to consider when an application outgrows the Rails way. From the perspective of layered architecture, the considered features can quickly turn into anti-patterns, since they tend to cross the boundaries between layers and lead to code that attracts many responsibilities (some of the patterns described in this chapter encourage developers to write code violating the single responsibility principle (or separation of concerns).

In other words, using these patterns leads to code with many responsibilities). Thus, the goal of this chapter is to learn how to prepare the code base to be layering-ready.

Technical requirements

In this chapter and throughout this book, the code given in code blocks is designed to be executed on Ruby 3.2 and Rails 7. Many of the code examples will work on earlier versions of the aforementioned software. You will find the code files on GitHub at `https://github.com/PacktPublishing/Layered-Design-for-Ruby-on-Rails-Applications/tree/main/Chapter04`.

Callbacks, callbacks everywhere

The callback functionality backs most Rails entities (controllers, models, channels, and so on). What is a callback? A **callback** is a piece of code executed when an operation is performed on the object. The execution of callbacks happens indirectly – that is, the operation only provides hooks but has zero knowledge of which callbacks are attached to it and their purposes.

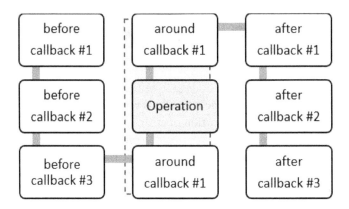

Figure 4.1 – The execution of an operation with callbacks

Callbacks might remind you of the plugin-based architecture we discussed in *Chapter 3, More Adapters, Less Implementations*, but on a micro-scale (defined within a single Ruby class). Although there are similarities, there is a crucial difference between these two concepts – unlike plugins, callbacks don't have to implement a particular interface, and they have no limits, neither technically nor conceptually. That makes them both powerful and dangerous.

Let's see how these properties express themselves in Rails controllers and models.

Callbacks under control (and in controllers)

Callbacks can help to move aside secondary or utilitarian functionality from an operation and only leave in the function's body what matters the most – its core purpose. In other words, if we think of callbacks as ad hoc middleware (see *Chapter 1, Rails as a Web Application Framework*, for the middleware pattern), we can benefit from using them. This type of thinking applies perfectly to Rails controllers.

Let's consider an example controller class – a typical resourceful Rails controller for the Post resource – and its #update action, responsible for modifying posts:

```
class PostsController < ApplicationController
  before_action :authenticate!
  before_action :load_post, only: [:show, :update]
  after_action :track_post_view, only: [:show]

  def update
```

```
      if @post.update(post_params)
        redirect_to @post
      else
        render action: :edit
      end
    end

    private
    def load_post = @post = Post.find(params[:id])

    def track_post_view
      # for example, enqueue a background job from here
    end
  end
```

The #update action only contains the code required to perform the actual record modification and generate a response, but the whole execution consists of the following phases:

1. Authenticating a user (before_action :authenticate!).

2. Looking up a post record in the database (before_action :load_post).

3. Performing the update operation (@post.update).

4. Preparing the response (redirect or render).

The first is an *action guard* (authentication and authorization are typical examples). The second one is responsible for data preloading. Only the latter two are essential for this action (#update action); thus, they're defined within the #update method.

We also have an after-action callback for the #show action (#track_post_view), but the #show method itself is missing. How so? We rely on the implicit behavior for this action – rendering the posts/show template.

Since preliminary checks and data loading happen within callbacks, we don't need to define the method itself. However, having an empty #show method would be nice to indicate which actions are available in this controller.

Without callbacks, we would have to write our actions like this:

Show action

```
def show
  authenticate!
  @post = Post.find(params[:id])
  track_post_view
end
```

Update action

```
def update
  authenticate!
  @post = Post.find(params[:id])
  if @post.update(post_params)
    redirect_to @post
  else
    render action: :edit
  end
end
```

The amount of action methods code got doubled and the code duplication increased, and that's just by unwrapping the callbacks defined in the `PostsController` class. Most applications define callbacks in the base controller class too.

While controller-specific callbacks usually deal with action requirements and data preloading, callbacks defined in the `ApplicationController` class (and other base classes) usually prepare the execution context for the current request. The following is an example of such context definitions – setting the current user's local and time zone for every request:

```
class ApplicationController < ActionController::Base
  around_action :with_current_locale
  around_action :with_current_tz, if: :current_user

  private

  def with_current_locale(&)
    locale = params[:locale] || current_user&.locale ||
      I18n.default_locale
    I18n.with_locale(locale, &)
  end

  def with_current_tz(&)
    Time.use_zone(current_user.time_zone, &)
  end
end
```

The critical rule for *contextual callbacks* is that deleting them shouldn't break the controllers inherited from the application controller. In other words, callbacks shouldn't introduce hidden dependencies.

One example of a hidden dependency is a global authentication (or authorization) callback:

```
class ApplicationController < ActionController::Base
  before_action :authenticate_user!
```

```
  private
  def authenticate_user!
    current_user || redirect_to(login_path)
  end

  def current_user
    # …
  end
end
```

Now, imagine that we decided to make some posts accessible to anonymous users. To accomplish that, we must modify the *callback chain* for a particular action by using the #skip_before_action method:

```
class PostsController < ApplicationController
  skip_before_action :authenticate!, only: [:show]

  def show
    authenticate! unless @post.is_public?
  end
end
```

Skipping a callback introduces the dependency on the internals of the parent class. Before this change, we might only depend on the presence of the current user, but now our code also depends on the actual method name and the callback, which guarantees the presence of the user.

For now, we can afford to skip a callback, but what if we add a new global callback, which relies on successful authentication? For example, we may want to add page view tracking functionality to every page:

```
class ApplicationController < ActionController::Base
  before_action :authenticate_user!
  after_action :track_page_view

  private
  def track_page_view
    current_user.track_page_view!(request.path)
  end
end
```

This addition will result in a NoMethodError exception for the posts#show action for public posts. To resolve it, we will have to either modify the #track_page_view code or add skip_after_action to the PostsController class.

Another option here is to add `if:  :current_user` to the `after_action` call. Either way, skipping a callback down the ancestor chain can trigger a chain reaction of modifications in parent classes. Lucky you if you have decent test coverage to catch them all before pushing code to production.

A similar problem with hidden dependencies can occur when callbacks are not scoped to specific actions (via the `only:` option). If that's the case, adding new actions to a controller class (explicitly or by including modules) can result in unexpected behavior or failures.

Apart from the aforementioned pitfalls, controller action callbacks are safe to use since they are only executed in the HTTP layer, and controller-specific callbacks are only triggered by a limited and small number of operations (HTTP requests). However, the deeper callbacks lie in the architecture layer hierarchy, the more dangerous they can be.

For example, callbacks defined in models can be triggered by various interactions and different layers; losing control of them is easy. Let's move on to the dark side of Rails callbacks and discuss how they affect Active Record models.

Active Record callbacks go wild

Similarly, as controller callbacks are hooked into the request handling phases, model-level callbacks are injected into an object's life cycle events. Unlike controllers, which only have three callback types for a single event (`before_action`, `around_action`, and `after_action`), Active Record provides 19 (nineteen!) different callbacks. You can list them all by looking at the following constant:

```
p ActiveRecord::Callbacks::CALLBACKS
#=> [:after_initialize, :after_find, :after_touch, :before_validation,
:after_validation, :before_save, :around_save, :after_save, :before_
create, :around_create, :after_create, :before_update, :around_update,
:after_update, :before_destroy, :around_destroy, :after_destroy,
:after_commit, :after_rollback]
```

You can go far in project development in Ruby on Rails by simply dropping callbacks into model classes. No additional abstractions or modifications in other application layers are required – it's as easy as that!

Let's consider a canonical example of using Active Record callbacks – sending welcome emails to new users:

```
class User < ApplicationRecord
  after_commit :send_welcome_email, on: :create

  private
  def send_welcome_email
    UserMailer.welcome(self).deliver_later
  end
end
```

With just a few lines of code, we've implemented a product feature. We don't even need to know when and how `User.create(params)` is called; we're assured that the email will be sent. So, let's move on to the next feature!

As our application evolves, new use cases appear, such as analytics or CRM software integrations, and prepopulating default data for new users. We want to stay productive, so we will use model callbacks again and again:

```
class User < ApplicationRecord
  after_create :generate_initial_project
  after_commit :send_welcome_email, on: :create
  after_commit :send_analytics_event, on: :create
  after_commit :sync_with_crm
end
```

Then, we are likely to introduce new concepts to our models, such as roles and privacy settings, which can affect the existing callback behavior. So, we will introduce conditions:

```
class User < ApplicationRecord
  after_create :generate_initial_project, unless: :admin?
  after_commit :send_welcome_email, on: :create
  after_commit :send_analytics_event,
               on: :create, if: :tracking_consent?
  after_commit :sync_with_crm
end
```

Eventually, the object life cycle becomes so entangled that it's hardly possible to predict the consequences of a single `User.create(params)` call.

With each added callback, the level of indirection grows, thus making the code base more error-prone – a change in one place can affect the other parts. From an architectural point of view, attaching side effects mixes new responsibilities into model classes, blending abstractions together (we discussed this problem in *Chapter 2, Active Models and Records*).

Another downside is test performance degradation – callbacks are executed whenever you create a record, but for most tests, you don't need all the side effects to take action. Want to skip a specific callback in a particular context? Different callbacks in different contexts? Everything is possible – just drop a few virtual attributes to control the callback execution. (And good luck with such code).

For example, let's skip the welcome email and interact with CRM independently:

```
class User < ApplicationRecord
  attr_accessor :skip_welcome_email, :skip_crm_sync
  after_create :generate_initial_project, unless: :admin?
  after_commit :send_welcome_email,
```

```
                on: :create, unless: :skip_welcome_email
    after_commit :send_analytics_event,
                on: :create, if: :tracking_consent?
    after_commit :sync_with_crm, unless: :skip_crm_sync
  end
```

Introducing new logical branches, as demonstrated in the preceding code, is like trying to use a band-aid to keep together broken bones – it is only helpful in the short term (i.e., to reach a hospital). For the long haul, more radical interventions are required to keep the code base healthy.

Since complexity grows with an increase in the number of callbacks and their conditions, a straightforward optimization is apparently to extract callbacks from the model. Some developers even advocate for avoiding model callbacks altogether. But where should we put the corresponding logic? To answer this question, let's try to categorize model callbacks first.

Transformers and utility callbacks

The variety of Active Record model callbacks you can meet in the wild deserves its own book or even an encyclopedia. For the purpose of this section, let's consider only the most common exemplars. Our goal is to devise a method of scoring model callbacks on a scale from *0* (*keep away from models*) to *5* (*good to keep in models*).

First, we'll take a look at **transforming callbacks**, or callbacks that modify data to be persisted. Such callbacks are usually used to populate default or computed values.

Let's consider a Post model with some transformer callback examples:

```
class Post < ApplicationRecord
  before_validation :compute_shortname, on: :create
  before_validation :squish_content, if: :content_changed?
  before_save :set_word_count, if: :content_changed?
  validates :short_name, :content, :word_count,
            presence: true

  private
  def compute_shortname
    self.short_name ||= title.parameterize
  end

  def squish_content
    content.squish!
  end

  def set_word_count
    self.word_count = content.split(/\s+/).size
```

```
      end
  end
```

In this example, we will use callbacks to provide a default value for the `#short_name` attribute during the post creation and calculate the number of words whenever the post contents change. Both attributes are required; hence, ensuring their presence in the model itself is a good way to go – I give these callbacks 5 out of 5.

In the preceding snippet, we also have a **normalization callback** – `#squish_content` (which removes unnecessary white space). Content is generated by users; thus, its value is *user input*, and handling input goes beyond the model layer's responsibility. However, without normalization in place, we will have to add a validation to ensure that the content's format is correct.

That sounds like a massive overhead with minimal value to maintain the code base, or *refactoring just for the sake of refactoring*. So, I give this normalization callback 4. By the way, Rails 7.1 introduced a new `.normalizes` API to declare attributes normalization rules without messing with callbacks:

```
class Post < ApplicationRecord
  normalizes :content, with: -> { _1.squish }
end
```

The new normalization interface can make normalization callbacks obsolete. Still, we have other use cases for callbacks. Let's continue exploring our example.

The `word_count` attribute can also be seen as an example of **denormalization**. That leads us to the second callbacks category – **technical/utility callbacks**. Such callbacks are added to solve some technical problems – for example, to help with caching or improve performance.

Usually, utility callbacks are defined by the framework or third-party Active Record extensions. Let's consider the `Comment` model representing comments on posts (backed by the `Post` model defined previously):

```
class Comment < ApplicationRecord
  belongs_to :post, touch: true, counter_cache: true
end
```

Although we haven't defined any callbacks, the `belongs_to` association added at least a couple for us. Here is the explicit version of the same class:

```
class Comment < ApplicationRecord
  belongs_to :post

  after_save { post.touch }
  after_create do
    Post.increment_counter(:comments_count, post_id)
  end
```

```
  after_destroy do
    Post.decrement_counter(:comments_count, post_id)
  end
end
```

We will touch (update the `updated_at` value) a post to bust the corresponding cache (for example, cached view partials or JSON responses). Keeping the current comments count in the post record (as `posts.comments_count`) helps us avoid expensive `SELECT COUNT(*)` queries. Thus, both features (caching and counter denormalization) are performance-oriented. On the other hand, we can see how particular use cases *leak* into the model. The responsibility is diluted briefly. But, again, as with normalization callbacks, we can afford it; it can bring significant value (in this case, a performance boost) with the least possible amount of work. So, 4 out of 5.

> **What a gem – activerecord-slotted_counters**
>
> On a larger scale, updating counter caches can result in noticeable lock contention at the database level. For example, when dozens of comments per second are created for the same post, all transactions with counter cache updates (triggered by callbacks) would *fall in line*, trying to acquire access to the same database record. The **Active Record Slotted Counters** library (`https://github.com/evilmartians/activerecord-slotted_counters`) provides an elegant solution to reduce this contention by spreading the counter value across multiple database rows in a dedicated table. This approach can help you to stay in the comfort zone of Rails callbacks for a longer time (but not forever).

Operations and event handlers

Let's go back to our `User` class and see what kind of callbacks we have there:

```
class User < ApplicationRecord
  after_create :generate_initial_project, unless: :admin?
  after_commit :send_welcome_email, on: :create
  after_commit :send_analytics_event,
               on: :create, if: :tracking_consent?
  after_commit :sync_with_crm
end
```

All four callbacks describe additional **operations** to be executed when a new user is created, or an existing one is updated. I would score all of them as 1 or 2 at most – that is, they'd better be moved away from the model class. Why so? From the layered Rails perspective, these operations *escape* from the model layer and cross the boundaries, thus resulting in the model becoming hyper-responsible (and turning into a God object). Let's for a moment forget about the layers and talk about how we can approach such callbacks without focusing on high matters.

The major indications of out-of-place model callbacks are conditions (`unless:  :admin?`) and collaboration with non-model objects (mailers, API clients, and so on), especially with **remote peers**. By *remote peers*, I mean peripheral *actors* (analytics and CRM integration) and non-adjacent domain entities.

Conditions usually imply some context. For example, the `generate_initial_project` callback is likely a part of the user registration process. Sending a welcome email is also a part of this process. Thus, we have two groups of callbacks in the `User` model – context-sensitive operations and remote peer communication. Let's talk about the possible ways to extract them from the model.

We will use the words *communication* and *remote peers* to describe the `send_analytics_event` and `sync_with_crm` callbacks, respectively. Alternatively, we can call them **event handlers**. An event handler reacts to a particular event type and performs a specific operation – for example, a `user.registered` (event), which tracks an analytics event (operation), and `user.updated` (event), which synchronizes with a CRM system (operation). Thinking about events is an important step toward better architecture. So, let's try to make it!

Pattern – event sourcing

Event-driven architecture shouldn't be confused with event sourcing. Event sourcing implies storing a domain object state as a stream of events (modifications), not as a single value. That allows us to navigate historical states and apply retroactive changes. So, event sourcing is about persistence, while event-driven architecture is about communication between system components.

An event-driven system includes publishers, subscribers, and a message bus (or broker). How they are represented in a Rails application depends on the chosen implementation (library). For demonstration purposes, we can build a simple pub/sub system on top of **Active Support Notifications** – the instrumentation framework built into Rails.

First, let's refactor the model and replace the CRM-related callback with the corresponding event publishing:

```
class User < ApplicationRecord
  after_commit do
    ActiveSupport::Notifications.instrument(
      "updated.user", {user: self}
    )
  end
end
```

Now, we need to create a subscriber and subscribe it to the corresponding event (`"updated.user"`):

```
class UserCRMSubscriber < ActiveSupport::Subscriber
  def updated(event)
    user = event.payload[:user]
    # …
```

```
    end
  end
```

Activate subscriber by attaching to "user" namespace

```
UserCRMSubscriber.attach_to :user
```

Congratulations! We just built a primitive event-driven system and used it to reduce the responsibility of our model class. Moreover, adding new event handlers can now be done by just creating a new subscriber.

> **What a gem – downstream/active_event_store**
>
> The `dowsntream` (https://github.com/bibendi/downstream) and `active_event_store` (P-Code) gems are twin gems twin gems that add event-driven capabilities to Rails applications (and in a *Rails-ish* way). They introduce the listener and event abstractions as well as provide testing utilities. Downstream uses an in-memory broker by default, while Active Event Store uses **Rails Event Store** (https://railseventstore.org).

Can we refactor the other three callbacks (`generate_initial_project`, `send_welcome_email`, and `send_analytics_event`) using events? Technically, we can. But, as we said before, user registration is a standalone business process, so we should consider representing it as a whole concept within the code base and not as a set of event subscribers.

Another question to consider is whether a model itself should be an event publisher. For example, if an event corresponds to a life cycle event (such as `"updated.user"`), keeping it in a model class doesn't cross the responsibility boundaries. In contrast, the presumed `"registered.user"` event goes beyond what the model should know.

This is what makes it necessary to introduce new abstractions to extract contexts from models. We will start talking about such upper-level layers in *Chapter 5, When Rails Abstractions Are Not Enough*. For now, let's consider a particular extraction pattern popular in Rails applications – moving logic into modules, or **Rails concerns**.

Concerning Rails concerns

In Ruby, we have classes and modules. Classes allow us to build object hierarchies via inheritance. Modules, technically, are just sets of methods (or mixins) that can be attached to classes or used independently. Semantically though, modules usually fall into one of the following categories:

- **Behavior**: This includes behavior modules that add new features or serve a particular purpose for the class. Examples of behavior modules include Enumerable and Comparable.

- **Builder**: These are modules extending Ruby class declaration capabilities via DSL – for example, Forwardable.

- **Static methods collection**: These are modules acting as containers for static methods.

- **Namespace**: These are modules that are used solely to isolate constants (classes, other modules).

This book will only talk about behavior modules (the first group), since they can be considered architectural elements.

Ruby on Rails, being an opinionated framework, treats modules in a special way. Instead of using pure Ruby modules, Rails advises using **concerns**. What is a Rails concern? A concern is an enhanced Ruby module; compared to plain modules, Rails concerns come with the additional functionalities:

- Concerns provide a DSL to simplify injecting standard Rails operations (defining callbacks, associations, and so on)

- Concerns support dependency resolution for included modules

To demonstrate these features, let's compare a concern with a plain Ruby module implementing the same functionality – so-called soft-deletion:

Rails concern

```
module SoftDeletable
  extend ActiveSupport::Concern
  include Discard::Model

  included do
    self.discard_column = :deleted_at
    belongs_to :deleted_by, class_name: 'User',
      optional: true
  end

  def discard(by: Current.user)
    self.deleted_by = by
    super()
  end
end
```

Ruby module

```
module SoftDeletable
  def self.included(base)
    base.include Discard::Model
```

```
      base.discard_column = :deleted_at
      base.belongs_to :deleted_by, class_name: 'User',
        optional: true
      base.include InstanceMethods
    end

    module InstanceMethods
      def discard(by: Current.user)
        self.deleted_by = by
        super()
      end
    end
  end
```

The `SoftDeletable` module defined previously (any version) can be used to add a soft deletion functionality to an Active Record model. The Rails version looks like a slice of a model class code (we only wrapped class-level code into the `included do...end` block); every line carries an application-specific meaning, and thus, it's easy to comprehend.

On the other hand, the Ruby version contains the code added solely to satisfy the Ruby object model – we had to extract instance methods into a separate module to include it after `Discard::Model` (since we rely on its `#discard` implementation).

So, the concerns simplify writing Ruby modules. But does using concerns improve your application design?

Remember that we're discussing controversial Rails patterns in this chapter, and concerns are at the top of the list.

> **Note**
> Although concerns can be used with all Rails abstractions, we will only consider models in this chapter.

Extracting behavior, not code

At the beginning of this section, we discussed Ruby modules and their types, but we haven't discussed using them (and, hence, concerns) for code deduplication and extraction. The reason is that refactoring for the sake of lexical code metrics satisfaction rarely helps to keep a code base under control. Nevertheless, in Rails projects, we can find something like this:

```
class Account < ApplicationRecord
  include Account::Associations
  include Account::Validations
  include Account::Scopes
```

```
    include Account::Callbacks
  end
```

As you can guess from the module names, each concern is responsible for a particular *slice* of the class definition – associations, validations, scopes, and so on. Although the class becomes *thin*, working with it gets harder – business-logic concepts are now spread across multiple files, and the conceptual cohesion is disrupted.

That was an example of overusing concerns. How can concerns be overused? It's probably because they are the only official Rails way to extract code from core entities (models and controllers). If an app/.../`concerns` folder exists, it will become full.

How can we reasonably fill the app/`models`/`concerns` folder? By extracting not code but behaviors. The distinctive features of behavioral modules are encapsulation and cohesiveness; they provide a concise and clear API that serves a single purpose (or being *atomic*).

For example, our `SoftDeletable` concern satisfies this definition, since it adds soft-deletion behavior to classes. Under the hood, `SoftDeletable` uses the `Discard` gem (`https://github.com/jhawthorn/discard`), but this implementation detail doesn't leak outside the concern. Thus, the provided behavior is owned by the application; it becomes a part of the application domain model – another sign of a good behavior extraction.

Extracting common atomic behaviors into concerns can help reduce the corresponding models' conceptual overhead. We do that a lot in Rails, sometimes without even realizing it. Whenever we use Active Record macros (built-in or provided by libraries), such as `has_secure_password`, `has_logidze`, and `has_ancestry`, we attach behaviors to models.

Concerns also help us to follow the **Don't Repeat Yourself** (**DRY**) principle, but that's not a necessary condition for extraction.

Non-shared concerns

Concerns are usually associated with common logic extraction from multiple models. However, even within a single model, we can detect multiple peripheral behaviors. Consider the following `User` model, for example:

```
class User < ApplicationRecord
  has_secure_password

  def self.authenticate_by(email:, password:)
    find_by(email:)&.authenticate(password)
  end
  # ...
end
```

We can clearly see the authentication behavior here, and it *doesn't seem part of the essence* of the User model. So, let's extract it into a concern:

User authentication concern

```
module User::Authentication
  extend ActiveSupport::Concern

  included do
    has_secure_password
  end

  class_methods do
    authenticate_by(email:, password:)
      find_by(email:)&.authenticate(password)
    end
  end
end
```

User class

```
class User < ApplicationRecord
  include Authentication
end
```

Note that we use the User class as a namespace for the Authentication concern. This way, we clearly indicate that this concern corresponds to a particular model. Moreover, we can store the concern in the app/models/user/authentication.rb file, thus keeping all the User related domain objects together.

Carving out a few lines of code into a separate file is overengineering, especially if the model is not bloated yet (let's say, contains less than a hundred lines of code). Of course, splitting a small class into tiny chunks is not as beneficial as refactoring God objects. Still, there is an advantage in early extraction – having concepts in isolated locations makes it harder to introduce dependencies between them accidentally.

Although extracting concerns can reduce the perceived complexity of a model and even encourage writing looser coupled code, the model's level of responsibility stays unchanged. So technically, it's still a single class with an enormous public (and private) interface. And that leads to consequences.

Concerns are still modules, with all the shortcomings

Concerns are Ruby modules; therefore, including them in a class injects their code. From a Ruby VM point of view, there is no significant difference between a class with dozens of included modules and a class that has the same code inlined. As a result, we must deal with the following caveats:

- **Lack of privacy**: Private methods are not private to other included concerns. Hence, you can make one module depend on another one, thus introducing a hidden (and sometimes even circular) dependency.

- **Naming is hard, and naming collisions are possible**: Leveraging a convention (for example, using namespace prefixes for methods) can help with this problem but can negatively affect readability.

- **Testing becomes more complicated**: Should you test a concern in isolation or test the concern's features for every model that includes it? Isolated tests are preferable, but can you guarantee that the concern's functionality won't interfere with a model or other included concerns code?

What a gem – with_model

Testing model concerns in isolation is not that simple if they rely on the database schema. The `with_model` (`https://github.com/Casecommons/with_model`) gem provides a convenient interface to create one-off Active Record models, backed by database tables for testing purposes.

Rails concerns also tend to contain callbacks with all the possible downsides but multiplied, since they are now scattered across the code base.

The key to avoiding the aforementioned problems is to keep concerns as isolated and self-contained as possible. There is a good rule of thumb for model concerns – if removing a concern from a model makes most of the tests involving this model fail, then this concern is an essential part of the logic. In other words, if a concern can't be detached, it's not a concern but just a piece of extracted code.

To sum up, Rails concerns can be efficiently used to separate the primary role of a class from peripherals (secondary support functionality). Isolating concepts should ideally be done at the object model level, not just by adding code to multiple files.

Now, let's see how we can extract objects from objects.

Extracting objects from objects

For demonstration, I picked a couple of concerns from real-life Ruby on Rails monoliths – `Contactable` and `WithMedia` (the code was slightly simplified and obfuscated).

Extracting models from models

Let's start with the `Contactable` module – a module that can be included in any User-like model to provide contact information-related features:

```ruby
module Contactable
  extend ActiveSupport::Concern

  SOCIAL_ACCOUNTS = %i[facebook twitter tiktok].freeze
  included do
    store_accessor :social_accounts, *SOCIAL_ACCOUNTS,
      suffix: :social_id

    validates :phone_number, allow_blank: true,
      phone: {types: :mobile}
    validates :country_code, inclusion: Countries.codes

    before_validation :normalize_phone_number,
      if: :phone_number_changed?
  End

  def region = Countries.region(country_code)

  def phone_number_visible?
    contact_info_visible && phone_number_visible
  end

  def normalize_phone_number
    return unless phone_number.present?
    self.phone_number = Phonelib.parse(phone_number).e164
  end
end
```

The concern tries to encapsulate the contact information aspect and is included in the `User` and `Company` models. We can imagine how it all started – first, it contained only phone numbers and country-related code; then, we added social network accounts to the mix.

Finally, visibility concerns were introduced. In total, at least five database table columns are involved, and more than a dozen API methods have been added. The concern clearly outgrew the notion of atomic behavior; let's promote it to a standalone model!

We can extract contactable columns into a separate table and use a `has_one` association to attach it to the original model:

New contact information model

```ruby
class ContactInformation < ApplicationRecord
  belongs_to :contactable, polymorphic: true

  SOCIAL_ACCOUNTS = %i[facebook twitter tiktok].freeze
  store_accessor :social_accounts, *SOCIAL_ACCOUNTS,
    suffix: :social_id

  validates :phone_number, allow_blank: true,
    phone: {types: :mobile}
  validates :country_code, inclusion: Countries.codes

  before_validation :normalize_phone_number,
    if: :phone_number_changed?

  # ...
end
```

Updated Contactable concern

```ruby
module Contactable
  extend ActiveSupport::Concern

  included do
    has_one :contact_information, as: :contactable,
      dependent: :destroy
  end
end
```

Keeping the concern around even if it consists of a single line of code is useful – the models still include `Contactable` behavior, and the association is an implementation detail. Moreover, we can add delegation for the most accessed APIs to make the refactored code *quack* like the previous one:

```ruby
module Contactable
  extend ActiveSupport::Concern

  included do
    has_one :contact_information, as: :contactable,
```

```
        dependent: :destroy
     delegate :phone_number, :country_code,
             to: :contact_information
   end
 end
```

This way, we make the `ContactInformation` model act as a **delegate object**.

Extracting value objects from models

Let's move on to the second example – the `WithMedia` concern. This concern contains methods to work with attached media objects (backed by Active Storage):

```
module WithMedia
  extend ActiveSupport::Concern

  SVG_TYPES = %w[
    image/svg
    Image/svg+xml
  ].freeze
  FONT_TYPES = %w[
    font/otf
    font/woff
  ].freeze

  included do
    has_one_attached :media

    delegate :video?, :audio?, to: :media
  end

  def font?() = FONT_TYPES.include?(media.content_type)
  def svg?() = SVG_TYPES.include?(media.content_type)
  # ... more <type>? methods
end
```

Active Storage provides objects encapsulating file information (`ActiveStorage::Attachment` and `ActiveStorage::Blob`) via `has_one_attached`, so we will use them as delegates. However, that's not enough for our application.

We need more granular control over media types, so we added a bunch of custom predicates and the corresponding constants. And now, all these methods and constants pollute the method sets of the models that include the concern. Can we avoid this? Yes, and we can use the **value object** pattern to do so.

> **Pattern – value object**
>
> A **value object** is an object that represents a simple entity and is distinguishable by the values of its properties. Immutability is often implied. Date, currency, and geometric points are typical examples of entities that can be represented as value objects. In Ruby, plain objects and structs that include the `Comparable` module are usually used to define value objects.

All the type predicates use only a single value from our media object – content type. So, let's extract a `MediaType` object. We can use the modern Ruby `Data.define` feature:

Media Type value object

```
MediaType = Data.define(:content_type) do
  SVG_TYPES = %w[…]
  FONT_TYPES = %w[…]
  include Comparable
  def <=>(other) = content_type <=> other.content_type

  def video?() = content_type.start_with?("video")
  def svg?() = SVG_TYPES.include?(content_type)
  def font?() = FONT_TYPES.include?(content_type)
  #
end

module WithMedia
  extend ActiveSupport::Concern
  included do
    has_one_attached :media
  end

  def media_type
    return unless media&.content_type

    MediaType.new(media.content_type)
  end
end
```

Value and delegate objects are examples of **downward extraction** – new concepts lie within the same abstraction layer (model or domain). This approach has an obvious limit in layered architecture – it's impossible to get rid of communication with upward layers. No matter how you extract one model from another, it cannot be done without carrying on the boundary violation.

We need **upward extraction** – adding an upper-level abstraction that won't cross the boundaries. We're just one chapter away from starting this journey, but let's first take a quick look at one more Rails peculiarity.

In the `SoftDeletable` example, we intentionally included a debatable piece of code – `Current.user`. That leads us to the third *anti-pattern* we want to talk about in this chapter – the **global state**.

On global and current states

Global state is evil – this is a typical phrase with regard to any usage of global variables or shared mutable state in software programs. It's hard to argue against this statement. Here are the most notable drawbacks of using globals:

- Global state introduces hidden dependencies between application components (and abstraction layers).

- Mutable global state makes code execution unpredictable, since it can be changed outside the current context. In multithreaded environments, that can lead to bugs due to race conditions.

- Understanding and testing code relying on globals is more complicated.

Doesn't this mean we should avoid global state as much as possible? The answer depends on what your goal is – building software products or creating ideal code (whatever that means for you). Ruby on Rails is a framework to build web products; thus, it can afford to use unpopular patterns to improve developers' productivity.

Let's see how Rails embraces global state and how we can keep it under control.

Current everything

The `Current` object from our example is a class defined as follows:

```
class Current < ActiveSupport::CurrentAttributes
  attribute :user
end
```

The interface provided by this `Current` class is like the one we can achieve with pure Ruby:

```
class Current
  class << self
    attr_accessor :user
  end
end
```

That is, we can write and read the value of the user attribute anywhere in the code base by using the `Current.user=` and `Current.user` methods, respectively. However, there are two crucial features of the `Current` attributes that make them more robust:

- The stored attribute values are thread-local (or fiber-local, depending on the execution model). Thus, race conditions between different execution contexts are impossible.

- The state is automatically reset at the end of every unit of work (a web request, background job, and so on). Hence, there is no state leakage.

So, technically, `Current` is only global within an execution context, not totally global. Still, that doesn't save us from potential global problems.

A typical usage example would be storing the current user object somewhere in the controller layer and access in the lower levels. Let's consider an example of tracking who is responsible for a record deletion:

Controller: setting current user

```
class ApplicationController < ActionController::Base
  before_action :set_current_user

  private
  def set_current_user
    Current.user = User.find_by(id: cookies[:user_id])
  end
end
```

Controller: calling a method which depends on the global state

```
class PostsController < ApplicationController
  def destroy
    post = Post.find(params[:id])
    post.destroy!
    redirect_to posts_path
  end
end
```

Model: using the global state

```
class Post < ApplicationRecord
  belongs_to :deleted_by, class_name: "User",
    optional: true
```

```
  def destroy
    self.deleted_by = Current.user
    super
  end
end
```

This example demonstrates the power of globals – the responsible user is encapsulated within the model class. Any component that can initiate a post deletion stays unchanged (the controller in the preceding example). However, our model class now depends on the execution environment – a higher-level concept from a layered architecture point of view. Let's see how it can play havoc in the future.

For performance reasons, we may decide to move post deletion to a background job, so we will update the controller's code as follows:

Updated controller class

```
class PostsController < ApplicationController
  def destroy
    post = Post.find(params[:id])
    PostDeleteJob.perform_later(post)
    redirect_to posts_path
  end
end
```

Job class

```
Class PostDeleteJob < ApplicationJob
  def perform(post) = post.destroy!
end
```

Moving the post.destroy! call to the background results in switching the execution context – all the Current information gets lost. Without decent integration test coverage, it might take a while before you realize that post.deleted_by is no longer being populated.

The missing global context is not the worst thing that could happen. Imagine a random value being stored in the Current instead. Curious about how that could happen? Let's consider another modification of the original example – deleting multiple posts at once and sending email notifications to the authors:

Controller: adding #destroy_all action

```
class PostsController < ApplicationController
  def destroy_all
    Post.where(id: param[:ids]).destroy_all
    redirect_to posts_path
```

```
    end
  end
```

Model: sending email notification after deleting

```
class Post < ApplicationRecord
  belongs_to :user
  belongs_to :deleted_by, class_name: "User",
    optional: true
  after_destroy :notify_author

  def destroy
    self.deleted_by = Current.user
    super
  end

  private
  def notify_author
    Current.user = user
    PostMailer.notify_deleted(post)
  end
end
```

Mailer: uses Current as a target user

```
Class PostMailer < ApplicationMailer
  default to: -> { Current.user.email }
  def notify_deleted(post)
    # ...
  end
end
```

The #destroy_all method is equal to calling #destroy on all found records consecutively – that is, Post.destroy_all == Post.all.map(&:destroy). Hence, overwriting the Current.user value in the after_destroy callback results in data inconsistency – the *deleter* is not the actual user performing the action; instead, it's the author of the post deleted in the previous iteration step.

Both demonstrated problems could be eliminated if we replace Current with explicit passing of all the dependencies (only the relevant parts of the Post class are shown):

```
class Post < ApplicationRecord
  def destroy_by(user: nil)
    self.deleted_by = user
```

```
      destroy
    end

    private
    def notify_author
      PostMailer.notify_deleted(user, post)
    end
  end
end
```

Now that our model doesn't depend on the execution environment, there are no more circular dependencies.

Switching from #destroy to #destroy_by can be expensive in terms of refactoring (since #destroy is a framework API and can be used in many places) – well, enforcing boundaries is not free, but it always pays off in the end.

Conceptually, Current attributes have three design flaws:

- Values can be written and read from anywhere, and no ceremony is required

- Reading unset values is possible (the result value would be nil)

- The same attribute can be written multiple times during the lifetime of the execution context

We can approach the multiple writes problem by using the Current.set method instead of attribute accessors. For example, we can fix the Post#notify_author like this:

```
def notify_author
  Current.set(user:) do
    PostMailer.notify_deleted(post)
  end
end
```

This workaround only works if we can ensure that no code within the block relies on the previous value of Current.user. However, we cannot give such guarantees due to the first downside.

A combination of conventions and, probably, code linters can help to keep Current usage under control. Here is an example set of rules to enforce:

- Keep the number of Current attributes as small as possible

- Always write attributes once within the same execution context

- Only write within the small number of abstraction layers (for example, only inbound layers)

- Only read within the small number of abstraction layers (and never from models)

> **What a gem – dry-effects**
>
> The `dry-effects` gem (`https://dry-rb.org/gems/dry-effects`) is an implementation of algebraic effects for Ruby. Putting aside the academics, you can use the *Reader* effect to pass context implicitly from upper to lower abstraction layers. Unlike `Current` attributes, working with an effect requires attaching a behavior (including a Ruby module), and there are separate writer and reader behaviors, so you always know how exactly a given object depends on global state. Finally, Reader prevents you from reading unset values by raising an exception, which is one less problem to worry about.

Summary

In this chapter, you learned about the Ruby on Rails trade-offs introduced by such design patterns as callbacks, Rails concerns, and `Current` attributes. You learned about different types of callbacks used in Rails controllers and models and how to assess their effect on maintainability. You got familiar with event-driven architecture and how it can be used to untangle models' responsibilities.

You learned how Rails concerns differ from Ruby modules and how they can be used to extract behaviors from models. You learned the limitations of splitting classes into models and how extracting domain objects can be used as an alternative approach to refactoring models. You also learned about the downsides of having global state and how to minimize them.

In the next chapter, we will take the first step toward new abstraction layers by introducing service objects.

Questions

1. What do callbacks and plugins have in common, and what are the differences?
2. How does having many callbacks in models affect test performance?
3. What are the key components of event-driven architecture?
4. What are the differences between plain Ruby modules and Rails concerns?
5. What are the key features of value objects?
6. What are the drawbacks of having a global state in an application?

Exercises

In the *Concerning Rails concerns* section of this chapter, we introduced a framework to evaluate a Rails concern's level of isolation (the drop and count failed tests ratio). Try to apply this technique to some of the concerns in your application. For concerns that didn't pass the test, think about possible refactoring strategies.

5

When Rails Abstractions Are Not Enough

In this chapter, we conclude our *Rails Way* research and prepare to enter the world of abstractions. First, we will discuss the limitations of the Rails MVC-based architecture layout, which lead to either controller- or model-layer bloats—an ever-increasing number of lines of code and growing conceptual overhead. Then, we'll take off the Rails Way and add *S* to the equation—*services*.

We will discuss how services can help in keeping controllers and models thin but, at the same time, turn into a chaotic or poor abstraction layer. Finally, we will discuss how breaking services further into more specialized abstractions could help keep the code base in a healthy state and how to design such abstractions following the layered architecture principles.

We will cover the following topics:

- The curse of fat/thin controllers and thin/fat models
- Generic services and granular abstractions
- Layered architecture and abstraction layers

The goal of this chapter is to define a conceptual framework for identifying abstraction layers in Ruby on Rails applications, which we will use in the second part of this book.

Technical requirements

In this chapter and all chapters of this book, the code given in code blocks is designed to be executed on Ruby 3.2 and Rails 7. Many of the code examples will work on earlier versions of the aforementioned software.

You will find the code files on GitHub at `https://github.com/PacktPublishing/Layered-Design-for-Ruby-on-Rails-Applications/tree/main/Chapter05`.

The curse of fat/thin controllers and thin/fat models

Controllers and models are two core abstractions in Ruby on Rails. If an application follows the Rails Way, most of the business logic code goes to either one of these two. Why so? Because that is all Rails gives us out of the box.

Having as few abstractions as possible has a significant benefit—a smooth learning curve. Every application looks the same; you can start working on a new code base quickly. Though, this is only a theory. In reality, having an insufficient number of abstractions (two, in our case—controllers and models) leads to a situation where business logic is distributed between the abstractions in an unpredictable manner.

Some applications prefer to keep logic in controllers, while others put everything into models. The latter approach, also known as **thin controllers and fat models**, became a best practice in the Rails community. But still, many applications follow it sparingly, and fat controllers appear there, then here. Therefore, the lack of abstractions results in a lack of consistency in terms of style in the code base, which negatively impacts maintainability and the developers' experience.

Even if we can enforce best practices and choose the main abstraction layer to keep our logic in, we would face the problem of responsibility bloat (and source code bloat usually comes along). Thus, there is no way to efficiently grow the application without introducing new, beyond-Rails concepts.

We have discussed over-responsible (or God) models in previous chapters; in the rest of this section, we will consider an example refactoring process of going from fat controllers and thin models to thin controllers and fat models and beyond.

From fat controllers to fat models

Before we dig deep into the Ruby code, let's try to figure out what is, in general, wrong with putting a lot of logic into controllers.

For that, we need to recall that the controller layer is an inbound layer, as we call it (see *Chapter 1, Rails as a Web Application Framework*). This means the controller layer *wraps* all other layers in the application, being an entry point for user actions. Controllers' primary responsibilities are building execution contexts (for example, authentication) and transforming Rack requests into business actions.

That's enough already; adding more responsibility would clearly violate the **separation of concerns** (**SoC**) principle and turn our abstraction into nothing but an interface. Good abstraction should include both generalization and simplification. Putting arbitrary code into controllers contradicts both.

A fat controller example

Let's consider a fictional GitHub Analytics application and one of its controllers that is responsible for handling webhooks and tracking user comments and pull requests:

Controller action code

```
class GithooksController < ApplicationController
  rescue_from JSON::ParserError do
    head :unprocessable_entity
  end

  def create
    verify_signature!
    event = parse_event(request.raw_params)
    case event
    in type: "issue", action: "opened",
       issue: {user: {login:}, title:, body:}
      track_issue(login, title, body)
    in type: "pull_request", action: "opened",
       pull_request: {
         user: {login:}, base: {label:}, title:, body:
       }
      track_pr(login, title, body, label)
    end
    head :ok
  end
end
```

We have a single action (#create), in which we verify params, parse input, and process it depending on the shape of the data. Some logic is extracted into helper methods, defined next:

Controller helper methods

```
def verify_signature!
  # Let's skip the payload signature verification
  # code, since it's irrelevant to our refactoring
end

def parse_event(payload)
  JSON.parse(payload, symbolize_names: true)
end

def track_issue(login, title, body)
  User.find_by(gh_id: login)
      &.issues.create!(title:, body:)
end
```

```
   def track_pr(login, title, body, branch)
     User.find_by(gh_id: login)
         &.pull_requests.create!(title:, body:, branch:)
   end
 end
```

We can see that each helper method is concise and single-purposed (though the purposes are different: from data parsing to domain object creation). We can imagine that these methods were extracted from the action method for readability.

How do we evaluate the maintainability of this code? One option is to perform the churn/complexity analysis we introduced in *Chapter 2, Active Models and Records*. Another option is the *specification test* that I introduce next.

Let's think about how we will test the functionality of the previous action. Without writing actual tests, we can define the structure of the test suite (or specification) as follows (using RSpec: https://rspec.info):

```
describe "/callbacks/github" do
  context "when event is pull_request"
  context "when event is issue"
  context "when user is not found"
  context "when signature is missing"
  context "when signature is invalid"
  context "when payload is not JSON"
end
```

This is the minimal number of tests we need to cover all the logical branches in the GithooksController#create action. Looking at the specification, we can see which scenarios correspond to our abstraction layer (that is, its primary responsibilities) and which are foreign. For example, testing signatures could be seen as authentication, which belongs to controllers.

All is good here. What about checking different event types and a user presence? These tests verify the business-logic operation and have nothing to do with the controller layer. Such tests (as well as the code they test) are highly coupled with the involved entities (models) from lower layers.

Also, request tests are harder to write and slower to execute; we need to populate the context (users, signatures) and perform actual HTTP requests (more precisely, calling the Rails Rack application). In general, the higher the abstraction lies in the layer hierarchy, the more expensive the tests become.

Specification test

We can formulate the specification test as follows: if the specification of an object (represented as tests) describes features beyond the primary responsibility of the object's abstraction layer, such features should be extracted into lower layers.

Refactoring the example controller following the thin controllers, fat models principle

Let's refactor the `GithooksController` class following the *thin controllers, fat models* principle, and see if it helps here. We can pick the `User` model to host the handling GitHub events logic and add a value object to represent webhook events:

GitHubEvent value objects

```
class GitHubEvent
  def self.parse(raw_event)
    parsed = JSON.parse(raw_event, symbolize_names: true)
    case parsed[:type]
    when "issue"
      Issue.new(
        user_id: parsed.dig(:issue, :user, :login),
        action: parsed[:action],
        **parsed[:issue].slice(:title, :body)
      )
    when "pull_request"
      PR.new(
        user_id: parsed.dig(:pull_request, :user, :login),
        action: parsed[:action],
        branch: parsed.dig(:pull_request, :base, :label),
        **parsed[:pull_request].slice(:title, :body)
      )
    end
  rescue JSON::ParserError
    nil
  end

  Issue = Data.define(:user_id, :action, :title, :body)
  PR = Data.define(
    :user_id, :action, :title, :body, :branch)
end
```

The `GithubEvent.parse` method takes raw JSON input from a GitHub webhook and transforms it into a domain-specific model (`GitHub::PR` or `GitHub::Issue`), as follows:

User class

```
class User < ApplicationRecord
  def handle_github_event(event)
```

```
    case event
    in GitHubEvent::Issue[action: "opened", title:, body:]
      issues.create!(title:, body:)
    in GitHubEvent::PR[
      action: "opened", title:, body:, branch:
    ]
      pull_requests.create!(title:, body:, branch:)
    end
  end
end
```

With the preceding additions to the model layer, our controller class now looks like this:

```
class GithooksController < ApplicationController
  def create
    verify_signature!

    event = GitHubEvent.parse(request.raw_post)
    return head :unprocessable_entity if event.nil?

    user = User.find_by(gh_id: event.user_id)
    user&.handle_github_event(event)

    head :ok
  end
end
```

The `GithooksController` class became much thinner. Did it become better? Sure—it now delegates some responsibilities to the model layer; for example, parsing the GitHub webhook payload and handling this event.

What about our specification test? We can leave only one example to test the happy path, issue, or pull request event since the controller no longer cares about particular event types. And that's it. We still need to test all the edge cases (invalid payload; missing user).

Let's discuss the model-layer changes.

The `GitHubEvent::Issue` and `GitHubEvent::PR` are pure data containers; also, they don't leak any third-party (GitHub) details and provide an application-specific interface. However, the `GitHubEvent.parse` method is coupled with the webhook payload format, which is not a part of our domain model.

Since we don't have any custom abstraction layers yet, we're good to keep it under `app/models`. But we should remember that it introduces a reverse dependency (bottom-to-top), and every reverse dependency contributes to the price of future refactoring.

The `User#handle_github_event` method deals only with domain objects, so it doesn't escape to the upper layers. This is also good. The downside to adding this method is the growing responsibility of the model, which will likely result in a higher churn and an increase in the overall complexity of the class. Unless handling GitHub events is the user-related functionality in the application, extracting this code into a different object would be reasonable.

In *Chapter 4, Rails Anti-Patterns?*, we discussed the Rails Way of splitting large models into smaller concepts (concerns) and its potential drawbacks. Now, let's look at a different pattern—extracting **service objects**.

From fat models to services

Although the service object pattern is very popular in the Ruby on Rails community, you can hardly find a definition on which all developers would agree. Probably, the most common definition of a service object in Rails is that it is an object representing a single business operation and lying in between controllers and models.

The definition could be violated in many ways: some developers define multiple (though relevant) operations within the same service objects, and others invoke service objects from models (thus, going upward in the layers). Similarly, the definition could be stricter. For example, there is a common practice to make all service objects callable objects. A **callable object** is any object responding to the `.call` method (including, for instance, `Proc` and `Lambda` objects).

> **What a gem – interactor**
>
> Interactor (`https://github.com/collectiveidea/interactor`) is the most popular library that helps you to standardize service objects and provides utilities to combine them. Interactors implement the callable interface and return specific result objects containing status (success or failure) information in addition to arbitrary data.

Whether a service object should return a specific result object, arbitrary data, or nothing is another debatable question, which could affect the way service objects are used by different teams. Finally, the way service objects deal with exceptions is a kind of third dimension, which reflects the actual definition of a service object in a particular project.

> **What a gem – dry-monads**
>
> The `dry-monads` library (`https://dry-rb.org/gems/dry-monads`) is a collection of common monads for Ruby. With regards to service objects, monads could be used to streamline exception handling and simplify method call chaining by using monadic return values (by using the result monad).

As you can see, service objects in the Ruby on Rails world are extremely diverse. (That's what happens when the framework doesn't provide an out-of-the-box abstraction to solve common design problems.) For simplicity, let's stick to the base definition we gave previously and continue our demo refactoring.

First, let's introduce a base class for service objects:

```
class ApplicationService
  extend Dry::Initializer

  def self.call(...) = new(...).call
end
```

Irrespective of whether you use a gem or craft your own service objects, having a base class with a common interface and utilities is the first thing you need to do. That will help you to keep service objects' style uniform and simplify adding extensions in the future (for example, logging or instrumentation features). We call the base class `ApplicationService` to follow the Rails conventions and store it in the `app/services` folder.

In the previous example, we use the `dry-initializer` gem (https://dry-rb.org/gems/dry-initializer/) to provide a DSL for declaring the object parameters. Let's move on to the actual service object to see it in action.

We can extract our first service object from the `User#handle_github_event` method:

```
class User::HandleGithubEventService < ApplicationService
  param :user
  param :event

  def call
    case event
    in GitHubEvent::Issue[action: "opened", title:, body:]
      user.issues.create!(title:, body:)
    in GitHubEvent::PR[
      action: "opened", title:, body:, branch:
    ]
      user.pull_requests.create!(title:, body:, branch:)
    end
  end
end
```

Note that we use the `-Service` suffix for the service object class name. This way, we introduce a naming convention that mimics the Rails Way. Of course, it's not necessary to follow the Rails naming principles; you can choose your own rules.

For example, one common practice is to use `<subject><verb>` or `<subject><verb><object>` patterns for service objects, such as `User::HandleGitHubEvent` or `Post::Publish`. One thing is important: *you must have a convention*. Otherwise, it would be hardly possible to form an abstraction layer from a set of objects.

Why did we choose the Rails naming rules? Rails is built on top of conventions, and there is no better way to extend the framework than to follow these conventions. We want to come along with Rails, not fight against it.

Let's finish this refactoring step and use our service object in the controller:

```ruby
class GithooksController < ApplicationController
  def create
    verify_signature!

    event = GitHubEvent.parse(request.raw_post)
    return head :unprocessable_entity if event.nil?

    user = User.find_by(gh_id: event.user_id)
    User::HandleGithubEventService.call(user, event)

    head :ok
  end
end
```

From the controller's point of view, there are no significant changes. We can go further and move the user lookup logic into a service object, too. That would also make our service user-independent since it will rely only on the GitHub event as input:

```ruby
class HandleGithubEventService < ApplicationService
  param :event

  def call
    user = User.find_by(gh_id: event.user_id)
    return unless user

    case event
      # This part stays the same
    end
  end
end
```

Now, the controller is getting thinner:

```ruby
class GithooksController < ApplicationController
  def create
    verify_signature!

    event = GitHubEvent.parse(request.raw_post)
    return head :unprocessable_entity if event.nil?

    HandleGithubEventService.call(event)
    head :ok
  end
end
```

We not only reduced the amount of code in the `GithooksController#create` action but also decreased the number of responsibilities (and thus, the number of tests in the specification)—we don't deal with users anymore. Should we proceed and move the event parsing code to the service object? Let's leave this question for the last section of this chapter.

The service object pattern is the first aid to prevent controller and/or model bloat. So, is extracting service objects the way to go? Despite being widespread, this approach got its portion of criticism. Let's look at the dark side of `app/services` and discuss the potential evolutionary branches for services.

Generic services and granular abstractions

Services appear to be powerful the first time you use them. Not sure where to put code for yet another use case? Just create a file under `app/services`. As simple as that. We can even notice a tendency: developers discuss where to put certain code in the application's file hierarchy.

This thinking-in-folders ideology is fundamentally broken. First, it usually implies that in any unclear situation, just create a service. Secondly, although a file structure positively affects developer experience and should be treated with respect, the place of the code in the application must be driven by its *role*, and the role is defined by the abstraction layer the code belongs to. Developers should *think in abstractions, not folders* when designing new features or refactoring legacy code.

> ### Anemic models
> Overusing service objects could lead to a situation when models do not carry any business logic (beyond **object-relational mapping (ORM)** or data encapsulation). This phenomenon is called the **anemic model**. Anemic models are considered an anti-pattern since we eliminate all the benefits of the **object-oriented (OO)** approach in favor of procedural-style code (because most services are procedures).

Extracting everything into services erodes the conceptual cohesion of this intermediate layer. It turns into a bag of random objects, not an abstraction layer. In the worst-case scenario, each service is the thing; thus, the conceptual complexity is proportional to the number of classes in the app/ services folder.

Introducing conventions and standard interfaces could help in decreasing complexity, but the problem is that it's hardly possible to come up with a generic interface for all service objects. Services are different by nature; the only thing they likely have in common is that they act as mediators between inbound layers and model layers.

If we cannot turn services into good abstractions, what should we do with them? Let's consider a train station analogy (we're on *rails*, right?).

The app/services folder could be seen as a waiting room for code. Until a corresponding abstraction (*train*) arrives, the code could comfortably sit in the app/services folder. But keep in mind that space is limited, so don't overcrowd your waiting room.

The *waiting room* interpretation implies a very important rule: *don't start early with abstractions*. A good abstraction involves both generalization and simplification (for example, boilerplate reduction). And generalization requires a bit of *aging*—give your code design ideas some time to prove they're helpful. Otherwise, you may end up with a bad abstraction (which is worse than no abstraction).

Decomposing app/services into a handful—say, K—of well-defined abstractions oddly enough decreases the conceptual complexity: we only have K concepts compared to the previous N—the number of service objects.

In the second part of this book, we will consider some common abstractions present in most Ruby on Rails applications. However, each application is as unique as the abstraction layers that could be identified. Apart from learning by example, are there other techniques we can apply to better see the abstractions?

One thing that could help in pulling out abstraction layers is the **layered architecture** pattern.

Layered architecture and abstraction layers

So far, we've been using the terms *abstraction layers* and *layered architecture* interchangeably. Now, it's time to put everything back into place.

Layered architecture is an established term for the architectural pattern, which implies the separation of application components/functions into horizontal logical layers. The data flows in one direction, from top to bottom; thus, layers do not depend on the layers on top of them.

Let's look at a layered architecture diagram example:

Figure 5.1 – Layered architecture example

The preceding diagram demonstrates a four-layer architecture typical for applications following the **domain-driven design** (**DDD**) paradigm. Surprisingly, this architecture fits Ruby on Rails applications, too.

Let's describe each layer mentioned in the preceding diagram:

- **Presentation layer**: Responsible for handling user interactions and presenting the information to users (via the UI).

- **Application layer**: Organizes domain objects to fulfill required use cases.

- **Domain layer**: Describes entities, rules, invariants, and so on. This layer maintains the state of the application.

- **Infrastructure layer**: Consists of supporting technologies (databases, frameworks, API clients, and so on).

Now, let's have a look at the relationships between them:

- The arrows in the diagram show how the layers can communicate with each other. For example, the presentation layer can only access the application- and domain-layer objects, while the application layer can access the domain and infrastructure layers. Finally, the domain layer can only access the infrastructure layer.

- One of the main ideas of layered architecture is to keep the number of arrows small and, thus, isolate layers from each other. This idea naturally leads to loose coupling and improves the testability and reusability of code. However, if we reduce the number of arrows to the minimum (so that each layer can only communicate with the adjacent one), we can hit the *architecture sinkhole* problem.

  This problem occurs when data is simply proxied through layers with little (or zero) modification—in other words, the situation when we introduce objects just to fill a gap between layers.

This is layered architecture in a nutshell. How does it relate to abstraction layers?

In general, abstraction layers describe reusable code concepts hiding the underlying implementation details. We can have many abstraction layers in each architecture layer, but what we must not have is an abstraction crossing the architecture layer boundary. In other words, every abstraction layer must belong to a single architecture layer. This rule alone can help in evaluating existing abstractions and identifying new ones.

The following diagram demonstrates how we can correspond Rails abstraction layers to architecture layers:

Figure 5.2 – Rails abstraction layers versus architecture layers

Using the diagram and the previously defined rule, let's go back to our `GithooksController` refactoring example and try to move the webhook parsing (`GitHubEvent.parse`) to the service object:

Updated service class: now accepts a request object

```
class HandleGithubEventService < ApplicationService
  param :request

  def call
    event = GitHubEvent.parse(request.raw_post)
    return unless event

    user = User.find_by(gh_id: event.user_id)
    return unless user

    case event
      # This part stays the same
    end
  end
end
```

Updated controller class

```
class GithooksController < ApplicationController
  def create
    verify_signature!
```

```
    if HandleGithubEventService.call(request)
      head :ok
    else
      head :unprocessable_entity
    end
  end
end
```

Does the `HandleGithubEventService` service object still belong to the application architecture layer? Not anymore. As soon as we made it dependent on the request object, which is from the presentation layer, we introduced a reverse dependency (from the application layer to the presentation layer). Our service became conceptually broken.

What if we passed not the request object but the raw request body to the service—that is, `HandleGithubEventService.call(request.raw_post)`? Technically, the payload is just a string, so we do not leak any presentation-layer abstractions. On the other hand, whether input conversion is acceptable or all service object arguments must be prepared is a matter of the convention in use. So, it's up to the author of the code (my personal preference would be to pass parsed data to the application layer, so we can deal only with Ruby objects and avoid deserialization).

Is there room for a new abstraction responsible for request params transformation? Yes—it would be worth considering if we had more use cases.

We completed the gradual refactoring of a single controller action and even tried to over-refactor it. We learned about the power of service objects and the need for more granular abstractions. It doesn't mean that, eventually, all service objects will emerge from their cocoons into something beautiful. Web applications are living things, and new requirements constantly appear; there won't always be a matching abstraction. Thus, there will always be some yet-uncategorized objects residing in the application layer.

Summary

In this chapter, you learned about the limitations of the Rails MVC design. You practiced refactoring fat Rails controllers and models. You learned about the service object concept and how it can be used to encapsulate business operations in code to lighten controllers and models. You also learned about the potential downsides to the growing number of services and how pulling out more specialized abstractions can help. Finally, you learned about the relationship between the layered architecture and abstraction layers and how to use the former to separate abstractions.

In the next chapter, we will take a closer look at domain services and the possible abstractions that could be found in this group of objects.

Questions

1. What are the negative consequences of having a low number of abstraction layers?

2. What is a *specification test*, and how could it be used to detect code worth refactoring?

3. What is a service object? What is a callable object? Are all service objects also callable objects?

4. What are the main features of a *good abstraction*?

5. What are the four standard layers in layered architecture?

Part 2:
Extracting Layers from Models

In this part, we will focus on Rails models and their maintainability. We will discuss how to keep models responsible only for the application's domain logic by pulling off upper-level abstractions into separate abstraction layers.

This part has the following chapters:

6

Data Layer Abstractions

This chapter opens *Part 2* of the book, in which we will talk about the particular patterns in extracting abstraction layers. As we discussed in *Part 1*, growing Rails applications feel too cramped within model-controller-view boundaries; introducing new abstractions allows your code to *breathe freely*. We start with the Rails model layer and its core component—**Active Record**.

In *Chapter 2*, *Active Models and Records*, we learned that Active Record models are by design responsible for representing domain objects and communicating with the persistence engine. In this chapter, we will discuss the techniques for reducing the responsibility of Active Record by introducing new abstraction layers. First, we will discuss how to keep the query-building functionality organized via query objects. Then, we try to leverage Data Mapper ideas and use repositories for Active Record models.

We will cover the following topics:

- Using query objects to extract (complex) queries from models
- Separating domain and persistence with repositories

The goal of this chapter is to learn about domain-layer abstractions with the aim of reducing Active Record model bloat, as well as getting practice in turning design patterns into well-defined abstractions.

Technical requirements

In this chapter and all chapters of this book, the code given in code blocks is designed to be executed on Ruby 3.2 and Rails 7.1. Many of the code examples will work on earlier versions of the aforementioned software.

You will find the code files on GitHub at `https://github.com/PacktPublishing/Layered-Design-for-Ruby-on-Rails-Applications/tree/main/Chapter06`.

Using query objects to extract (complex) queries from models

Active Record provides an extensive API for querying database data. Without writing a pinch of SQL, you can achieve most of your data reading goals using the **fluent API** (a smart term for method chaining). In simple scenarios, the code is very easy to comprehend as it is read in plain English. Here is how we can load published posts ordered by their creation date (from newest to oldest):

```
Post.where(draft: false).order(created_at: :desc)

#=> SELECT * FROM posts WHERE draft = 'f'
   ORDER BY created_at DESC
```

In recent versions of Rails, even complex queries can be constructed solely with Active Record methods. Let's consider an example—loading a list of users whose posts published in the previous week have been bookmarked at least once:

```
User.with(
  bookmarked_posts: Post.
      .where(created_at: Date.current.prev_week.all_week)
      .where.associated(:bookmarks)
      .select(:user_id).distinct
).joins(:bookmarked_posts)

#=> WITH "bookmarked_posts" AS (
   SELECT DISTINCT "posts"."user_id"
   FROM "posts" INNER JOIN "bookmarks" …
) SELECT "users".* FROM "users"
   INNER JOIN "bookmarked_posts"
   ON "users"."id" = "bookmarked_posts"."user_id"
```

We can assume that the first query (loading published posts) is used in some controller and the second one (loading users with bookmarked posts) in a background job (for example, sending weekly email digests to these users). Let's further assume that we put the query-generation code (from the previous examples) right into a controller and a job class, respectively. How would this affect their maintainability?

One of the key maintainability characteristics is *churn rate* (see *Chapter 2, Active Models and Records*), or how often we need to change the code. Code modifications may be triggered by business logic changes—we can't avoid them. However, there are also modifications required to handle incompatible changes in the dependencies.

For example, we may introduce soft deletion to posts, thus changing the domain model logic. Such a change would require us to update the controller's query building code as follows:

```
Post.where(deleted_at: nil)
  .where(draft: false).order(created_at: :desc)
```

Prior to this change, the controller has no knowledge of whether we soft- or hard-deleted posts—it is out of its scope. Now, we have increased the coupling between the controller and the underlying domain.

Similar ad hoc query patches are likely to be required in other parts of the application's code base. There is a non-zero chance of missing one, and thus, letting bugs escape to production.

Another important characteristic of code is **testability**. Almost every method calls in an Active Record query chain represents a logic branching and, thus, should be covered by a test (ideally). Also, when querying code in a controller, we have to write slower integration tests, thus leading to longer test runs (which negatively affect productivity).

Finally, logic, as well as code duplication, might occur, which could lead to divergence in the future.

The more complex a query is, the more it affects the surrounding code's maintainability and thus the application stability. In Rails, there is a common pattern of moving complex queries into model class methods or scopes. Here is how we can refactor our queries:

Post class scopes

```
class Post < ApplicationRecord
  scope :ordered, -> { order(created_at: :desc) }
  scope :published, -> { where(draft: false) }
  scope :kept, -> { where(deleted_at: nil) }
  scope :previous_week, -> {
    where(created_at: Date.current.prev_week.all_week)
  }
end

Post.kept.published.ordered
```

We introduced named scopes and now can use them instead of explicit conditions. We can also use class methods, as in the following example, to move complex query construction into a model class:

User class method

```
class User < ApplicationRecord
  def self.with_bookmarked_posts(period = :previous_week)
    bookmarked_posts =
      Post.kept.public_send(period)
```

```
          .where.associated(:bookmarks)
          .select(:user_id).distinct
    with(bookmarked_posts:).joins(:bookmarked_posts)
  end
end

# Now we can use this query as follows
User.with_bookmarked_posts
```

Extracting queries into models can help with code deduplication and better isolation, but it turns the model class into a God object. It also increases the churn rate since the model becomes responsible for many different user-facing features, which are highly volatile.

Let's see how we can avoid bloating models by introducing a new abstraction layer—query objects.

Extracting query objects

`User.with_bookmarked_posts` is a good candidate for being extracted into a separate object. First, the method is self-contained and is not coupled with the model definition itself. Secondly, the logic is context-specific, that is, it's only used by a single (or a few) application component(s), and we should prefer to keep only generic logic in model classes.

So, let's move it as is into a new class—UserWithBookmarkedPostsQuery:

```
class UserWithBookmarkedPostsQuery
  def call(period = :previous_week)
    bookmarked_posts =
      Post.public_send(period)
          .where.associated(:bookmarks)
          .select(:user_id).distinct
    User.with(bookmarked_posts:).joins(:bookmarked_posts)
  end
end
```

Now we can use this object as follows:

```
UserWithBookmarkedPostsQuery.new.call
```

Congratulations – we've just extracted a query object from the model.

> **Pattern – query object**
>
> **A query object** is an object responsible for building a query (usually SQL, but not necessary) by using domain-level objects as input. Thus, the primary responsibility of a query object is to separate the persistence layer from the domain.

Even such a simple extraction is beneficial: we isolated a business logic concept and slimmed down the model; we can freely use all OOP patterns (such as method extraction) without worrying about potential conflicts with the model code. However, still, creating a standalone class is not enough to introduce a new abstraction layer.

An abstraction requires a signature or convention; it also should provide solutions to common problems (for instance, reducing boilerplate when creating new objects). Let's see how we can turn the pattern into a good abstraction by creating a base query class step by step.

From pattern to abstraction

Let's start with the signature. What API makes sense for query objects? These objects are single-purpose—they build and resolve a query against a data store. So, we need a single public interface method. Let's pick a good name for it.

In the previous example, we used the #call method. It's a common practice in Ruby and Rails to name the only API method call (a so-called callable interface). However, this naming poorly communicates the object's purpose; it's too generic. Let's use a more descriptive interface for our abstraction, such as #resolve:

```
class ApplicationQuery
  def resolve(...) = raise NotImplementedError
end
```

To make our signature complete, we need to decide on the public method parameters and return values. We have just two methods, #initialize (constructor) and #resolve. The arguments passed to a constructor should represent an initial state or context. Since we're building query objects for Active Record, a good initial state could be an Active Record relation object.

This would make it possible to apply a query object to any scope, not just Model.all. Similarly, the return value of the #resolve method should also be an Active Record relation so that we can modify it further with other query objects or Active Record methods. Let's update our base class according to these ideas:

```
class ApplicationQuery
  private attr_reader :relation
  def initialize(relation) = @relation = relation
  def resolve(...) = relation
end
```

What about the #resolve method arguments? We can use them to provide query parameters or control the query-building logic. Let's rewrite the UserWithBookmarkedPostsQuery class to inherit from ApplicationQuery and implement our common interface:

```
class UserWithBookmarkedPostsQuery < ApplicationQuery
  def resolve(period: :previous_week)
```

```
    bookmarked_posts = build_bookmarked_posts_scope(period)
    relation.with(bookmarked_posts:)
      .joins(:bookmarked_posts)
  end

  private

  def build_bookmarked_posts_scope(period)
    return Post.none unless Post.respond_to?(period)

    Post.public_send(period)
      .where.associated(:bookmarks)
      .select(:user_id).distinct
  end
end
```

And here is how we can use this updated query object:

```
UserWithBookmarkedPostsQuery.new(User.all).resolve
UserWithBookmarkedPostsQuery.new(User.where
  (name: "Vova")).resolve(period: :previous_month)
```

Since our #resolve method returns a relation object, we can re-write the latter example as follows:

```
UserWithBookmarkedPostsQuery.new(User.all).resolve
  (period: :previous_month).where(name: "Vova")
```

Notice that in most cases, we pass the same object to the constructor—User.all. We can reduce this boilerplate by adding a default value to the constructor:

Updated query object

```
class UserWithBookmarkedPostsQuery < ApplicationQuery
  def initialize(relation = User.all) = super(relation)
  # …
end
```

Updated usage example

```
UserWithBookmarkedPostsQuery.new.resolve
```

Finally, we can also get rid of the .new call by adding a class-to-instance delegation:

```
class ApplicationQuery
  class << self
```

```
      def resolve(...) = new.resolve(...)
   end
end
```

```
UserWithBookmarkedPostsQuery.resolve
```

This is our final abstraction signature. Now let's talk about the convention.

A convention is a set of rules on how to name and organize things (code or files, for example), which can be used by the program to implicitly infer functionality. In other words, following a convention helps us to reduce the amount of code and also simplify the design process (since we don't need to reinvent the wheel every time we want to add a new entity).

Let's see how we can introduce a convention into our query objects. For that, let's take a look at `UserWithBookmarkedPostsQuery` and its constructor:

```
class UserWithBookmarkedPostsQuery < ApplicationQuery
   def initialize(relation = User.all) = super(relation)
   # …
end
```

As humans, we can infer from the query object class name that this query object deals with the `User` model. Can we make our program do the same? Sure, we can do that by adding some naming rules. For example, we can require storing query object classes under the corresponding model namespace:

```
class User
   class WithBookmarkedPostsQuery < ApplicationQuery
      # …
   end
end
```

Now, we can update our base class constructor to automatically infer a default relation from the class name:

```
class ApplicationQuery
   class << self
     def query_model
       name.sub(/::[^\:]+$/, "").safe_constantize
     end
   end

   def initialize(relation = self.class.query_model.all)
     @relation = relation
   end
end
```

Using this convention, we can define and use query objects as follows:

```
class Post::DraftsQuery < ApplicationQuery
  def resolve = relation.where(draft: true)
end


Post::DraftsQuery.resolve #== Post.all.where(draft: true)
```

The convention could also be used to simplify testing (custom matchers or shared contexts) or apply static code analysis (for example, writing custom RuboCop cops). Linters could be used to enforce query object usage, but there is a question: when do we use query objects and when do we use Rails's built-in features, such as scopes, for instance?

Let's try to answer this question.

Scopes versus query objects

Active Record has a built-in feature that resembles query objects in some sense—**scopes**. We already used scopes for the Post class in the previous examples; let's recall them:

```
class Post < ApplicationRecord
  scope :ordered, -> { order(created_at: :desc) }
  scope :published, -> { where(draft: false) }
  scope :kept, -> { where(deleted_at: nil) }
  scope :previous_week, -> {
    where(created_at: Date.current.prev_week.all_week)
  }
end
```

Compared to using where (…) or order (…) explicitly, scopes carry semantical meaning; they don't leak implementation details. This makes using scopes more robust to potential changes to the underlying model or schema. In this sense, scopes are like query objects, but not all scopes are like that.

The scopes in the example are atomic. They add just a single modification each and can be easily combined. However, there may be complex scopes: either combining multiple scopes, relying on complicated query building, or both. Let's consider an example of over-scoping—an extensive usage of scopes that could lead to unexpected behavior.

Imagine we noticed that in many places, we use the .ordered and .published scopes together, so we decided to add .ordered to the .published scope by default:

```
class Post < ApplicationRecord
  scope :ordered, -> { order(created_at: :desc) }
  scope :published, -> { ordered.where(draft: false) }
end
```

Now, we can write `Post.published` instead of `Post.published.ordered`. That's good – less typing. Assume that now you want to show published posts in alphabetical order for a certain feature:

```
Post.insert_all([
  {title: "A", created_at: 1.day.ago},
  {title: "B", created_at: 1.hour.ago}
])
Post.published.order(title: :asc).pluck(:title)
#=> ["B", "A"], but we expect ["A", "B"]
```

Why doesn't the code work as expected? We have already added the `order` clause to the query within the `.published` scope:

```
Post.published.order(title: :asc) == Post.where
  (draft: true).order(created_at: :desc).order(title: :asc)
```

Sure, we can find a workaround: change the order of the `.published` and `.order` calls, use `.reorder`, or avoid using the scope. Any of these options will mean that this code now knows about internals it doesn't really use.

This is a simple example of overusing scopes and how it can lead to conflicts. In real life, the dependencies could be much more entangled and harder to resolve. Sticking to atomic scopes and query objects for complex queries helps to avoid this.

There is, however, a benefit in using scopes or class methods compared to query objects from a readability point of view. Consider the following examples:

```
# Using a scope
account.users.with_bookmarked_posts
# Using a query object
User::WithBookmarkedPostsQuery.new(account.users).resolve
```

We can achieve the same level of readability with query objects by attaching them to models:

```
class User < ApplicationRecord
  scope :with_bookmarked_posts, WithBookmarkedPostsQuery
end
```

A scope body could be any callable object, not only `Lambda` or `Proc`. Hence, all we need is to make our query class respond to the `.call` method. We can make this by creating an alias for the `.resolve` method:

```
class ApplicationQuery
  class << self
    def resolve(...) = new.resolve(...)
    alias_method :call, :resolve
```

```
    end
  end
```

That's it. Now we can extend Active Record models with query objects without sacrificing the *Rails Way* interface.

So far, we've only considered specific model queries and the corresponding query objects. Let's see how we can use query objects to share the querying behavior between multiple models.

Reusable query objects and Arel

When we construct queries with Active Record, we can fall back to plain old SQL and go very far with it. However, when switching from ORM to raw strings, we lose a lot of features, such as automatic type casting and quoting, to name a few. The risk of introducing bugs increases, especially when the code is re-used by multiple models (and, thus, database tables).

Let's assume that we added tags support to the `Post` model from our examples. Now, a post can be created with a list of arbitrary tags as follows:

```
post = Post.create!(
  title: "Query Objects on Rails",
  tags: ["rails", "active_record"]
)
```

Since tags can have any value, we decided to store them as a JSON array in the database. To make it possible to select posts matching a given tag, we added a scope:

```
class Post < ApplicationRecord
  scope :tagged, ->(tag) {
    where("EXISTS ("\
      "SELECT 1 FROM json_each(tags) WHERE value = ?"\
    ")", tag)
  }
end
```

This query is specific to SQLite 3, which we use for demonstration purposes. We can use it like this:

```
Post.tagged("rails")
#=> [#<Post id: 1, title: "Query Objects..."]
```

Then, we decided to add tags support for bookmarks in a similar fashion:

```
user.bookmarks.create!(post: post, tags: %w[ruby todo])
```

The same scope code could be used for the `Bookmark` model, too:

```
class Bookmark < ApplicationRecord
  scope :tagged, ->(tag) {
    where("EXISTS ("\
      "SELECT 1 FROM json_each(tags) WHERE value = ?"\
    ")", tag)
  }
end
```

```
user.bookmarks.tagged("ruby")
```

The querying logic and code for both `.tagged` scopes are the same, so why not extract it and reuse it? Let's try to use a query object for that:

```
class TaggedQuery < ApplicationQuery
  def resolve(tag)
    relation.where("EXISTS ("\
      "SELECT 1 FROM json_each(tags) WHERE value = ?"\
    ")", tag)
  end
end
```

Now, we can use this query object with any model:

```
# For posts
TaggedQuery.new(Post.all).resolve("rails")
# For bookmarks
TaggedQuery.new(user.bookmarks).resolve("ruby")
```

Note that since the query is not model-specific, we cannot infer a `model` class automatically, and thus cannot attach the query object to a model via scopes. To overcome this problem, we can enhance the `ApplicationQuery` class with the ability to explicitly specify a model:

```
class ApplicationQuery
  class << self
    attr_writer :query_model_name

    def query_model_name
      @query_model_name ||= name.sub(/::[^\:]+$/, "")
    end

    def query_model
      query_model_name.safe_constantize
    end
```

```
      end
  end
```

Now, to reuse the same query object class for different models, we need to create a copy of it and define a model class. For that, we can use a **parameterized module** approach:

Attaching a query object as a parameterized class

```
class Post < ApplicationRecord
  scope :tagged, TaggedQuery[self]
end

class Bookmark < ApplicationRecord
  scope :tagged, TaggedQuery[self]
end
```

Parameterization implementation

```
class ApplicationQuery
  class << self
    def [](model)
      Class.new(self).tap {
        _1.query_model_name = model.name
      }
    end
  end
end
```

The use of a parameterized module is a metaprogramming technique, which implies generating Ruby modules or classes dynamically with some predefined configuration passed as an input parameter. Usually, the # [] = method is used as a constructor, so it looks like a regular module or class with a modifier. Such an API resembles generics in typed languages.

Now we can use our query object via an Active Record scoping interface:

```
Post.tagged("rails")
user.bookmarks.tagged("ruby")
```

We isolated the querying logic and made this logic pluggable into any model requiring this functionality. The query object code might look too simple to justify the extraction, but let's see how it will evolve to reflect changing requirements.

Let's assume that we decided to allow users to select the bookmarked posts matching any given tag. For that, we can create a through association:

```
class User < ApplicationRecord
  has_many :bookmarked_posts, through: :bookmarks,
                             source: :post
end
```

However, using this association and the query object defined here together doesn't work:

```
user.bookmarked_posts.tagged("rails")
#=> SQLite3::SQLException: ambiguous column name: tags
```

This is one of the caveats of using plain SQL—we need to take care of quoting column names ourselves.

As a quick fix, we can update our SQL string to include a table name for the tags column:

```
class TaggedQuery < ApplicationQuery
  def resolve(tag)
    relation.where("EXISTS ("\
      "SELECT 1 FROM
       json_each(#{relation.table_name}.tags)
       WHERE value = ?"\
    ")", tag)
  end
end
```

The preceding fix will work in most cases (it will break if a table name contains spaces or other special symbols); the query is still readable. However, what if we introduce a new requirement? For example, we may want to support filtering by multiple tags or modify the structure of the JSON field containing tags.

When building reusable queries by wiring plain SQL parts, it's easy to get to a point where the source code is barely understandable due to a heavy mix of string literals and interpolation. Introducing errors becomes easier while debugging turns into a nightmare.

Luckily, Rails has a tool for building queries in an object-oriented manner— **A Relational Algebra (Arel)**. Arel is a part of the Active Record library, and it is what drives all SQL generation under the hood. We can use it when existing Active Record APIs are not enough (as in our example).

Arel is a SQL abstract syntax tree manager. Instead of writing raw strings, you build a tree from SQL operation and value nodes, and Arel compiles it into a valid SQL. It performs proper quoting and typecasting along the way, so you don't have to do it yourself.

Arel is an advanced tool that should be used with caution, but once you get the hang of it, you will never come back to manual SQL string stitching.

> **What a gem – arel helpers**
>
> The `arel-helpers` gem (`https://github.com/camertron/arel-helpers`) is a collection of extensions for Arel to reduce the amount of boilerplate (especially for complex JOIN conditions).

Let's see how we can rewrite our query object with Arel:

```
class TaggedQuery < ApplicationQuery
  def resolve(tag)
    subquery = tags.project(1).where(tags[:value].eq(tag))
    relation.where(subquery.exists)
  end

  private

  def tags
    @tags ||= Arel::Nodes::NamedFunction.new(
      "json_each", [arel_table[:tags]]
    ).then do
      name = Arel.sql(_1.to_sql)
      Arel::Table.new(name, as: :json_tags)
    end
  end

  def arel_table = self.class.query_model.arel_table
end
```

The code may look more sophisticated, but at the same time, it's more robust. Although it may be unclear from this example, using nodes to construct queries brings better composability and flexibility: all Ruby features are available to use since we operate on objects.

The good thing about using query objects along with Arel is that we can physically isolate advanced code from the rest of the application code base. By physically, I mean that the code lives in a separate file, not in your model. But where to put this file? Let's finish discussing query objects by answering this question.

Code organization with query objects versus architecture layers

In *Chapter 5, When Rails Abstractions Are Not Enough*, we learned about layered architecture and how it relates to abstraction layers. Models belong to the domain layer. What about query objects? From the layered architecture point of view, they also belong to the domain layer since they operate only on the entities from this layer. On the other hand, query objects clearly lie above the domain models, thus comprising an upper sub-layer. We can borrow the **domain-driven design (DDD)** terminology and call this architecture sub-layer **domain services**.

Since the domain services layer is not a real architecture layer, we have more freedom in how to organize the corresponding code. For Rails apps, that means that query objects can be stored under the `app/models` folder; no need to separate them from models.

The convention we introduced here works well in this case: query objects are grouped under the corresponding model folder; the filename suffixes (`*_query.rb`) help to differentiate between abstraction layers. Introducing a new top-level folder (`app/queries`) is justified in case most query objects are reusable and not model-specific.

We can say that the query object layer is weak. We do not enforce using query objects every time we need to read data – only when the logic is quite complex (which is very subjective). Otherwise, a plain Active Record scope or even in-place queries can be used. This way, we try to balance simplicity and maintainability.

However, you can go further and turn the domain services into a standalone (and require) layer, thus enforcing all querying as well as persistence-related operations on domain models to be performed via dedicated objects. Let's take a quick overview of this approach and how it can be implemented in Rails.

Separating domain and persistence with repositories

In *Chapter 2, Active Models and Records*, we discussed two object-relational mapping abstractions, Active Record and Data Mapper, and their differences. Rails obviously goes with the first approach, but that doesn't mean we cannot derail and use Data Mapper concepts in our code.

To recall, the main difference between Active Record and Data Mapper is that Data Mapper separates models from persistence: models are just enhanced data containers, and other objects are used for querying and storing data (repositories and relations). Thus, there is a clear separation between the domain layer and domain services. This separation gives you more control over data access and transformation at the cost of losing Active Record's (the library's) simplicity.

Usually, switching to the Data Mapper paradigm in Ruby on Rails applications comes along with migrating to some other ORM instead of Active Record – for instance, Ruby **Object Mapper** (`https://rom-rb.org`). As the purpose of this book is to explore the *Extended Rails Way*, we will try to apply Data Mapper ideas to Active Record models by introducing **Active Record Repository** abstraction.

Pattern – repository

A **repository object** is an intermediate object between domain models and data sources (persistence). It abstracts data access by providing collection-like access to domain objects, so the upper abstraction/architecture layers operate on plain objects without relying on their persistent nature.

The good thing about building repositories on top of Active Record is that we can gradually migrate models one by one to this new concept without changing everything else. Let's start with the `Post` model from the previous examples.

Here is the list of data access-related operations over posts we had and the corresponding Rails code:

- **Creating a post**: `Post.create(post_params)`

- **Publishing a post**: `post.update!(draft: false)`

- **Showing all posts**: `Post.all`

- **Showing a single post**: `Post.find(id)`

- **Searching posts by tags**: `Post.tagged("rails")`

We need to migrate all these actions to use a repository. Thus, our repository needs at least four public methods:

```
class PostsRepository
  def all = Post.all.to_a
  def find(id) = Post.find_by(id:)
  def add(attrs) = Post.create!(attrs)
  def publish(post) = post.update!(draft: false)
  def search(tag: nil)
    Post.where("EXISTS (" \
      "SELECT 1 FROM json_each(tags) WHERE value = ?)",
      tag
    )
  end
end
```

We can use our repository like this:

```
repo = PostsRepository.new
post = repo.add(
  title: "Repositories on Rails",
  tags: %w[orm data_mapper])
repo.publish(post)
repo.search(tag: "orm")
```

Even such a basic repository example highlights the differences from Active Record.

First, update operations are no longer generic; the repository pattern encourages us to use an action-specific interface (#publish instead of #update). Having dedicated methods for different update operations better reflects the business logic and helps us to understand how an entity is used in the application. Thus, unlike Active Record, which provides universal data access, repositories provide an application-specific interface to data (which is usually much more concise).

Secondly, complex querying is extracted from the model by design. The #search method acts similarly to a query object from the previous section. We can say that a repository is a collection of queries and transformations (or commands). Does this mean that repositories are at risk of becoming God objects now? Not really. We can create multiple repositories for the same model but for different contexts, and thus organize code according to product features.

Finally, note that we added #to_a to the #all method of the PostRepository class defined here. This is because a repository must return only domain objects (collection-like access). Returning an Active Record relation would mean leaking internals. For the same reason that the #find method doesn't raise an exception if a record is not found but returns null, it's up to the calling code to decide how to handle a missing object.

Similar to the ApplicationQuery class, we can introduce an ApplicationRepository class to implement a common behavior and introduce a convention:

```ruby
class ApplicationRepository
  class << self
    attr_writer :model_name

    def model_name
      @model_name ||=
        name.sub(/Repository$/, "").singularize
    end

    def model
      model_name.safe_constantize
    end
  end

  delegate :model, to: :class

  def all = model.all.to_a
  def find(id) = model.find_by(id:)
  def add(attrs) = model.create!(attrs)
end
```

Now, our PostsRepository class looks like this:

```ruby
class PostsRepository < ApplicationRepository
  def publish(post) = post.update!(draft: false)
  def search(tag: nil)
```

```
   model.where(
      "EXISTS (SELECT 1 FROM json_each(tags) "\
      "WHERE value = ?)", tag)
  end
end
```

This is the simplest repository pattern implementation on top of Active Record. It still lacks some important features:

- Returned objects are Active Record objects; they still have access to the persistence layer. Ideally, we need to map Active Record objects to some plain Ruby models. Otherwise, we're not really *data-mapping*.

- We have to explicitly instantiate a repository object every time we need it. In practice, a dependency injection/inversion system must be used instead. See, for example, the `dry-container` gem (`https://dry-rb.org/gems/dry-container`).

- One particular motivation for introducing repositories into a Ruby on Rails application could be the desire to migrate from a monolithic architecture to a modular one. Repositories help to eliminate hidden dependencies between models and define clear public interfaces for components.

Summary

In this chapter, you learned about the query objects and repository abstractions and how they could be used to reduce Active Record models' responsibility. You practiced turning a design pattern into an abstraction layer. You also learned about the domain services layer and its place in the layered architecture.

In the next chapter, we will further explore how to reduce Active Record models' responsibility by introducing abstractions from the upper architecture layers, such as the presentation layer.

Questions

1. What is a query object?
2. What is the difference between a query object and an Active Record scope?
3. What is an atomic scope?
4. What is the difference between a query object and a repository?

7

Handling User
Input outside of Models

In this chapter, we'll continue discussing abstractions related to Rails models. This time, we will talk about user-driven operations and the corresponding design patterns. First, we'll talk about modifying operations (creating or updating models) and introduce the concept of a **form object**, which is an object representing a user interface form in the code base. Then, we'll discuss how to read (or filter) data based on user-provided parameters with the help of **filter objects**.

You will learn how to identify functionality that can be moved to form and filter objects, so you can introduce new abstraction layers and reduce the responsibility of the existing ones (especially the model layer).

We will cover the following topics:

- Form objects – closer to the UI, farther from persistence
- Filter objects or user-driven query building

This chapter aims to give you practice in extracting the presentation layer abstractions from Rails models so you learn which properties they have in common and how and when to use them in your code base.

Technical requirements

In this chapter, and all chapters of this book, the code given in code blocks is designed to be executed on Ruby 3.2 and Rails 7. Many of the code examples will work on earlier versions of the afore mentioned software.

You will find the code files on GitHub at https://github.com/PacktPublishing/Layered-Design-for-Ruby-on-Rails-Applications/tree/main/Chapter07.

Form objects – closer to the UI, farther from persistence

From a user interaction point of view, using almost any web application could be seen as a sequence of interleaving form submissions and link clicks. Although this is a very rough definition, it's good enough to demonstrate that there are two primary ways an application deals with user-provided information: *consuming incoming payloads* and *answering user-generated queries*.

Let's start with the first one.

In most cases (at least for Ruby on Rails applications), *consuming a payload* means creating or updating domain objects backed by Active Record models. The built-in `#create`, `#update`, and `#destroy` Active Record methods can get us far beyond simple **Create**, **Read**, **Update, and Delete** (**CRUD**) operations, especially *spiced* with conditional or contextual validations and model callbacks—almost any sophisticated form could be processed without leaving the boundaries of a model object. But wait, didn't we discuss the downsides of such an approach in *Chapter 4, Rails Anti-Patterns*? Let's recall these downsides and see how we can avoid them by introducing a new abstraction.

UI forms versus models

Here is the question: should a model be aware of the UI? The layered architecture (see *Chapter 5, When Rails Abstractions Are Not Enough*, in particular the *On layered architecture and abstraction layers* section) answers this question quickly: no, it's *illegal* to go up the architecture stack (a model lies somewhere at the bottom, while the UI is at the top).

Why am I asking this question? In Rails, it's easy to introduce an implicit connection between models and the UI. For example, when we try to make a model responsible for processing non-trivial form submissions or when there are multiple contexts in which we create or update the model objects.

Let's consider an example of a model evolution reflecting ever-changing business-logic requirements.

Scaffolding a form-controller-model relationship

Let's imagine we build a new Rails application from scratch. One of the productivity tools the framework gives us is generators. With the help of generators, you can quickly scaffold the application without writing any code by hand but executing command-line commands.

For example, here is how you can add a `User` resource to your application:

```
$ bin/rails g scaffold user name:string email:string
   invoke   active_record
   create      db/migrate/20230130220042_create_users.rb
   create      app/models/user.rb
   invoke   resource_route
   route       resources :users
   invoke   scaffold_controller
```

```
   create      app/controllers/users_controller.rb
 invoke   erb
   create      app/views/users
   create      app/views/users/index.html.erb
   # ...
   create        app/views/users/_form.html.erb
   # ...
 invoke test_unit
   # ...
```

The preceding command creates a model class and a corresponding controller class implementing all CRUD actions and HTML templates. Finally, it configures the application routes and generates test stubs.

By default, Rails generates a single form template (users/_form.html.erb) for both the #create and #update actions. Let's look at the generated code for these actions:

```
class UsersController < ApplicationController
  # ...
  def create
    @user = User.new(user_params)
    if @user.save
      redirect_to @user, notice: "User was successfully
        created."
    else
      render :new, status: :unprocessable_entity
    end
  end

  def update
    if @user.update(user_params)
      redirect_to @user, notice: "User was successfully
        updated."
    else
      render :edit, status: :unprocessable_entity
    end
  end
  # ...
end
```

They look similar: the same filtered parameters are used, and the actual creation/modification is delegated to the model class. We use the generic User#save and User#update methods. No UI (that is, form) context is leaking to the model. The form itself is also generic: it allows you to set/update all the available attributes.

New user

Name

Vova

Email

palkan@evl.ms

[Create User]   **Back to users**

Figure 7.1 – A form UI created by the scaffold generator (using the tailwindcss-rails gem)

However, such generic forms are not very common. There are usually different contexts in which model entities can be modified. Let's see how our user form evolves and splits into multiple context-specific forms.

From generic creation to invitation and registration

When it comes to application users, we're likely to deal with operations such as inviting users and signing up. Unfortunately, neither of these two actions matches the auto-generated `UsersController` class and the form we created in the previous step. So, let's create two new controllers, `InvitationsController` and `RegistrationsController`, to render and process the invitation and registration forms, respectively:

InvitationsController

```ruby
class InvitationsController < ApplicationController
  def new
    @user = User.new
  end

  def create
    @user = User.new(params.require(:user).permit(:email))

    if @user.save
      redirect_to root_path
    else
      render :new, status: :unprocessable_entity
    end
  end
end
```

RegistrationsController

```ruby
class RegistrationsController < ApplicationController
  def new
    @user = User.new
  end

  def create
    @user = User.new(params.require(:user).permit
      (:email, :name))
    @user.confirmed_at = Time.current

    if @user.save
      redirect_to root_path
    else
      render :new, status: :unprocessable_entity
    end
  end
end
```

The difference between the two #create actions here is subtle but important from a business-logic perspective: to invite a user, we only need an email address, whereas during self-registration, we require both an email address and name to be provided. Model-level validations enforce the requirement:

```ruby
class User < ApplicationRecord
  validates :email, presence: true, uniqueness: true
  validates :name, presence: true, if: :confirmed?
  def confirmed? = confirmed_at.present?
end
```

Note that we use the #confirmed_at attribute to distinguish invited users from users who completed registration. We must use conditional validations to support both invitation and registration scenarios. Though, at a stretch, we can say that the User model became coupled with the UI (through this conditional validation).

Let's enhance our scenarios to make the connection between the model and the presentation layer clearer.

Adding notifications to the equation

Our invitation functionality lacks one important feature—sending an email to the newly invited user. The simplest way to add this feature is to introduce a model-level callback:

```ruby
class User < ApplicationRecord
  after_create_commit :send_invitation, unless: :confirmed?
```

```
  def send_invitation
    UserMailer.invite(self).deliver_later
  end
end
```

The callback connects the invitation feature to the `#confirmed_at` attribute. Similarly, we can add another callback to send a welcome email to a just-registered user:

```
class User < ApplicationRecord
  after_create_commit :send_invitation, unless: :confirmed?
  after_create_commit :send_welcome_email, if: :confirmed?

  def send_invitation
    UserMailer.invite(self).deliver_later
  end

  def send_welcome_email
    UserMailer.welcome(self).deliver_later
  end
end
```

Now, whenever we create a `User` record, we send an email (either invitation or registration), even if the user is created, say, from the Rails console. In *Chapter 4, Rails Anti-Patterns?*, in the *Active Record callbacks go wild* section, we learned about a potential workaround to better control callback execution—virtual attributes:

```
class User < ApplicationRecord
  attribute :should_send_invitation, :boolean
  attribute :should_send_welcome_email, :boolean

  after_create_commit :send_invitation, if:
    :should_send_invitation
  after_create_commit :send_welcome_email, if:
    :should_send_welcome_email
  # ...
end
```

We can update our controllers (`InvitationsController` and `RegistrationsController`) to explicitly tell the model to send notifications:

InvitationsController

```
class InvitationsController < ApplicationController
  def create
```

```
    @user = User.new(params.require(:user).permit(:email))
    @user.should_send_invitation = true
    if @user.save
      # ...
    end
  end
end
```

RegistrationsController

```
class RegistrationsController < ApplicationController
  def create
    @user = User.new(params.require(:user).permit(:email, :name))
    @user.confirmed_at = Time.current
    @user.should_send_welcome_email = true
    if @user.save
      # ...
    end
  end
end
```

Let's add the icing on the cake—adding the **Send me the copy** checkbox (and the implementation of the corresponding feature – sending the email copy) to the invitation form. The form UI will look as follows:

Figure 7.2 – Invitation form with the Send me the copy checkbox

How can we handle this checkbox value? Should we add yet another virtual attribute to the User model? At this point, it becomes clear that putting everything into the model isn't a clever idea. Let's make our controller responsible for dealing with it!

```
class InvitationsController < ApplicationController
  def create
    @user = User.new(params.require(:user).permit(:email))
```

```ruby
      @user.should_send_invitation = true
    if @user.save
      if params[:send_copy] == "1"
        UserMailer.invitation_copy(current_user, @user)
          .deliver_later
      end
      redirect_to root_path
    else
      # ...
    end
  end
end
```

The preceding solution is far from ideal. The invitation logic is now spread across two classes; there are multiple logical branches and magic constants (like "1" here). (We could move all the logic to the controllers and go the *fat controllers* way—let me leave this interesting exercise to you, the reader.)

The conceptual complexity we introduced into our code base is incomparable to the size of the feature—a couple of tiny forms with a handful of fields. Let's see how we can compress the complexity by introducing a new abstraction—**form objects**.

Form objects to the rescue

One important thing we need to learn about Rails development: when struggling with whether to put new logic into a model class or a controller class, always remember there is a third way—creating a new object in between. In *Chapter 5, When Rails Abstractions Are Not Enough*, we discussed the phenomenon of service objects (and how they're often used as universal intermediate objects).

We concluded that service objects could comprise a standalone architecture layer (application services) right below the presentation layer and above the domain layer. Abstraction layers are only good if they respect architecture layers' boundaries. Thus, we cannot use our *silver bullets*, service objects, to implement form-handling logic. We need something new. So, here come form objects.

Pattern — form object

A **form object** is responsible for handling a specific user interaction involving data submission (usually through an HTML form interface or something similar). Form objects validate user input and trigger interaction-specific business-logic rules and side effects.

Since form objects belong to the presentation layer (see the following), they could also be used by views (for example, to dynamically render form fields). However, form objects must be distinguished from form builders and form view components, whose sole responsibility is building a UI (for instance, producing an HTML representation of the form). We will discuss view-layer abstractions in *Chapter 11, Better Abstractions for HTML Views*.

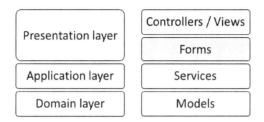

Figure 7.3 – The location of form objects in the layered architecture

Let's extract the invitation form-related functionality into a standalone Ruby class—our first form object.

Let's start with the public interface:

```ruby
class UserInvitationForm
  attr_reader :user, :send_copy, :sender
  def initialize(params, send_copy: false, sender: nil)
    @user = User.new(params)
    @send_copy = send_copy.in?(%w[1 t true])
    @sender = sender
  end

  def save
    validate!
    return false if user.errors.any?

    user.save!
    deliver_notifications!
  end

  # ...
end
```

Our class has only two public methods: a constructor (#initialize) and a *form submission* method (#save). The constructor accepts user input (form params) and the context (a sender). Note that due to the structure of input parameters, we had to split them into two method parameters (send_copy is passed separately). The #save method mimics the Active Record API: it returns false when the input is invalid and performs the required actions otherwise.

The private part of our form object class is responsible for validation and side effects:

```ruby
class UserInvitationForm
  # ...

  private
```

```
    def validate!
      user.errors.add(:email, :blank) if user.email.blank?
    end

    def deliver_notifications!
      UserMailer.invite(user).deliver_later
      if send_copy
        UserMailer.invite_copy(sender, user).deliver_later
      end
    end
  end
```

We collect validation errors in the Active Model Errors object (user.errors) to make our form object compatible with Rails form helpers (to render user.errors.full_messages in the response).

This is how we use the UserInvitationForm class in our controller:

```
class InvitationsController < ApplicationController
  def create
    form = UserInvitationForm.new(
      params.require(:user).permit(:email).to_h,
      send_copy: params[:send_copy],
      send_copy_to: current_user
    )

    if form.save
      redirect_to root_path
    else
      @user = form.user
      render :new, status: :unprocessable_entity
    end
  end
end
```

We've implemented a UI form-driven feature without touching our model class and have kept our controller slim. However, the form object extraction we just conducted has many rough edges:

- Form initialization is ad hoc (the #initialize signature)

- The controller is still responsible for filtering params (params.require(:user).permit(:email))

- We have to typecast user input ourselves (send_copy.in?(%w[1 t true])) and perform validations manually

- We leak form object internals (form.user) for rendering

Let's see how we can standardize form objects with the help of Active Model.

Using Active Model to abstract form objects

Which common tasks does our form object abstraction need to solve? Looking at the previous example, we can form the following list:

- Input parameter filtering, typecasting, and validation
- Triggering actions on successful form submission
- Compatibility with Action View helpers

Active Model provides features to implement all of this. Let's start with the core functionality—attributes, validations, and the public API (#save):

```
class ApplicationForm
  include ActiveModel::API
  include ActiveModel::Attributes

  def save
    return false unless valid?

    with_transaction { submit! }
  end

  private
  def with_transaction(&)
    ApplicationRecord.transaction(&)
  end

  def submit!
    raise NotImplementedError
  end
end
```

Including ActiveModel::API automatically gives us validation support, while ActiveModel::Attributes provides DSL for defining a form object schema along with parameter types. Finally, we define a generic #save method, which performs validations and invokes a submission action only if they succeed. We wrap the submission action in a database transaction by default (since performing multiple mutating database queries within a form object is common).

Let's see how can we rewrite our invitation form object using the newly created abstraction (via the `ApplicationForm` class):

```ruby
class InvitationForm < ApplicationForm
  attribute :email
  attribute :send_copy, :boolean

  attr_accessor :sender

  validates :email, presence: true

  private
  attr_reader :user

  def submit!
    @user = User.new(email:)
    user.save!
    deliver_notifications!
  end

  def deliver_notifications!
    UserMailer.invite(user).deliver_later
    if send_copy && sender
      UserMailer.invite_copy(sender, user).deliver_later
    end
  end
end
```

We use the `.attribute` method to declare form inputs—this is our convention. If we need to provide some additional context, we use regular Ruby attribute accessors. We use a familiar validations API with no mental overhead added.

We've just laid the foundation for our form object abstraction. Let's see how we can make it more powerful.

Adding callbacks to decompose submission actions

In the preceding example, the `#submit!` method becomes a single entry point for all the actions to be performed. We can decompose it by moving side effects to callbacks! Let's add `after_save` and `after_commit` callback support to the `ApplicationForm` class:

```ruby
class ApplicationForm
  include ActiveModel::API
  include ActiveModel::Attributes

  define_callbacks :save, only: :after
```

```ruby
  define_callbacks :commit, only: :after

  class << self
    def after_save(...)
      set_callback(:save, :after, ...)
    end

    def after_commit(...)
      set_callback(:commit, :after, ...)
    end
  end

  def save
    return false unless valid?

    with_transaction do
      AfterCommitEverywhere.after_commit { run_callbacks
        (:commit) }
      run_callbacks(:save) { submit! }
    end
  end
end
```

The callbacks behave the same way as the corresponding Active Record callbacks (see *Chapter 4, Rails Anti-Patterns?*). To implement the `after_commit` callbacks outside of Active Record, we use the `after_commit_everywhere` gem (`https://github.com/Envek/after_commit_everywhere`).

Let's update our `InvitationForm` class to use callbacks:

```ruby
class InvitationForm < ApplicationForm
  # ...
  after_commit :deliver_invitation
  after_commit :deliver_invitation_copy, if: :send_copy

  private
  def submit!
    @user = User.new(email:)
    user.save!
  end

  def deliver_invitation
    UserMailer.invite(user).deliver_later
  end
```

```
    def deliver_invitation_copy
      UserMailer.invite_copy(sender, user).deliver_later if sender
    end
  end
```

On the one hand, our #submit! method now implements only the primary logic of this form. On the other hand, we can easily see all the additional actions from the declarations at the beginning of the class.

Let's move on to the presentation part of a form object's responsibility.

Making form objects Action View-friendly

Form objects belong to the presentation layer; thus, they can be used in view templates. Building on top of the Active Model allows us to use form objects with Action View helpers just like regular models. We already explored this feature in *Chapter 2, Active Models and Records*, so let's briefly demonstrate how it can be applied to our example.

First, look at the HTML template for the original invitation form (styling omitted):

```
<%= form_for(@user, url: invitations_path) do |form| %>
  <%= form.label :email %>
  <%= form.text_field :email %>

  <%= label_tag :send_copy, "Send me the copy" %>
  <%= check_box_tag :send_copy %>

  <%= form.submit "Invite" %>
<% end %>
```

We mix two APIs: form.<field> and <field>_tag. That's because the send_copy attribute is not defined on the model, so we have to fall back to *plain* form helpers, not backed by a model instance. We also specified the URL explicitly since we need to submit this form via the custom controller (InvitationsController, not UsersController).

With our form object, we can fully leverage Rails APIs and conventions and avoid workarounds:

```
<%= form_for(@invitation_form) do |form| %>
  <%= form.label :email %>
  <%= form.text_field :email %>

  <%= form.label :send_copy, "Send me the copy" %>
  <%= form.check_box :send_copy %>

  <%= form.submit "Invite" %>
<% end %>
```

Form helpers recognize attributes, and URL helpers can automatically infer a correct action URL. The latter feature requires a tiny modification to the `ApplicationForm` class—overriding the `#model_name` method:

```ruby
class ApplicationForm
  # ...
  def model_name
    ActiveModel::Name.new(
      nil, nil, self.class.name.sub(/Form$/, "")
    )
  end
end
```

We override the `#model_name` method used for inference to cut the `Form` suffix from the resource name represented by a form object. Thus, `InvitationForm` represents the (virtual) *Invitation* resource. This is another convention we use to define the form object abstraction.

At this point, our abstraction seems rather complete. There are multiple directions in which we can evolve it depending on the application's needs. One common power-up is integrating form objects with strong parameters.

Form objects versus strong parameters

Let's see how the `InvitationForm` class fits the corresponding controller:

```ruby
class InvitationsController < ApplicationController
  def new
    @invitation_form = InvitationForm.new
  end

  def create
    @invitation_form = InvitationForm.new(
      params.require(:invitation)
            .permit(:email, :send_copy)
    )
    @invitation_form.sender = current_user

    if @invitation_form.save
      redirect_to root_path
    else
      render :new, status: :unprocessable_entity
    end
  end
end
```

The code is as simple as the scaffolded controller's code, which we saw at the beginning of this chapter (in the *Scaffolding a form-controller-model relationship* subsection). And we can make it even simpler by removing the duplication: **params filtering**.

By convention, a form object class declares all the acceptable form fields as attributes (via the .attribute method). We can reuse this information to infer the filtering pattern (arguments passed to the #permit method). The basic implementation would be as follows:

```ruby
class ApplicationForm
  class << self
    def from(params)
      new(params.permit(attribute_names.map(&:to_sym)))
    end
  end
end
```

Active Model keeps the information about defined attributes, so we can use, for example, the .attribute_names method to get their names. It's good enough for simple attributes. However, for nested attributes, a more sophisticated technique would be required (which is beyond the scope of this book).

Finally, let's simplify our controller by delegating parameter filtering to a form object:

```ruby
class InvitationsController < ApplicationController
  def new
    @invitation_form = InvitationForm.new
  end

  def create
    @invitation_form = InvitationForm.from(
      params.require(:invitation)
    )
    @invitation_form.sender = current_user

    if @invitation_form.save
      redirect_to root_path
    else
      render :new, status: :unprocessable_entity
    end
  end
end
```

The preceding example demonstrates how form objects can help controllers serve their primary purpose of routing user requests to business-logic operations without taking too much responsibility.

The form object abstraction we created mimics an Active Record model and, thus, reduces the developer's conceptual overhead—it follows the Rails Way. But form objects allow us to go beyond a standard *controller-model* correspondence and deal with more complex scenarios.

A form object is more than a model wrapper

So far, we have only considered using form objects for interactions involving a single model. But the number of models affected by a user action (such as form submission) could be any whole number *N* (yes, including zero), and form objects fully *awake* when *N* is not equal to one.

Multi-model forms

Let's recall the example `User` model from *Chapter 4, Rails Anti-Patterns?* (in the *Active Record callbacks go wild* section):

```ruby
class User < ApplicationRecord
  after_create :generate_initial_project, unless: :admin?
  # ...
end
```

We added a callback to create a project record for a user on creation (or *registration*). Thus, user registration is a multi-model operation, which we encapsulated within a `User.create` call. This is a perfect candidate for form object extraction, so let's do that.

We can define our `RegistrationForm` class as follows:

```ruby
class RegistrationForm < ApplicationForm
  attribute :name
  attribute :email
  attribute :should_create_project, :boolean
  attribute :project_name

  validates :project_name, presence: true, if: :should_create_project

  attr_reader :user

  after_save :create_initial_project, if: :should_create_project

  private
  def submit!
    @user = User.create!(email:, name:)
  end

  def create_initial_project
    user.projects.create!(name: project_name)
```

```
    end
  end
```

We moved the project creation step into a callback, which is only invoked if a user opts in. Similarly, we added conditional validation for the project name presence. What about user-related attribute validation? We can assume that the model itself validates email and name presence:

```
class User < ApplicationRecord
  validates :email, :name, presence: true
end
```

One important feature of a form object is that *it should handle invalid input gracefully*. Right now, if we try to submit a form without any email or name provided, an exception is raised:

```
RegistrationForm.new(name: "Test").save
#=> ActiveRecord::RecordInvalid: Validation failed:
  Email can't be blank
```

One option is to duplicate validations in the form object class. Alternatively, we can delegate validation to a model instance:

```
class RegistrationForm < ApplicationForm
  # ...
  validate :user_is_valid

  def initialize(...)
    super
    @user = User.new(email:, name:)
  end

  def user_is_valid
    return if user.valid?
    merge_errors!(user)
  end
end
```

We override the default constructor to create a user instance immediately upon initialization. Then, during validation, we check whether the user object is valid and merge its validation errors into a form object's errors set otherwise. The #merge_errors! method can be implemented in the ApplicationForm class:

```
class ApplicationForm
  # ...
  def merge_errors!
    other.errors.each do |e|
```

```
        errors.add(e.attribute, e.type, message: e.message)
      end
    end
end
```

Now we can show validation errors to a user:

```
form = RegistrationForm.new(name: "Test")
form.save #=> false
puts form.errors.full_messages
#=> Email can't be blank
```

Similarly, we can delegate project attribute validation to the corresponding model. However, we should never do the opposite: add model-level validations required for a specific form object (and, thus, a context).

To finish this section, let's consider a case of an *N* model form where *N* is zero.

Model-less forms

There could be user actions unrelated to any model but still requiring input validation and/or transformation. Form objects proved to be priceless for such use cases.

Let's consider a feedback form example:

Share your feedback!

Name

Andy

Email

andy@rails.test

Message

How to use form objects in Rails?

Send

Figure 7.4 – A feedback form UI

We want to provide feedback functionality, which simply sends an email to the support team. Using our form object abstraction, we can achieve this with the following code:

```
class FeedbackForm < ApplicationForm
  attribute :name
  attribute :email
  attribute :message

  validates :name, :email, :message, presence: true
  validates :message, length: {maximum: 160}

  after_commit do
    SystemMailer.feedback(      email, name, message
    ).deliver_later
  end

  def submit! = true
end
```

Note that we enqueue the delivery from within the `after_commit` callback and stub the `#submit!` method. This way, we guarantee that a mailer background job would be enqueued outside a database transaction, even if we wrapped the form object execution in a transaction somewhere in the upper layers.

Form objects can be seen as a universal abstraction to represent non-trivial form-like interfaces in your application (for simple CRUD operations, using models directly is good enough). The main goals of a form object are to *translate user input* into an application-level object for propagation to lower layers (services or domain objects) and to *provide meaningful feedback to a user*.

These responsibilities are specific to the presentation-layer abstractions, but not every abstraction requires carrying them both. Sometimes, we just need to react to user-provided data to generate the desired response.

Filter objects or user-driven query building

If we continue our *web development simplification* that we started at the beginning of this chapter, we can say that besides forms and links, we build data tables and lists. For example, a list of repositories on GitHub or an inbox in a web email client. What do these interfaces have in common? They all have filtering, sorting, and search controls available to users. Whenever we display a large amount of homogeneous data to a user, we want to make their life easier and allow narrowing down the scope.

Such user-driven querying requires processing input parameters and applying transformations to the base dataset based on the values provided. Let's see how we can implement this in a Ruby on Rails application.

Filtering in controllers

Just like before, we start with a pure Rails way of solving this problem. For parameter-based filtering, that means putting transformation logic right into the controller class.

Let's consider, for example, a controller responsible for providing a filtered view of *projects* based on query params:

```
class ProjectsController < ApplicationController
  def index
    projects = Project.all.order(sort_params)

    if params[:type_filter].in?(%w[published draft])
      projects.where!(
        status: params[:type_filter]
      )
    end

    if params[:time_filter] == "future"
      projects.where!(started_at: Time.current...)
    end

    projects.where!(
      Project[:name].matches("%#{params[:q]}%")
    ) if params[:q].present?

    render json: projects
  end
end
```

In the #index action, we take the base scope, Project.all, and depending on the user query, we add additional conditions to the resulting query. Every condition is built in a different way (we even use Arel and the arel-helpers gem here).

The sorting logic is extracted into a private method due to its complexity:

```
def sort_params
  col, ord = params.values_at(:sort_by, :sort_order)

  col = :started_at unless col.in?(%w[id name started_at])
  ord = :desc unless ord.in?(%w[asc desc])

  {col => ord}
end
```

In the end, we have more than 20 **lines of code** (LOC) and half a dozen logical branches here. And that's just a single controller's action. Can you imagine writing tests for this action? And don't forget that *controller tests are integration tests* and, thus, rather slow. Maybe we can move some responsibility to the model. Let's see.

Moving filtering to models

One popular technique for dealing with filters is to create an Active Record scope for each filterable parameter. Here is how it will look for our example:

Model with scopes

```ruby
class Project < ApplicationRecord
  scope :filter_by_type, -> {
    where(status: _1) if _1.in?(%w[published draft])
  }
  scope :filter_by_time, -> {
    where(started_at: Time.current...) if _1 == "future"
  }
  scope :searched, -> {
    where(arel_table[:name].matches("%#{_1}%")) if
      _1.present?
  }
  scope :sorted, (lambda do |col, ord|
    col = :started_at unless
      col.in?(%w[id name started_at])
    ord = :desc unless ord.in?(%w[asc desc])

    order(col => ord)
  end)
end
```

We added a scope for each parameter group we accept in a query. Note that we're using the `where(<condition>) if <validation>` pattern. This is an important feature of Active Record scopes: if a nil value is returned, the scope is skipped. That makes scopes chainable. We rely on this property to make our controller's code more readable:

```ruby
class ProjectsController < ApplicationController
  def index
    projects = Project.all
      .filter_by_type(params[:type_filter])
      .filter_by_time(params[:time_filter])
      .searched(params[:q])
```

```
          .sorted(params[:sort_by], params[:sort_order])

      render json: projects
    end
  end
```

Now the controller's code looks much better. The filtering functionality looks like a pipeline—a good visualization of the underlying logic. However, our model's code is now full of functionality required for the particular interface. And we clearly have an *over-scoping* problem (see *Chapter 6, Data Layer Abstractions*). Let's lighten both the model and the controller by extracting filtering-related functionality into a new object—a **filter object**.

Extracting filter objects

As the title of this chapter states, our primary goal is to reduce the model's responsibility. In other words, we want to extract scopes. But what will we use in the controller if we extract scopes from the model? We will use a new object, which will encapsulate all the transformations (or scopes) and will take only the base scope (`Project.all`) and the user query as its input.

> Pattern — filter object
>
> A **filter object** is an object responsible for transforming a dataset based on the parameters provided by a user. Filter objects are responsible for sanitizing user input, extracting known values, providing defaults, and performing the required transformations.

Let's start with refactoring the `ProjectsController` class:

```
class ProjectsController < ApplicationController
  def index
    projects = ProjectsFilter.filter(Project.all, params)
    render json: projects
  end
end
```

That's what using a filter object in a controller looks like—a single expression. Such code design drastically simplifies testing: we only need to test that the controller's action uses a correct filter, and there is no need to test all the combinations in controller tests. Here is an example RSpec test:

```
RSpec.describe ProjectsController, type: :request do
  before do
    allow(ProjectsFilter)
      .to receive(:filter).and_call_original
  end
```

```
  it "uses ProjectsFilter" do
    get "/projects.json"
    expect(response.status).to eq(0)
    expect(ProjectsFilter).to have_received(:filter)
      .with(Project.all,
            an_instance_of(ActionController::Parameters))
  end
end
```

Let's move on to the most interesting part—defining a filter object class. As always, you can implement it in pure Ruby and iterate until you figure out how to form an abstraction out of it. Let me skip this thought process and propose the final solution. This time, I suggest using a third-party gem—Rubanok.

> **What a gem — rubanok**
>
> Rubanok (`https://github.com/palkan/rubanok`) is a library that helps to build parameter-based transformation pipelines. It's a universal library, meaning that it could be used for any kind of data (not only Active Record models) and transformation scenarios. The key feature of Rubanok is its DSL, which allows you to define transformation rules in a very descriptive manner.

The filter classes built on top of Rubanok's `Processor` class look as follows:

ApplicationFilter

```
class ApplicationFilter < Rubanok::Processor
  class << self
    alias filter call
  end
end
```

The `ApplicationFilter` class only adds the `.filter` alias. We want to use the more descriptive `#filter` API instead of the generic `.call` provided by Rubanok. Now we can create a specific filter object using the base class:

ProjectsFilter

```
class ProjectsFilter < ApplicationFilter
  TYPES = %w[draft published].freeze
  SORT_FIELDS = %w[id name started_at].freeze
  SORT_ORDERS = %w[asc desc].freeze
```

```
    map :type_filter do |type_filter:|
      next raw.none unless TYPES.include?(type_filter)

      raw.where(status: type_filter)
    end

    match :time_filter do
      having "future" do
        raw.future
      end
    end

    map :sort_by, :sort_order do |sort_by: "started_at",
      sort_order: "desc"|
      next raw unless SORT_FIELDS.include?(sort_by) &&
        SORT_ORDERS.include?(sort_order)

      raw.order(sort_by => sort_order)
    end

    map :q do |q:|
      raw.where(Project[:name].matches("%#{q}%"))
    end
  end
```

The code looks like pattern matching. Each modification block is activated only when the corresponding parameters or defaults are present. Despite using a custom DSL, we can use all of Ruby's OOP features: extract common functionality into modules or use inheritance, to name a couple.

Note that our filter object implementation is a bit stricter than the previous versions: we return .none if the provided value is incorrect (for the time_filter parameter, Rubanok does it automatically).

Another detail worth mentioning is the usage of the .future scope within the filter object:

```
match :time_filter do
  having "future" do
    raw.future
  end
end
```

I intentionally used the scope here to demonstrate that filter objects can reuse *atomic* scopes already defined on the model (and used elsewhere).

We can iterate further and make our abstraction more *Rails-ish*. For example, we can use a naming convention to automatically infer a filter object from a model and introduce the `ApplicationRecord.filter` method:

```
class ApplicationRecord < ActiveRecord::Base
  def self.filter_by(params, with: nil)
    filter_class = with ||
      "#{self.name.pluralize}Filter".constantize
    filter_class.filter(self, params)
  end
end


rails_projects = Project.filter_by({q: "Rails"})
```

We also allow specifying a custom filter class via the `with` parameter. That would help us to prevent the attempts to make a single universal filter object per model and encourage us to define filter objects for each respective filtering interface.

Filter objects versus form objects versus query objects

In conclusion, I'd like to draw the lines between filter objects and other abstractions we have introduced so far.

Filter objects may be confused with query objects (see *Chapter 6, Data Layer Abstractions*). Indeed, they serve a similar purpose: building queries. However, let's recall that query objects belong to the domain (or domain services) layer. They operate only with domain objects, while filter objects consume user input. Filter objects may use query objects, but query objects should never deal with the presentation layer entities (request parameters, and so on)—they are from the lower architectural layer (domain or domain services).

Filter objects are close to form objects. However, they differ in two aspects. First, form objects perform actions and return the status of the execution, while filter objects must return filtered data used to display the information. Secondly, form objects must provide feedback in case of failure (for example, invalid input); filter objects can ignore unknown parameters. However, there can be situations when hybrid objects, both form and filter, are a good fit.

The most crucial similarity between form and filter objects is that they play a role in *application security*: both must validate user input and reject malicious content, so the lower layers of the application can assume that data is correct and safe.

Summary

In this chapter, you've learned about the presentation layer abstractions, form objects, and filter objects and how they can extract context-specific logic from Active Record models closer to the user interface. You've learned about key features of presentation architectural layer abstractions. Finally, you've practiced using Active Model as a basis for custom Rails abstractions.

In the next chapter, we will finish the topic of reducing Active Record models' responsibility and talk about moving view-specific code to the presentation layer.

Questions

1. Why does a form object abstraction belong to the presentation layer and not the services layer (or lower)?

2. Which common tasks does form object abstraction solve?

3. How do models and form objects relate to each other? Can we create a form object not backed by a model?

4. What is the difference between filter objects and form objects?

5. What is the difference between filter objects and query objects?

Exercise

Consider the invitation and registration scenarios from the *UI forms versus models* section. We tried to enhance the model to support both scenarios (the *fat models* approach). Try moving as much functionality as possible to controllers (the *fat controllers* approach). Look at the resulting code and think of its maintainability properties: readability, testability, and extensibility.

8

Pulling Out
the Representation Layer

This chapter finishes the journey of reducing Active Record models' responsibility by discussing representation-specific logic, which we sometimes put into our model classes. First, we will consider view-template-related helpers and how we can extract them into decorating objects or **presenters**. Then, we will discuss the concept of serialization in API-only applications and how we can organize the corresponding logic using **serializers**.

We will cover the following topics:

- Using presenters to decouple models from views
- Serializers are presenters for your API

The aim of this chapter is to show you how to extract representation-related logic from models to eliminate the coupling introduced by mixing presentation and domain logic in the same architectural layer. By doing so, we will keep our code base maintainable.

Technical requirements

In this chapter, and all chapters of this book, the code given in code blocks is designed to be executed on Ruby 3.2 and Rails 7. Many of the code examples will work on earlier versions of the previously mentioned software.

You will find the code files on GitHub at `https://github.com/PacktPublishing/Layered-Design-for-Ruby-on-Rails-Applications/tree/main/Chapter08`.

Using presenters to decouple models from views

In *Chapter 1, Rails as a Web Application Framework*, we discussed the basics of the MVC paradigm and how Ruby on Rails employs it. Specifically, we mentioned that in Rails, views read from models to render the UI. This naturally introduces a unidirectional connection between the two layers: views depend on models.

However, it's possible to introduce a reverse dependency and make a model aware of (and, thus, responsible for) a particular UI feature. Such a dependency would violate the core principle of the layered architecture—not having upward dependencies (views belong to the presentation layer, the topmost one).

Now, let's move from theory to practice and consider a couple of examples demonstrating such upward dependencies. In other words, let's see how representation logic can leak into the domain layer by looking at the following `User` model:

User

```
class User < ApplicationRecord
  def short_name
    name.squish.split(/\s/).then do |parts|
      parts[0..-2].map { _1[0] + "." }.join + parts.last
    end
  end
end
```

In the preceding code snippet, we can see a situation very typical for a `User` model: adding some name-formatting methods to the class. All that the `#short_name` method does is turn `Ruby Crystal` into `R.Crystal`, so we can print abbreviated names in views:

Post

```
class Post < ApplicationRecord
  def status_icon
    "fa-#{draft? ? 'hourglass-start' : 'calendar-check'}"
  end
  def author_name = user&.short_name
end
```

The `Post` class goes further and adds a helper method (`#status_icon`) to control a page's style by providing a CSS class. Thus, we're mixing our design system with a domain model! Can you imagine that? In Rails, everything is possible, even writing CSS in models.

Here is an example HTML template using the preceding code:

```
<div>
  <i class="fa <%= post.status_icon %>"></i>
  <span><%= post.title %><span>
  <span> (by <%= post.author_name %>)</span>
</div>
```

The preceding methods all serve a single purpose: *the representation of data*. They don't add anything to the domain logic; they're just helpers used in views. However, even discarding architectural principles, keeping such code in models contributes to code bloat and churn, increases high coupling, and, thus, negatively affects maintainability. Let's see how we can move representation logic out of models.

Leave helpers for libraries

Before we jump into off-Rails abstractions, let's first consider a built-in Rails one—**view helpers**.

Rails helpers are Ruby methods, which (mostly) are used by templates and have access to the current rendering context (for example, instance variables defined in controllers). If you add a new resource to a Rails application (via a generator), a corresponding helper module is created by default. Rails assumes that you put some view-related logic for the resource there.

Let's refactor our examples to use helpers:

UsersHelper

```
module UsersHelper
  def user_short_name(user)
    user.name.squish.split(/\s/).then do |parts|
      parts[0..-2].map { _1[0] + "." }.join + parts.last
    end
  end
end
```

PostsHelper

```
module PostsHelper
  def post_icon(post)
    if post.draft?
      "fa-hourglass-start"
    else
      "calendar-check"
    end
```

```
    end

    def post_author(post) = user_short_name(post.user)
  end
```

The actual implementation stayed the same; only the method names changed. We added the `user_` and `post_` prefixes, respectively. This tiny difference signals an important feature—*helpers are global*. Yes, it's possible to disable the *include all helpers* behavior via a configuration option (`config. action_controller.include_all_helpers`), but that would require specifying every module explicitly in the controller class.

The problem is that you need to know which partials (and, thus, helpers) are going to be used by each controller, which is hardly possible when you have a decent amount of deeply nested partials.

There is also no good way to organize helpers. We just have modules and methods, no objects, and other OOP features. So, the more helpers we have, the harder it becomes to maintain them.

Helpers are great for extracting reusable *utility code for views*. That's how Rails itself uses them: form builders, `link_to`, and so on. For application-specific view extensions, we can use better abstractions.

Presenters and decorators

Let's recall that our goal is to extend a domain object for a particular view context. We can say that we want to create a *projection* of an object, something that *represents* a model instance within a view. This is exactly how the **presenter pattern** works.

Basic presenters in plain Ruby

A **presenter** is an object that encapsulates another object (or multiple objects) to provide an interface (*representation*) for the view layer. A presenter acts as a bridge between the model and the view layers, thus increasing loose coupling. A presenter is a *semantical* pattern specifying the role of such objects. The actual structural patterns used to define presenters may vary.

Let's create the simplest possible presenter for a `User` class object:

```
  class UserPresenter
    private attr_reader :user
    def initialize(user) = @user = user
    def short_name
      # The same code as in the examples above
    end
  end
```

Now, whenever we want to represent a user in a view, we can use its presenter:

```
<div id="user-<%= user.id %>">
  <%= link_to UserPresenter.new(user).short_name, user %>
</div>
```

In the preceding example, we used both a raw model instance and its presenter. That's because we may need to access some domain-level information (for example, IDs) and make it possible to use presenters with Rails helpers (so #link_to will generate a correct URL).

We can avoid mixing objects by adding delegation to our presenter class:

```
class UserPresenter
  delegate :id, :to_model, to: :user
  # ...
end
```

Now, in the view, we can only rely on the presenter object:

```
<%- user = UserPresenter.new(user) -%>
<div id="user-<%= user.id %>">
  <%= link_to user.short_name, user %>
</div>
```

This is a basic example of a *closed presenter*: it exposes only a subset of a model's interface (via delegation) to the view layer and hides the implementation details. Closed presenters are better from a layer isolation point of view but they increase the development effort.

First, we need to keep track of methods to delegate, and that can be tricky if the *rendering tree* (made of templates and partials) is complex. Second, we must expose utility methods, which are not actual parts of the representation logic, to make presenters work great with built-in helpers (like we did with the #to_model method).

To improve developer ergonomics, we can use *open presenters* by using the **decorator pattern**.

Presenting decorators

Although the decorator pattern is not view-specific, it could be used as a basis for presenters.

A **decorator** wraps a given object and adds new behavior to it dynamically without affecting other instances of a given class or creating new classes. The decorated object's interface is a superset of the original interface; the methods not explicitly defined by the decorator are delegated to the wrapped object. Thus, decorators could be stacked to add multiple behaviors without breaking the original object's interface.

Decorators are used to extend an object's behavior for a particular context. It shouldn't necessarily be a view context; decorators can be useful in every architecture layer. However, in the Rails community, the word *decorator* is usually used to describe presenting decorators or presenters acting as decorators.

In Ruby, we have a built-in mechanism to create decorators—`SimpleDelegator`:

```ruby
class UserPresenter < SimpleDelegator
  def short_name
    name.squish.split(/\s/).then do |parts|
      parts[0..-2].map { _1[0] + "." }.join + parts.last
    end
  end
end
```

We inherit from the `SimpleDelegator` class to delegate (or proxy) all methods to the underlying object. Now we can use our presenter interchangeably with a model instance (thus, our representation follows the Liskov substitution principle—the L in SOLID). And we don't need to specify methods to expose manually.

Open or closed presenters – which to choose?

The *open/closed presenter* terminology is not common (if it existed before this book). However, in the author's opinion, it communicates the difference between the two most common types of presenters very well: open presenters allow method calls to pass through and reach the target object, while closed presenters do not. The terminology shouldn't be confused with OOP's open/closed principle (although open presenters could be seen as a demonstration of this principle).

Whether to use closed or open presenters is up to you. If you follow the Rails way, it can be reasonable to start with decorating presenters, so you can gradually extract presentation logic from models. For new UI logic, it makes sense to use stricter closed presenters. Yes, it's okay to mix presenter types while you're in the process of adopting the pattern and growing a new abstraction layer on top of it.

Irrespective of the presenter type you choose, you benefit from the significant advantage of keeping representation logic outside of models: this logic knows about the context it is used within.

Models and helpers have no knowledge of the context in which they're being used; if there are multiple different contexts, we must differentiate between methods by using composed names (for example, `Post#admin_status_icon` or `#report_user_short_name`). With presenters, we can have multiple projections by creating different classes—that's it!

So far, we've considered only single-model presenters. However, this pattern is not limited to dealing with a single object representation. Let's see how we can use presenters to project multiple entities at once.

Multi-model presenters, page objects, facades, or...

The concept of the presenter can be easily applied to multiple objects at once. Presenters should be extracted according to UI needs (since they belong to the presentation layer). And sometimes, we have complex interfaces involving multiple objects. Common use cases for such presenters are dashboards, various reports, and similar pages.

Let's consider an example—a page containing information about the books read by a user:

Figure 8.1 – User's books interface

For each book, we show user-specific information: the date when the user read the book, how the user rated the book, and so on. The representation of a book pulls the information from two models: Book and BookRead. The following is the models' code, simplified:

Book

```
class Book < ApplicationRecord
  has_many :book_reads
end
```

BookRead

```
class BookRead < ApplicationRecord
  belongs_to :user
  belongs_to :book

  def read? = !!read_at
end
```

User

```
class User < ApplicationRecord
  has_many :book_reads
end
```

Then, to represent a book in the context of a particular user, we can write a `User::BookPresenter` class, as follows:

```
class BookPresenter < SimpleDelegator
  # some common book representation logic
end

class User::BookPresenter < BookPresenter
  private attr_reader :book_read
  delegate :read?, :read_at, :score, to: :book_read
  def initialize(book, book_read)
    super(book)
    @book_read = book_read
  end

  def progress_icon
    read? ? "fa-circle-check" : "fa-clock"
  end

  def score_class
    case score
    when 0..2 then "text-red-600"
    when 3...4 then "text-yellow-600"
    when 4... then "text-green-600"
    end
  end
end
```

We inherit our presenter from the base `BookPresenter` class. This way, we leverage the benefits of object-oriented presenters (compared to view helpers). We also delegate some methods to the `BookRead` object and add a couple of UI-specific methods—#`progress_icon` and #`score_class`.

Now, we can use our presenter in the view template (styling is omitted):

```
<% user.book_reads.preload(:book).each do |book_read| %>
  <%- book = User::BookPresenter.new(book_read.book, book_read) %>
  <div id="book-#{book.id}">
    <h1>
      <%= book.title %>
```

```
      <i class="fa <%= book.progress_icon %>"></i>
    </h1>
    <%- if book.read? %>
      <div>
        <span>Read at: <%= l(book.read_at) %></span>
        <span class="<%= book.score_class %>">
          <%= book.score %> / 5
        </span>
      </div>
    <% end %>
    </div
  </div>
<% end %>
```

Technically, we could avoid using a multi-model presenter and create a `BookReadPresenter` class instead. The problem with this approach is that the presenter becomes vaguely connected to the interface: we display books, not virtual reads. Also, we cannot use inheritance anymore.

The idea of multi-object presenters can be found in technical literature under different names, such as **page objects** or **facades**. Usually, more specialized naming is a result of additional constraints and conventions on top of the presenter pattern. This brings the pattern one step closer to becoming an abstraction.

Presenters as an abstraction layer

Let's talk about how we can turn the presenter pattern into a full-featured abstraction layer. Which conventions do we introduce? What are the common tasks to be solved by a good abstraction?

Naming conventions and code organization

As always, in Rails, we can employ a naming convention to both communicate the role of an object and reduce boilerplate in the source code.

In the preceding examples, we already used the `Presenter` suffix for presenter classes. This is a common Rails naming pattern, and it brings the following benefits right away:

- We can automatically infer presenter classes from model entities (`"#{self.class.name} Presenter".constantize`).

- We naturally get an answer to the question *Where do we keep presenters?* —`app/presenters`! (Or even `app/views/presenters`; see *Chapter 11, Better Abstractions for HTML Views*.)

- One common way to leverage the naming convention for presenters is by creating a universal helper method to convert objects into their representations. For example, we can create a #present helper:

```
module ApplicationHelper
  def present(obj, with: nil)
    presenter_class = with ||
      "#{obj.class.name}Presenter".constantize
    presenter_class.new(obj)
  end
end
```

Note that we allow specifying a presenter class explicitly—that will help us to use different presenters for the same class.

Now, we can update our template to use the helper:

```
<%- user = present(user) -%>
<div id="user-<%= user.id %>">
  <%= link_to user.short_name, user %>
</div>
```

Our #present helper provides just basic functionality. In a real-world application, you may want to make it smarter. You can add a cache to avoid allocating new presenters to the same objects (for example, when you render templates in a loop).

Another useful modification would be making the #present helper namespace-aware, that is, preserve the controller namespace (for example, use Admin::UserPresenter in Admin::WhateverController).

Another option is to pick an existing library to manage the presenters layer in the application. Let's consider, for example, the keynote gem.

What a gem — keynote

Keynote (https://github.com/rf-/keynote) is a library that provides a consistent interface to define presenters and use them in the application (via helpers). It also comes with test helpers so that you can test presenters in isolation. Presenters created with Keynote are closed presenters by design. A distinctive feature of this gem is the built-in caching mechanism, which allows reusing presenters for the same object (that is, present(obj).equal?(present(obj)) is true).

Let's rewrite our original example using Keynote:

PostPresenter

```
class PostPresenter < Keynote::Presentor
  presents :post
  def status_icon
    if post.draft?
      "fa-hourglass-start"
    else
      "fa-calendar-check"
    end
  end
end
```

UserPresenter

```
class UserPresenter < Keynote::Presenter
  presents :user

  def short_name
    user.name ...
    # The same code as before
  end
end
```

In views, we use the #k helper to get a presenter for an object:

```
<div>
  <i class="fa <%= k(post).status_icon %>"></i>
  <span><%= post.title %><span>
  <span> (by <%= k(post.user).short_name %>)</span>
</div>
```

Note that unlike in previous examples, we do not instantiate a presenter beforehand but do that right when we need to use it. So, we call #k multiple times, and we can do that for the same object: Keynote's caching mechanism will create and reuse only a single presenter object.

Using a shortcut method to initialize presenters in views has one more advantage: we can pass additional context to the presenter object implicitly. For example, we can make the current view context (and, thus, view helpers) accessible from a presenter.

View helpers in presenters

In the preceding example template, we have the logic of rendering an icon spread across two files, the HTML template and the presenter. What if we could keep this logic in one place?

One option is to add conditionals to the template and render different icons depending on the value of post.draft?. That would increase the template complexity. In general, we should tend to minimize logical branches in HTML templates to improve readability. And that's where presenters are especially helpful.

With Keynote, each presenter has access to the view context and view helpers. That is, we can generate HTML programmatically using Rails helpers in presenters.

Let's upgrade our PostPresenter class to become responsible for the whole icon rendering:

```
class PostPresenter < Keynote::Presenter
  presents :post
  def status_icon
    icon = post.draft? ?  "hourglass-start" : "clock"
    content_tag(:i, nil, class: "fa fa-#{icon}")
  end
end
```

And now, in the template, we can render the result of the presenter's method call:

```
<div>
  <%= k(post).status_icon %>
  <span><%= post.title %><span>
</div>
```

Beware of playing too much of the *HTML-in-presenter* game. A presenter should act as a template helper, not a substitute. A presenting object is still connected to the underlying domain object; it's not an abstraction for organizing templates (for that, we have view components; see *Chapter 11, Better Abstractions for HTML Views*).

Avoid leaking presenters

Presenters belong to the presentation layer. Thus, we shouldn't let them escape to lower layers. That means you shouldn't replace real objects with their representations too early. You should be especially careful with decorators since it may be tempting to decorate an object right after its instantiation in a controller.

Consider the following example:

```
class PostController < ApplicationController
  before_action :set_post, only: [:show]
```

```
    def show
      Analytics.track_event("post.viewed", @post)
    end

    private
    def set_post = @post = present(Post.find(params[:id]))
  end
```

We track post views by invoking the `Analytics` module—it belongs to the services (or, maybe, infrastructure) layer. However, by decorating the `Post` object in the `#set_post` method (via the `#present` helper), we introduce a *leakage*: the decorator from the presentation layer is passed to the lower layer.

Although the decorator behaves like the original object, it's a different one. For instance, if the `Analytics` service uses the object class to generate an event's metadata, it would be corrupted:

```
module Analytics
  def self.track_event(name, obj)
    puts("event=#{name} id=#{obj.id} class=#{obj.class}")
  end
end

get "/posts/1"
↳ event=post.viewed id=1 class=PostPresenter
```

Thus, it's better to create representations right within views or pass them as explicit rendering arguments (via template locals).

Let's stop discussing HTML views for a moment (we will continue to talk about them in *Chapter 11, Better Abstractions for HTML Views*) and talk about the presentation layer in API-only applications.

Serializers are presenters for your API

Ruby on Rails is popular for both HTML-first and API-first applications. So far in this chapter, we've only considered HTML-driven applications, with templates, view helpers, and so on—all the frontend things. What about pure backend Rails applications? Is there a representation layer? Sure, there is.

Although API-only Rails applications delegate most of the browser-related work to frontend frameworks, it's still the responsibility of the application's presentation layer to prepare responses to HTTP requests.

In most cases, we deal with JSON responses. So, let's discuss how we can turn our application's data into JSON strings and how the presenter pattern could be used here, too.

From model to JSON

In Rails, there are a couple of built-in options for generating JSON responses. Let's first discuss them.

Using #as_json

Rails makes it dead simple to respond with JSON from controllers. All you need to do is to call the `#render` method with the `json` option:

```
class PostsController < ApplicationController
  def show
    post = Post.find(params[:id])
    render json: post
  end
end
```

That's it! Rails will automatically turn your model object into a hash first and into a JSON afterward:

```
get "/posts/1"
↳ {"id":1,"title":"Serialize all the things","user_id":1,
"draft":true,"created_at":"…","updated_at":"…"}
```

However, the default behavior is to include all model attributes in the resulting hash. Chances are low that you want to expose all the model fields to the client application (imagine rendering a `User` record with password hashes and salts).

We can modify this logic by overriding the `#as_json` method:

```
class Post < ApplicationRecord
  belongs_to :user
  def as_json(options)
    super({
      only: [:id, :title, :draft],
      include: {user: {only: [:id, :name]}}
    }.merge(options))
  end
end
```

With `#as_json`, we can specify which attributes to include and can even include associations:

```
get "/posts/1"
↳ {"id":1,"title":"Serialize all the
things","draft":true,"user":{"id":1,"name":"J Son"}}
```

Note that we used the `super({...}.merge(options))` expression in `#as_json`. This will allow us to pass custom configuration, if necessary, as in the following example:

```
def show
  post = Post.find(params[:id])
  render json: post.as_json({only: [:id]})
end
```

Although we reached some flexibility, our JSON is still highly coupled with the model. In theory, it's possible to rename fields or add virtual ones, but that would make the resulting code quite complex. No worries, Rails has you covered—we can use templates to render JSON!

Templatifying JSON via Jbuilder

The Rails way of dealing with non-trivial JSON schemas is using a custom template engine called **Jbuilder** (`https://github.com/rails/jbuilder`). Jbuilder is a template engine (like ERB, Haml, or Slim). Hence, all the problems discussed in the first part of this chapter could apply to Jbuilder as well.

And yes, we can use presenters to isolate representation logic, too. But then the question arises: does it make sense to keep JSON representation logic in two abstractions, presenters and templates? The answer is *no*. Templates would be redundant; we can cover all the JSON representation needs with presenters.

Serializers as API presenters

In the Ruby world, presenters used to generate JSON responses are usually called **serializers**, thus communicating that their purpose is to serialize domain objects to JSON format.

Strictly speaking, **serialization** is the process of converting an object into some transferrable form (for example, into a JSON string), which can be used to *restore* the object. When we serialize a Ruby object to JSON sent to a client application, we transfer the representation requested by the client application. We never transfer original objects. Thus, serializers are just specialized presenters.

Plain Ruby serializer

We can turn any presenter from the first part of the chapter into a serializer by simply defining the `#as_json` method. Take the following example:

UserSerializer

```
class UserPresenter < SimpleDelegator
  def short_name
    # ...
  end
```

```ruby
  def as_json(...)
    {id:, short_name:}
  end
end
```

PostSerializer

```ruby
class PostPresenter < SimpleDelegator
  def as_json(...)
    {
      id:, title:,
      is_draft: draft?,
      user: UserPresenter.new(user)
    }
  end
end
```

The approach is straightforward: define helper methods when necessary and build a resulting hash manually. With the Ruby 3.1 hash shorthand syntax, the resulting code even looks readable enough. But we can do better if we treat serializers as a specific abstraction to render JSON responses.

Serializer as an abstraction

Defining the #as_json method by hand is far from being developer-friendly. We can avoid this routine by introducing some configuration methods or DSL. Let's consider a particular library for defining serializers—Alba.

> **What a gem — alba**
>
> The alba gem (https://github.com/okuramasafumi/alba) is a performant JSON serializing library for Ruby (not only Rails) applications. It provides a convenient and powerful DSL for defining serializer objects with support for nested attributes and associations.

The main purpose of the serializer is to declare which fields to include in the resulting JSON. The most intuitive way of doing this is to specify them as a list. Using Alba, the serializer definition will look as follows:

```ruby
class PostSerializer < ApplicationSerializer
  attributes :id, :title
  attribute :is_draft, &:draft?
end
```

Delegating attributes to an underlying object could be configured via a single expression. Renaming is also plain and clear. Let's add an association:

```
class PostSerializer < ApplicationSerializer
  # ...
  one :user
end
```

Just one line to include a serialized user to the post's JSON representation. Without any options, the `UserSerializer` class will be used. This is possible with the help of some extensions we defined in the base class:

```
class ApplicationSerializer
  include Alba::Resource
  class << self
    def one(name, **options)
      options[:resource] ||= proc {
        "#{_1.class.name}Serializer".constantize
      }
      super(name, **options)
    end
  end
end
```

We provide the default resource class as a `Proc` instance, which infers a serializer class from a given object class name. Using `Proc` intstances is required to make code reload work in development (so that the latest version of a serializer class is used every time).

Since Alba is not a Rails-specific library, some tuning is required. We also deviate from Alba's terminology and use *Serializer* instead of *Resource* as a class name suffix. This is how we form an abstraction layer for our Rails application and don't simply use a library.

In the controller, we also use a custom helper to look up a serializer class:

```
class PostsController < ApplicationController
  def index
    render json: serialize(Post.all)
  end
end
```

The `#serialize` helper is defined as follows:

```
class ApplicationController
  private
  def serialize(obj, with: nil)
```

```
      serializer = with || begin
        model = obj.try(:model) || obj.class
        "#{model.name}Serializer".constantize
      end
      serializer.new(obj)
    end
  end
```

Using a custom base class and a helper to infer serializers (such as `ApplicationSerializer` and `#serialize` from the previous snippets) makes our serializers less coupled with the implementation. It also helps us to turn serializers into first-class application citizens and form a full-featured abstraction layer out of them.

Summary

In this chapter, you learned about the presenter pattern and how it can be used to move representation logic closer to views. You now understand the drawbacks of keeping presentation logic in models and the downsides of using view helpers. You learned about open and closed presenters, as well as about the general decorator pattern.

You familiarized yourself with the common practices and conventions used to form/shape an abstraction layer from presenters. You've learned about representation patterns used in API applications, such as serializers, and how they're common to presenters.

This chapter finishes the topic of reducing models' responsibility. In the next chapter, we will talk about one of the vital security concerns and the corresponding abstractions—authorization.

Questions

1. What are the pros and cons of moving presentation logic from models to helpers?
2. What is the difference between a closed presenter and an open presenter (or decorator)?
3. Can presenters be used to generate HTML for views?
4. What is the leaking decorator problem?
5. What is the difference between serializers and presenters?
6. How do Rails serializers relate to the concept of serialization?

Further reading

Polished Ruby Programming (Chapter 2, Designing Useful Common Classes): `https://www.packtpub.com/product/polished-ruby-programming/9781801072724`

Part 3:
Essential Layers
for Rails Applications

In this part, we will discuss the most common abstraction layers that can help to keep your Rails code base maintainable and your team productive.

This part has the following chapters:

- *Chapter 9, Authorization Models and Layers*
- *Chapter 10, Crafting the Notifications Layer*
- *Chapter 11, Better Abstractions for HTML Views*
- *Chapter 12, Configuration as a First-Class Application Citizen*
- *Chapter 13, Cross-Layers and Off-Layers*

Authorization
Models and Layers

Authorization is a crucial security aspect and, thus, it's important for any web application. This chapter explores the concept of authorization in Ruby on Rails applications. First, we will discuss the role and place of authorization in an application's security.

Then, we'll introduce the two fundamental concepts of authorization: the **authorization model** and the **authorization layer**. Finally, we'll discuss the problem of authorization enforcement and how it relates to an application's performance.

This chapter touches on an important topic of application security. The robustness of its implementation is doubly important. Every user action must be authorized, and every input verified. You can achieve such a level of robustness by designing proper abstractions in your application. This is exactly what we will try to accomplish in this chapter.

We will cover the following topics:

- Authorization, authentication, and friends
- Authorization models
- Authorization enforcement, or the need for authorization abstractions
- The performance implications of authorization

The goal of this chapter is to learn how authorization can be integrated into a Rails web application according to the layered architecture principles.

Technical requirements

In this chapter, and all chapters of this book, the code given in code blocks is designed to be executed on Ruby 3.2 and Rails 7. Many of the code examples will work on earlier versions of the aforementioned software.

You will find the code files on GitHub at `https://github.com/PacktPublishing/Layered-Design-for-Ruby-on-Rails-Applications/tree/main/Chapter09`.

Authorization, authentication, and friends

The security of a web application is a vast topic. Although (web) frameworks often offer built-in security measures to overcome some common vulnerabilities such as XSS attacks and SQL injections, various other aspects of web application security are the responsibility of engineers building on top of the framework. In this book, we focus on the latter group.

Let's begin by differentiating between the two most popular and commonly confused concepts: *authorization* and *authentication*.

Authentication versus authorization

The meaning of life of every web application is to serve user requests (note that a user is not necessarily a human), and, in most cases, we restrict which requests are available to a particular user and which must be forbidden. The underlying decision-making process could be divided into two phases, which can be represented by the following questions:

- **Who's there?**: Or, on behalf of which domain entity (User, Account, or Customer) is this request made? This is known as **identification**. Usually, we also verify that provided information is valid—that is, the user is who they say they are. For instance, we can ask for a password. This is known as **verification**. But we don't ask for a password on every request, right?

  As soon as we have identified and verified a user, we issue some kind of *token* to use for subsequent requests to transparently identify and verify the current user. This is known as authentication, technically speaking. However, the term **authentication** is commonly used to describe all three: identification, verification, and authentication.

- **Am I allowed to do that?**: This question assumes that we already have *I*, an acting subject, and we know which action this subject wants to perform. Depending on the subject, the action, and—in most cases—the action's target object, we respond to the question with *yes* or *no*. This is known as **authorization**.

We can say that the responsibility of authentication is to enrich the execution context with the current actor (verified), while the responsibility of authorization is to ensure that the actor has enough permissions to execute the request. In some sense, authorization validates the execution context.

Let's look at an example controller action—deleting a post:

```
class PostsController < ApplicationController
  before_action :authenticate! # authentication
  def destroy
    post = Post.find(params[:id])
    if post.user_id == current_user.id # authorization
      # context has been validated,
      # feel free to perform the action
      post.destroy
      redirect_to posts_path, notice: "Post has been
       deleted"
    else
      redirect_to posts_path, alert: "You are not allowed
        to delete this post"
    end
  end
end
```

We have two guard clauses in the code, and we can easily recognize authentication and authorization in them by asking the right questions.

Both authorization and authentication protect the application at the presentation level (since both require the current actor). For regular HTTP requests, both are performed within the controller abstraction layer—as early as possible.

To see a better picture of Rails applications security, we must also mention similar concepts from the lower architecture layers.

Lines of defense for a web application

Let me first make a statement: each architectural (or abstraction) layer of an application must be secured. Even though we said that authorization validates the context, we shouldn't be careless down the execution path. We still have a lot of things to be careful about: user input, data consistency, and so on.

In the services layer, we can verify system constraints. System constraints describe which business operations can be performed independently of the current actor. Thus, we exclude the *user* element from the authorization triple of *user-action-target* .

Here are some examples of system constraints:

- An organization with a *Free* tier may only have one project
- A user can generate only 100 images per day
- The system is not allowed to publish chat messages with links to websites from the blocklist

Note that even in the second example, we talk about a user; we still call this rule a system constraint because it doesn't depend on user permissions but on the feature limits. Moderation (the third example) is another common use case for system constraints.

Finally, at the domain level, we verify data consistency through validations (see *Chapter 2, Active Models and Records*).

The process is illustrated in the following diagram:

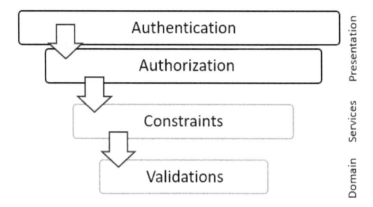

Figure 9.1 – Lines of defense in a web application

From the layered architecture point of view, it's important to keep each kind of protection (authentication, authorization, system constraints, and validations) in a single layer. That is, performing authorization sometimes in a controller and sometimes in a service object should be considered a design smell. Why? By requiring (and allowing) each kind of protection only within a particular layer, we guarantee consistency.

Also, we make it easier to reason about arguments and the context at the lower level. For example, if a service object was called with a user and some record as input, we can freely assume that the corresponding action has been verified, and we don't need to double-check permissions.

In this chapter, we focus only on authorization, though similar ideas (to the ones described shortly) can be applied to other security concerns (for example, system constraints).

Authorization models

Although the act of authorization happens in the presentation layer, its roots lie much deeper—in the domain layer. To answer the question *Am I allowed to…?*, we usually rely on some properties of the domain objects. Thus, we rely on the domain model. The subset of the domain model responsible for authorization logic is called the **authorization model**. Let's do a quick overview of common authorization models.

Domain-less authorization models

Technically, to perform authorization, we mustn't have a dedicated model. For example, if you build an application in which a user can only work with their own data (for example, personal notes management), there is no need to introduce roles, permissions, and so on.

All you need is to verify that a target object belongs to the current user. We did this in the previous example, reproduced here:

```
class PostsController < ApplicationController
  def destroy
    post = Post.find(params[:id])
    if post.user_id == current_user.id
      post.destroy
      redirect_to posts_path
    else
      redirect_to posts_path, alert: "Forbidden"
    end
  end
end
```

This is a very basic authorization scenario. We may also have special admin users in the application, and to differentiate between regular and admin users, we need to enhance our model. For example, we can add the User#is_admin attribute—and an authorization model is born!

Although there are no formal restrictions on how to implement an authorization model, in most cases, developers tend to pick one of the classic ones.

Classic authorization models

Formal authorization models describe relationships between subjects and objects, which can be used to perform access checks. That's why they are usually called *some kind of access control*, and there are plenty of abbreviations such as DAC, MAC, RBAC, and so on.

Let's decipher some of them!

> **Note**
>
> We will use the User model as the authorization subject in the rest of the chapter for simplicity.

Role-based access control (RBAC)

Role-based access implies that each user has a role or multiple roles. Roles give users privileges to perform specific operations on different domain entities (or resources), as depicted in the following diagram:

Figure 9.2 – RBAC diagram

There are multiple ways to introduce roles into the application's domain model, as follows:

- Roles can be static (a fixed set) or dynamic (created by users)

- Roles can be backed by a model or just an attribute in the User model

Let's consider, for example, a library application using RBAC. We have three types (and, thus, roles) of users: administrators, librarians, and regular users.

We can add the User#role attribute to represent roles:

```
class User < ApplicationRecord
  enum :role, regular: "regular", admin: "admin",
    librarian: "librarian"
end
```

We declared the possible role value using the .enum feature of Active Record. This feature also generates useful helper methods, such as #admin? and #librarian? predicates.

We can now use them in a controller to perform authorization:

```
class BooksController < ApplicationController
  before_action :require_access, only: [:new, :create,
    :edit, :update, :destroy]

  private
  def require_access
    return if current_user.librarian? ||
      current_user.admin?
    redirect_to books_path, alert: "No access"
  end
end
```

The authorization check is a simple logical expression. However, this simplicity vanishes as our authorization logic evolves. With every new role added, we need to update a lot of places in the code to take this new role into account. We can avoid this by denormalizing roles into permissions.

Roles as permission sets

As we stated in the RBAC definition, roles define sets of privileges or permissions for users. Thus, permissions always exist in a role-based authorization model, even if we don't define them explicitly in the code. For example, in our library application example, we may have the following permissions:

Role/Permission	Regular	Librarian	Administrator
Browse catalog	X	X	x
Borrow books	X	X	x
Manage books		X	x
Manage librarians			x

Permissions communicate business logic concerns, not design or implementation details. That's why, for example, we have identical (in terms of inclusion into roles) permissions—*Browse catalog* and *Borrow books*. These permissions represent two independent (though related) user actions; they can diverge in the future.

By introducing permissions into authorization-related code, we can simplify logical expressions in access checks:

```
class BooksController < ApplicationController
  # ...
  private
  def require_access
    return unless current_user.permission?(:manage_books)
    redirect_to books_path, alert: "No access"
  end
end
```

We only allow the action if a user has the required permission; our controller's code no longer depends on actual roles. Here is a straightforward implementation of the `User#permission?` method:

```
class User < ApplicationRecord
  enum :role, regular: "regular", admin: "admin",
    librarian: "librarian"
  REGULAR_PERMISSIONS = %i[
   browse_catalogue borrow_books
  ].freeze
```

```
LIBRARIAN_PERMISSIONS = (
  REGULAR_PERMISSIONS + %i[manage_books]
).freeze
ADMIN_PERMISSIONS = (
  LIBRARIAN_PERMISSIONS + %i[manage_librarians]
).freeze
PERMISSIONS = {
  regular: REGULAR_PERMISSIONS,
  librarian: LIBRARIAN_PERMISSIONS,
  admin: ADMIN_PERMISSIONS
}.freeze

def permission?(name) =
  PERMISSIONS.fetch(role.to_sym)
           .include?(name)
end
```

Careful readers would have probably noticed that authorization-related logic flooded the model class, and that's not what we aim for in this book. We can refactor this code by introducing a role value object (see *Chapter 2, Active Models and Records*), for example. I will leave this exercise to the reader.

Too many roles

A typical RBAC model problem is **role explosion**. This is a situation when a new action requires specific permissions that can't be covered by existing roles. So, we create a new one, and again and again. To break this cycle, we can upgrade to a more flexible access control model.

Attribute-based access control (ABAC)

The ABAC model can be seen as a generalization of RBAC. With RBAC, we only take into account roles, while with ABAC, any attributes of objects and subjects can be used to define the set of permitted actions. In addition, the authorization environment or context can also play a role in making an access decision, as depicted in the following diagram:

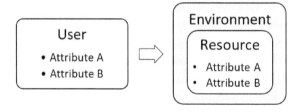

Figure 9.3 – ABAC diagram

To demonstrate ABAC in action, let's enhance our library example and add another authorization constraint: librarians can only delete books from the departments they belong to. For simplicity, let's use enums again to add departments:

User model

```
class User < ApplicationRecord
  enum :dept, fic: "fic", nonfic: "nonfic",
              ref: "ref"
end
```

Book model

```
class Book < ApplicationRecord
  enum :dept, fic: "fic", nonfic: "nonfic",
              ref: "ref"
end
```

Now, in the controller, we also need to check for matching departments for librarians in addition to the permission check:

```
class BooksController < ApplicationController
  def destroy
    book = Book.find(params[:id])
    if current_user.permission?(:manage_all_books) || (
      current_user.permission?(:manage_books) &&
      book.dept == current_user.dept
    )
      book.destroy!
      redirect_to books_path, notice: "Removed"
    else
      redirect_to books_path, alert: "No access"
    end
  end
end
```

Note that we also added a new permission, `:manage_all_books`. It's a new permission for admins since they may manage all the books in the library. Could we use the `current_user.admin?` check? Technically, yes—the result would be the same. But mixing roles and permissions when performing authorization checks eliminates the pros of denormalization.

The flexibility of the ABAC model is limited only by the expressiveness of the language we use to define authorization rules—that is, the rules and the corresponding code can be as sophisticated as we can imagine. Keeping access rules logic in an inbound layer (such as controllers) quickly leads to duplication and overall higher complexity of both the application and test code.

Let's discuss how we can separate authorization rules from authorization enforcement and why we must do that.

Authorization enforcement, or the need for authorization abstractions

From the layered architecture point of view, defining authorization rules right in the presentation layer doesn't seem right. Authorization rules must describe your business logic.

They do not and should not depend on the delivery mechanism (HTML, APIs, WebSockets, and so on) and, thus, can be used by different presentation-layer abstractions (or different inbound abstraction layers). Only **authorization enforcement**, the act of performing authorization, must stay in the presentation layer, and the enforcement must rely on the rules defined lower in the architecture stack. How much lower?

Putting authorization rules into models can look attractive. For each model, we can define a method encapsulating authorization rules (say, `Post#can?(user, action)`) and use it in controllers. This approach has at least two problems. First, as always with models, such methods are not context-aware; we should either add separate, context-specific methods or try to add modifying parameters, thus increasing the complexity of the `#can?` method.

Secondly, authorization rules are not part of the domain layer. Domain objects do not need authorization; they live in the authorized context. By moving authorization rules up (say, to the services layer), we disallow authorization checks in the domain layer by design.

Thus, we need a new abstraction at the services layer. If we look up the ABAC article on *Wikipedia* (`https://en.wikipedia.org/wiki/Attribute-based_access_control`), we can find that it is also referred to as **policy-based access control** (**PBAC**). That's because, typically, authorization rules are described as policies. Unsurprisingly, there is a design pattern with a similar name that we can utilize for authorization purposes.

Extracting policy objects

Policy objects are not specific to authorization and even security features; they can be used for any business rules in your application. When it comes to authorization, a single policy object usually corresponds to a single resource in your application. In most cases, a resource is a domain model entity.

Pattern – policy object

A **policy object** encapsulates a business rule or a set of related business rules describing which operations can be performed or not within a given context. Its main purposes are hiding the implementation details (usually, a bunch of *ifs* and *elses*) and reducing duplication. A policy object public interface usually contains one or a few predicate methods—that is, methods returning `true` or `false`.

In our library application example, we have a `Book` resource (and the corresponding model). Thus, we can create a `BookPolicy` class to encapsulate authorization rules related to the `Book` model.

Let's do that using plain Ruby:

```ruby
class BookPolicy
  attr_reader :user, :book
  def initialize(user, book)
    @user, @book = user, book
  end

  def destroy?
    user.permission?(:manage_all_books) || (
      user.permission?(:manage_books) &&
      book.dept == user.dept
    )
  end
end
```

We moved our expression to check the permissions to delete a book into the `#destroy?` predicate method. We also made a `book` instance a part of the policy object's state along with a `user` object.

Thus, each policy object is associated with a particular resource entity and the current authorization context (user). Alternatively, we might make a policy object independent of a resource instance and pass it as an argument to predicate methods, like so:

```ruby
def destroy?(book)
  # ...
end
```

This approach makes sense if you need to perform authorization against many resources during a single unit of work, so you can avoid the overhead of creating many policy objects. In practice, such a situation is not common.

Usually, we authorize a single resource, and making it a part of the policy object's state can be beneficial in terms of code readability (no need to propagate parameters to internal methods).

Let's see how we can use our newly created policy object in the controller:

```
class BooksController < ApplicationController
  def destroy
    book = Book.find(params[:id])
    if BookPolicy.new(current_user, book).destroy?
      book.destroy!
      redirect_to books_path, notice: "Removed"
    else
      redirect_to books_path, alert: "No access"
    end
  end
end
```

The controller's code has now become more readable. We can clearly see the phases of the action's execution: look up a target record, perform authorization, and execute the operation. The controller looks like an actual controller orchestrating data flow. The actual logic is delegated to lower abstraction layers.

Even adding such a simple policy object is beneficial from a maintainability perspective. We not only improved readability but we also made it possible to reuse the code responsible for authorization. Let's see what we can achieve by building an authorization policy object abstraction layer.

Shaping an abstraction layer for authorization

Technically, authorization spreads across multiple architecture layers: policy objects (services), enforcement points, and view filtering (presentation). Thus, the primary goal of policy abstraction is to provide seamless integration with the presentation layer. Here, *seamless* means that authorization should act as a pluggable concept for inbound layers, not be highly coupled with the host code.

Let's see what such abstraction can look like by using the Action Policy library as an example.

> **What a gem – action_policy**
>
> Action Policy (`https://github.com/palkan/action_policy`) is an authorization framework for Ruby and Rails applications that uses policy objects to define authorization rules. The framework focuses on performance, scalability, and developer experience (via enhanced debugging and testing support).

Action Policy provides a standardized interface for policy classes and comes with extensions (Ruby modules) to inject authorization enforcement into any Ruby class. Let's see how these two aspects (policy classes and authorization enforcement modules) work together to help you integrate policy-driven authorization into your code base.

Conventions for policy classes

As with other abstractions, employing naming conventions serves two purposes: interface unification and boilerplate reduction.

As we already learned in the previous chapter, there is a common pattern to naming model-related classes by adding suffixes. We agreed that policies should be resource-based; hence, we can use "`<Model>Policy`" class names for policy objects. We already did this in the plain Ruby example shown previously (`BookPolicy`).

To name predicate methods, we can rely on the fact that authorization enforcement usually happens in controllers. Thus, we can borrow the naming from Rails controllers: `#show?`, `#update?`, and `#destroy?`. This way, our policy classes will provide a hint on where they're used. This correspondence can also be used to simplify the enforcement code (see the code in the *Seamless authorization enforcement* section).

On the other hand, defining all CRUD-based rules in each policy can be redundant. From an authorization point of view, many actions are conceptually the same. For example, `#edit?`, `#update?`, and `#destroy?` usually answer the same question: does a user have write access to the resource?

Similarly, `#show?` and `#index?` can be seen as read operations. Thus, we can design our policy based on the two fundamental permission types and define action-specific predicates when needed. In Action Policy, we can use the `#view?` and `#manage?` methods for that:

```ruby
class BookPolicy < ApplicationPolicy
  def view?() = true
  def manage?
    permission?(:manage_all_books) || (
      permission?(:manage_books) &&
      book.dept == user.dept
    )
  end
end
```

Under the hood, aliases are created to route read actions (show, index, and so on.) to the `#view?` rule and everything else to the `#manage?` rule.

Note that our policy class has no initialization (constructor) code. That's because we assume that every policy object is created for a given authorization context (usually, the current user, but it can be a composite) and a resource instance being authorized. Thus, we made both the context and the resource being authorized a part of the object's state and exposed via attribute readers (`#user` and `#book`, respectively). The name of the resource attribute (`book`) is inferred from the policy class name.

To sum up, here are the things to consider when you define an abstraction for authorization policy objects:

- Name policies according to the resources they're attached to

- Choose predicate names reflecting the authorization nature (read, write, execute, and so on) and provide aliases to connect to the presentation layer

- Standardize the constructor/state interface

The idea of adding CRUD aliases to policy classes may look controversial: aren't we introducing a reverse dependency with the presentation layer? To answer this question, let's see how authorization enforcement works with our abstraction.

Seamless authorization enforcement

As we already mentioned a few times, we commonly perform authorization checks in controllers. Let's see how this can be accomplished if we follow the conventions described previously (using Action Policy):

Authorization enforcement with Action Policy

```
class BooksController < ApplicationController
  def destroy
    book = Book.find(params[:id])
    authorize! book
    book.destroy!
    redirect_to books_path, notice: "Removed"
  end
end
```

The injection of authorization requires just a single line of code. However, under the hood, the #authorize! helper does a lot, as outlined here:

- A policy class is identified from the passed record (book → BookPolicy)

- A policy rule is inferred from the controller's action name (#destroy → #destroy?)

- Finally, the rule is invoked with #current_user as a context, and an exception is raised if the authorization fails

All three items from the preceding list rely on the abstraction we defined previously, thus demonstrating its power.

There are a couple more things worth paying attention to in the *Authorization enforcement with Action Policy* snippet, so let's have a look at what these are.

First, we trigger the `destroy?` policy rule, which resolves to the `manage?` rule under the hood. By not calling the `manage?` rule directly, we *decouple common actions from rules*. A controller shouldn't know whether there is a difference between, say, an update or destroy action for a particular resource—that's the responsibility of the policy object. Thus, if later we enhance our policy and add a custom `#destroy?` method, no change in the presentation layer will be required.

The corner case in this approach is using custom, non-RESTful actions. Should there be corresponding aliases in policy classes? It depends, but in general, this will mean that a policy becomes aware of the presentation, and thus should be avoided. The CRUD-based rules (`#index?`, `#show?`, `#create?`, and so on) are generic enough not to be considered presentation-specific.

The only thing that makes our policies somehow coupled with controllers is the Rails naming convention for action names. But here, we can say that we reuse the naming convention as an abstract idea, not the fact that it's used by controllers.

The second noticeable feature of our authorization enforcement implementation is the exception-driven control flow. It's also a typical authorization pattern: break out from the execution flow by raising an exception. Even more, treating authorization failures as exceptions is natural.

Why? An application shouldn't allow the execution of unauthorized actions in the first place (for example, we should avoid showing certain buttons or links to users that they aren't allowed to click); that is, a regular user (not a hacker) shouldn't be able to do that at all.

Authorization can be implemented with a single line of code. Let's see how this line affects the testability of the object it's injected into.

Authorization versus testability

Policy objects can be tested in isolation as units. Unit tests are faster and require less setup than integration tests, so extracting policy objects has a positive impact on the application's testability. However, we still need to figure out how to test the act of authorization enforcement.

Testing authorization only in policy tests is not enough to make sure your application is properly secured. You should always test authorization at the level at which it's enforced. In other words, for every controller action, there should be a corresponding test that ensures that an expected authorization was performed. How to do that?

A naïve way to test authorization is to cover all permissions-related scenarios in integration tests (for example, controller tests). Although this approach may seem the most robust, it leads to duplication and redundancy. Moreover, since the amount of code needed to thoroughly test all actions is huge, it's much easier to miss some edge cases and, thus, introduce breaches.

Rephrasing the question can help us to come up with a better testing technique: what does it mean to verify that authorization has been performed as expected? Since we use a well-defined abstraction and a standard enforcement mechanism, we can say that verifying authorization is equal to checking that a particular policy has been used to authorize a given resource with a given user as a context. If we can write such a test, the actual authorization logic can only be tested in policy tests.

Action Policy comes with a built-in solution to this problem—custom RSpec and Minitest matchers:

```
class BooksTest < ActionDispatch::IntegrationTest
  include ActionPolicy::TestHelper

  test "is authorized" do
    assert_authorized_to(:view?,  Book) do
      get "/books"
    end
    assert_response :success
  end
end
```

The `#assert_authorized_to` matcher verifies that the specified policy and rule were used to authorize the request via the `#authorize!` helper.

A good authorization abstraction should take testability into account and make it easier to test both policies and points of enforcement.

Let's go back to the application code and discuss another abstraction layer using authorization policies—views.

Authorization in views

When we talked about authorization exceptions, we discussed that users ideally shouldn't be able to perform unauthorized actions using the application UI. Thus, we need a way to *filter* UI components depending on the current user's permissions. For that, we can also rely on policy objects.

A typical use case is to hide a control corresponding to an action that is not allowed for the current user. With Action Policy, for example, we can declare view templates as follows:

```
<li>
  <%= book.name %>
  <% if allowed_to?(:destroy?, book) %>
    <%= button_to "Delete", book, method: :delete %>
  <% end %>
</li>
```

The `#allowed_to?` helper is provided by Action Policy. It works similarly to the `#authorize` method we explored previously, but instead of raising an exception, it returns `true` or `false`.

The situation when we need to conditionally show an action-triggering element depending on the permission to perform this action fits our authorization-layer abstraction well. The view layer relies on policies, but policies have no presentation-specific logic. All is good (from the layered architecture point of view).

Sometimes, however, presentation-layer details can leak into policies, thus breaking the separation of abstraction and architecture layers.

Form fields versus authorization

A common scenario where we may want to enhance policy classes with presentation-specific logic is dealing with conditional form fields. Let's continue exploring our library application example.

Imagine that we have a search form where users can type a query (author or book name) to find the matching books. For librarians, we also want to add another search form field to search by ISBN.

Finally, we can add another field to look up a book by a database ID and make it available to administrators only. We can write the corresponding view template as follows:

```
<%= form_for Books::SearchForm.new do |f| %>
  <%= f.text_field :q, placeholder: "Type a query.." %>
  <% if current_user.librarian? || current_user.admin? %>
    <%= f.text_field :isbn, placeholder: "ISNB" %>
  <% end %>
  <% if current_user.admin? %>
    <%= f.text_field :book_id, placeholder: "Book ID" %>
  <% end %>
<% end %>
```

Using an authorization model (role, permissions) in views directly is technically acceptable, but has all the downsides we discussed with regard to authorization logic in controllers. Also, mixing policies with checking roles directly within the same layer increases the conceptual overhead—we need to keep in mind two authorization-related abstractions (policies and models).

Let's explore how we can implement this logic with policies. The first approach is to add custom rules to the policy class, as follows:

```
class BookPolicy < ApplicationPolicy
  def search_by_isbn?() = user.librarian? || user.admin?
  def search_by_id?() = user.admin?
end
```

Now, we can use the #allowed_to? helper in the template:

```
<%= form_for Books::SearchForm.new do |f| %>
  <%= f.text_field :q, placeholder: "Type a query.." %>
  <% if allowed_to?(:search_by_isbn?, Book) %>
    <%= f.text_field :isbn, placeholder: "ISNB" %>
```

```
  <% end %>
  <% if allowed_to?(:search_by_id?, Book) %>
    <%= f.text_field :book_id, placeholder: "Book ID" %>
  <% end %>
<% end %>
```

From the view-layer perspective, everything is great. However, our policy class got new functionality that's required just for a single form—the policy object became presentation-aware. If we continue adding new rules for any UI-related occasion, we'll quickly end up with bloated policy classes.

There is an alternative approach: make policy objects responsible for the list of permitted form parameters. This way, we define a single helper method (probably, per form) and use it in views:

```
class BookPolicy < ApplicationPolicy
  def search_params
    [].tap do
     _1 << :isbn if user.admin? || user.librarian?
     _1 << :book_id if user.admin?
    end
  end
end
```

In the view, we can no longer use the #allowed_to? helper and must call #search_params explicitly:

```
<%- policy = BookPolicy.new(user: current_user) -%>
<%= form_for Books::SearchForm.new do |f| %>
  <%= f.text_field :q, placeholder: "Type a query.." %>
  <% if policy.search_params.include?(:isbn) %>
    <%= f.text_field :isbn, placeholder: "ISNB" %>
  <% end %>
  <% if policy.search_params.include?(:book_id) %>
    <%= f.text_field :book_id, placeholder: "Book ID" %>
  <% end %>
<% end %>
```

This approach reduces the potential policy class bloat but still doesn't solve the main problem: making policies aware of presentation logic. Also, in this example, it's questionable whether the BookPolicy class is the right place to define this logic.

Remember—we discussed that policy objects are usually associated with domain models, but not always. For example, we could create a standalone SearchPolicy object to describe authorization rules related to the form. That leads us to an interesting idea I'd like to explore slightly in this chapter.

Both solutions we discussed previously demonstrate the same disadvantage—presentation logic leaks into the policies layer. What if we look at the problem from the other side and, instead of trying to adjust existing policies to ever-changing representation requirements, we move the authorization logic for the presentation layer up the stack?

For the library search example, extracting a standalone policy class responsible for the form representation and submission (we must verify submitted params, too) looks like a reasonable option. We can call this concept a **view policy object**, an object that encapsulates authorization-related logic for a particular UI. Such objects must delegate non-presentation authorization logic to regular policy objects; thus, they could be wrappers or decorators for resource policy classes.

We can go further and integrate view policy objects into form objects (see *Chapter 7, Handling User Input outside of Models*). The final interface may look like this:

```
<% search_form = Books::SearchForm.new %>
<%= form_for search_form do |f| %>
  <%= f.text_field :q, placeholder: "Type a query.." %>
  <% if search_form.field_allowed?(:isbn) %>
    <%= f.text_field :isbn, placeholder: "ISNB" %>
  <% end %>
  <% if search_form.field_allowed?(:book_id) %>
    <%= f.text_field :book_id, placeholder: "Book ID" %>
  <% end %>
<% end %>
```

I will leave it up to the reader as an exercise to implement this functionality. Now, let's move on to the final topic related to authorization abstractions—application performance.

Performance implications of authorization

As with any abstraction, we also need to take performance into account. Sometimes, abstractions providing great developer experience may do so at the price of poor performance. That's especially critical for authorization since, as we learned, it permeates the whole application.

Let's discuss a couple of the most common performance implications related to authorization.

The N+1 authorization problem in the representation layer

Let's imagine a typical table-like interface showing many records along with the possible actions the current user can trigger for each one. For example, that could be a list of blog posts, and the possible actions could be *publish*, *delete*, and *edit*.

The corresponding view template could look like this:

```
<%= posts.each do |post| %>
  <div>
    <%= link_to post.title, post %>
```

```
    <% if allowed_to?(:publish?, post) %>
      <%= button_to "Publish", publish_post_path(post), method: :patch
%>
    <% end %>
    <% if allowed_to?(:edit?, post) %>
      <%= link_to "Edit", edit_post_path(post) %>
    <% end %>
    <% if allowed_to?(:destroy?, post) %>
      <%= button_to "Delete", post, method: :delete %>
    <% end %>
  </div>
<% end %>
```

For each row in the list, we perform three authorization checks. Thus, for 40 posts, we perform 120 checks. And each check, in its turn, performs many operations under the hood: looking up a policy class, initializing a policy object, invoking a predicate method, and evaluating the result. The policy class lookup is the responsibility of the abstraction. We must ensure it has the smallest possible overhead compared to initializing a policy object explicitly.

The overhead from performing pure Ruby calls can likely stay unnoticeable. Now, imagine that one of the rules—say, `publish?`—requires querying a database; we hit the N+1 query problem. That's where authorization can start negatively affecting the application performance. Let's see what options we have to prevent this.

The first option is to leverage common preloading techniques (`#preload`, `#eager_load`, and so on.) if possible. If the authorization rule executes queries not related to associations, we'll need to come up with some custom preloading mechanism. In either case, it makes sense to make the preloading logic a part of the policy class implementation since it depends on the rules. The interface could look like this:

```
<%= PostPolicy.preload_for(posts, :publish?, :update?, :destroy?).each
do |post| %>
  # ...
<% end %>
```

Preloading can be too complicated and hard to apply to policies relying on other sources of data (for example, HTTP APIs). An alternative approach to resolving N+1 authorization is to add caching.

There are multiple levels at which we can add caching, from view partials (Russian doll caching) to authorization rules. Caching at the policy level can be especially useful. Users' permissions usually do not change frequently, so cached values can last for a long time. For example, Action Policy provides different caching mechanisms out of the box. One advantage of a policy-level cache is that adding it doesn't require changing the code using policies.

Finally, we can use scoping to pre-authorize records. This approach can be used only in situations when all records are homogenous from the authorization perspective. That means we know beforehand that the result of the `publish?` check is `true` for all the records (for example, when the list contains the current user's post).

For that, we first use the policy to load the filtered view of the data, and then we mark the resulting records as pre-authorized for the specified actions, telling the authorization layer to pass the checks. At the time of writing, no known author libraries implement this approach.

Thus, let's come up with an interface proposal based on the `#authorized_scope` method from Action Policy:

```erb
<%= authorized_scope(posts, as: :own, preauthorize: %i[publish?
update? destroy?]).each do |post| %>
  # …
<% end %>
```

No solution fits all the use cases (the caching approach is probably the closest). Just as authorization rules vary a lot depending on the application business logic, so do the ways to overcome N+1 authorization.

The permissions-based scoping we just mentioned can also cause performance issues when overused.

The case of scoping-based authorization

Scoping-based authorization is an authorization-layer design pattern that implies combining data loading with authorization into one step. That means, instead of per-record rules, we define scopes to filter collections.

Here is, for example, how we can rewrite our `BooksController` example to follow this pattern:

```ruby
class BooksController < ApplicationController
  def destroy
    book = authorized_scope(Book.all, as: :destroyable)
      .find(params[:id])
    book.destroy!
    redirect_to books_path, notice: "Removed"
  end
end
```

We can still use policies to define scopes, as in the following example:

```ruby
class BookPolicy < ApplicationPolicy
  relation_scope(:destroyable) do |scope|
    next scope.all if permission?(:manage_all_books)
    next scope.where(dept: user.dept) if
      permission?(:manage_books)
    scope.none
```

```
    end
  end
```

The scope defined in the preceding snippet provides the same authorization guarantees as the #destroy? method we had before, but there is a significant difference due to the implementation. Scoping-based authorization enforcement is considered more secure since no data is loaded in case access is denied. However, it comes at a price of performance overhead.

Scoping rules and the corresponding database queries can grow complex, involving joins and sub-queries. Such queries are always slower than looking up by a primary key. Now, imagine the N+1 authorization situation in conjunction with the scoping-based authorization—it can slow down the application drastically.

Crafting a good abstraction is always a case of balancing between developer experience and an application's vital characteristics, such as performance. Authorization is one example of when you should pay additional attention to the corresponding abstraction designs.

Summary

In this chapter, you learned about the concept of authorization and its role in a web application's security. You familiarized yourself with security concerns such as authentication, authorization, system, and data constraints. You learned about the authorization model and its common designs, such as RBAC and ABAC.

You also learned about the policy object design pattern and how it can be used to decouple authorization enforcement from authorization rules. Finally, you learned about the potential performance implications related to authorization abstractions.

In the next chapter, we will talk about the notification layer of the application and discuss how to keep notification logic under control in the world beyond emails.

Questions

1. What is the difference between authentication and authorization?
2. What is the main disadvantage of the RBAC authorization model?
3. What is authorization enforcement, and where should it happen?
4. What is a policy object, and how can it be used to design an authorization layer in web applications?
5. What is a view policy object, and how does it differ from a regular policy object?
6. How do we solve the N+1 authorization problem?
7. What is scoping-based authorization? What are the pros and cons of this authorization pattern?

Exercise

Implement the concept of the view policy object integrated into form objects based on the library search example from the *Authorization in views* section of this chapter.

Further reading

Polished Ruby Programming (Chapter 17, Robust Web Application Security), *Jeremy Evans, Packt Publishing*: `https://www.packtpub.com/product/polished-ruby-programming/9781801072724`

10

Crafting the Notifications Layer

In this chapter, we will touch on the topic of user notifications and how to organize the corresponding code in a Rails application. We will start by discussing the built-in abstraction for sending emails—Action Mailer. Then, we will demonstrate how adding notification *channels* increases the code base's complexity and how we can tackle this complexity by introducing a new abstraction layer (with and without third-party libraries). Finally, we will talk about the part of the domain model responsible for managing notifications.

We will cover the following topics:

- From Action Mailer to multiple notification channels

- Extracting the notifications layer

- Modeling user notification preferences

This chapter aims to familiarize you with the idea of the notifications layer and how it improves the maintainability of applications relying on different communication channels.

Technical requirements

In this chapter, and all chapters of this book, the code given in code blocks is designed to be executed on Ruby 3.2 and Rails 7. Many of the code examples will work on earlier versions of the previously mentioned software.

You will find the code files on GitHub at `https://github.com/PacktPublishing/Layered-Design-for-Ruby-on-Rails-Applications/tree/main/Chapter10`.

From Action Mailer to multiple notification channels

Notifying a user about the events happening asynchronously in the system (for example, *the order has been delivered* or *a new message has been received*) is a crucial feature of most web applications. Users do not have your application open 24/7 (well, maybe some might), so you need a way to inform them.

For many years, the primary and only way of informing web application users was by sending an email. Rails has covered this use case via Action Mailer since the beginning.

Let's do a quick tour of this Rails sub-framework.

Action Mailer in action

Action Mailer provides an abstraction to manage (route or generate) emails in a Rails application—**mailers**. A mailer is an object that encapsulates the generation of email messages and provides an API to deliver them. Each mailer may describe multiple kinds of related messages, usually bound by a context such as a domain model.

Let's consider an example—a `UserMailer` class with the `#welcome` notification action defined:

```
class UserMailer < ApplicationMailer
  def welcome(user)
    @user = user
    mail(
      to: @user.email,
      subject: "Welcome to the club!"
    )
  end
end
```

The `#mail` method builds an internal email representation object, which will be used to perform the actual delivery. Note that we only specify the *To* address and email subject, not the contents. Action Mailer uses the Action View rendering mechanism under the hood to generate content from HTML or text templates.

The convention is the same as for controllers—we put a template with the name corresponding to the notification method name into the mailer's class folder in the `app/views` folder. For our example, that is `app/views/user_mailer/welcome.html.erb`:

```
<h1>Welcome to the club, <%= @user.name %>!</h1>
<p>We hope you will enjoy working with us!</h1>
```

As with controller templates, we can access the instance variables defined in the mailer object (`@user`).

Finally, let's demonstrate how to use our mailer:

```
UserMailer.welcome(user).deliver_later
```

We generate a mail object and invoke the #deliver_later method to perform the delivery in the background (via Active Job). The #deliver_now method is also available to send an email immediately.

Like other Rails built-in components, Action Mailer supports callbacks and comes with testing utilities and developer tools (such as previews). In other words, a mailer is a well-designed abstraction to solve the problem of notifying users via email.

Now, let's think about where this abstraction, mailers, lies in the layered architecture.

Mailers in the layered architecture

According to the layered architecture definition (see the *Layered architecture and abstraction layers* section in *Chapter 5, When Rails Abstractions Are Not Enough*), mailers must be in the Application or Services layer since they don't belong to either the Presentation or Domain layer. However, it might not be clear why we don't consider mailers to be a part of the Presentation layer given that they may use templates. Let's try to figure this out.

We can say that the primary role of a mailer is to coordinate the delivery process and prepare the content, and the rendering itself is secondary. Or we can point out that email templates are independent of the UI templates. Or we can try to find another excuse, but from the *strictly layered architecture* point of view, using views in mailers still would be a violation.

Let's just call it a compromise and move on.

The layered architecture is not limited to the four layers we usually refer to. Some developers, for example, split the Application layer into two layers, Business and Services. The Business layer encapsulates the business rules in a framework-agnostic way, while the Services layer knows more about the implementation details, though it still describes the application's business logic.

So, if we consider that we're talking about the *two-story* Application layer as described previously, authorization policies (see *Chapter 9, Authorization Models and Layers*) belong to the Business layer, while mailers belong to the Services layer since they're coupled with the actual notification method (email).

Finally, we should mention that Action Mailer delivery adapters (SMTP, file, and so on) belong to the Infrastructure layer.

Figure 10.1 – Action Mailer abstractions in a layered architecture

Even though there can be different approaches in defining architecture layers, there is an invariant: mailers always belong to a layer above the Domain layer. Now, let's take a look at the very typical Rails application code:

```
class User < ApplicationRecord
  after_commit :send_welcome_email, on: :create

  private
  def send_welcome_email
    UserMailer.welcome(self).deliver_later
  end
end
```

Although the preceding code demonstrates a popular technique—invoking mailers from model callbacks—it violates the layered architecture principles (introduces the coupling between layers) and, thus, must be avoided. Instead, we should either move the mailer invocation to the upper layer or to an event handler (see the *Active Record callbacks go wild* section in *Chapter 4, Rails Anti-Patterns?*, for possible ways to separate domain models from business operations).

For the rest of the chapter, let's assume that we have a service object triggering a notification as a part of its execution. For example, that could be an object responsible for publishing a post:

```
class Post::Publish < ApplicationService
  param :post

  def call
    post.update!(
      published_at: Time.current,
      status: :published
    )
    notify_subscribers
  end
```

```
  private
  def notify_subscribers
    post.user.subscribers.each do |user|
      next unless user.email_notifications_enabled?
      PostMailer.with(user:)
          .published(post).deliver_later
    end
  end
end
```

As a part of the post-publication operation, we also notify the author's subscribers (only with notifications enabled) about a new post via email. The `PostMailer` class implementation is not particularly interesting to us, except that we use mailer parameters, `.with(user:)`, to separate the context, a notification recipient, from the notification arguments.

This example is good enough to demonstrate what happens when we introduce other notification methods beyond email to our application.

Not only emails or adding more notification channels

With the appearance of mobile phones and applications, new notification channels emerged, such as SMS and push notifications. Today, push notifications are widely supported by web browsers, making it possible to deliver time-sensitive messages almost instantly. Moreover, we can add messaging applications to the list as potential communication channels. Finally, many applications also have in-app-integrated notifications (usually hidden behind a *bell* button in the window's top-right corner).

Let's see how adding more notification delivery channels affects our code base.

We will continue using our post-publishing example. Assume we also want to notify subscribers via SMS and through the application's built-in notification system (powered by Action Cable).

The updated code of the `Post::Publish` class will look as follows:

```
class Post::Publish < ApplicationService
  param :post

  def call
    post.update!(
      published_at: Time.current,
      status: :published
    )
    notify_subscribers
  end

  private
```

```ruby
  def notify_subscribers
    payload = post.slice(:id, :title)
      .merge(event: "post.published")
    post.user.subscribers.each do |user|
      NotificationsChannel.broadcast_to(user, payload)
      next unless user.notifications_enabled?
      if user.email_notifications_enabled?
        PostMailer.with(user:)
          .published(post).deliver_later
      end
      if user.sms_notifications_enabled?
        SMSSender.new(user.phone_number).send_later(
          body: "Post has been published: #{post.title}"
        )
      end
    end
  end
end
```

The size (the number of source code lines) of the service object has almost doubled. Most of its code is now responsible for coordinating notifications, although the primary role (as declared by the class name) is to publish a post. If we follow the idea of the Business and Services layers separation, we could say that the Post::Publish class has been *demoted* from the Business to the Services layer since now it knows too much about the notification delivery mechanism.

This situation can be easily extrapolated to all the places in the code where you used mailers initially since, in most cases, you want to use all available notification channels. That leads to code duplication, more complicated testing, and other maintainability troubles caused by low cohesion.

To keep concerns separated, we need to extract the communication details from the business logic operations while leaving *notification triggers*. In other words, we need to put delivery logic into its own abstraction layer—the notifications layer.

Extracting notifications layer

What is the notifications layer? We can define it as an abstraction layer responsible for orchestrating user notifications. The responsibilities of this layer are as listed here:

- Deciding which communication channels to use for a given notification and a user

- Preparing notification payloads (email subjects and bodies, SMS contents, and so on)

- Interacting with *delivery services* (mailing servers, third-party APIs, and so on)

A notifications layer may be comprised of multiple abstractions or sub-layers. For example, we still can (and should) use Action Mailer for emails, but we need a higher-level entry-point abstraction, which would delegate the specific channel logic to lower abstractions.

As the first step toward a new abstraction, let's refactor our Post::Publish class using a simple object (or class) extraction technique.

Ad hoc abstraction

Let's start by moving the #notify_subscribers method implementation into a separate class, say, Post::NotifyPublished:

```
class Post::NotifyPublished < ApplicationService
  param :post

  def call
    payload = post.slice(:id, :title)
      .merge(event: "post.published")
    post.user.subscribers.each do |user|
      NotificationsChannel.broadcast_to(user, payload)
      next unless user.notifications_enabled?
      if user.email_notifications_enabled?
        PostMailer.with(user:)
          .published(post).deliver_later
      end
      if user.sms_notifications_enabled?
        SMSSender.new(user.phone_number).send_later(
          body: "Post has been published: #{post.title}"
        )
      end
    end
  end
end
```

We haven't changed anything in the source code yet. It's not really a refactoring; it's more like a *re-arranging*. However, even such a simple manipulation improves the maintainability of the host object, Post::Publish:

```
class Post
  class Publish < ApplicationService
    param :post

    def call
```

```ruby
      post.update!(
        published_at: Time.current,
        status: :published
      )

      NotifyPublished.call(post)
    end
  end
end
```

Now we clearly see that the Publish operation consists of two steps: modifying the record's state and notifying users about the event.

Testing also becomes less complicated: we only need to test the primary functionality and the fact that the NotifyPublished class has been called. Here is how we can write such tests with RSpec:

```ruby
RSpec.describe Post::Publish do
  let(:post) { Post.create!(title: "Test") }

  subject { described_class.call(post) }

  before { allow(Post::NotifyPublished).to receive(:call) }

  it "marks post as published and sets published_at" do
    subject
    expect(post.reload.published_at).not_to be_nil
    expect(post).to be_published
  end

  it "triggers notification via NotifyPublished" do
    subject
    expect(Post::NotifyPublished)
      .to have_received(:call).with(post)
  end
end
```

However, tests for the NotifyPublished class still must cover all the sophisticated logic of notifying users: taking into account notification settings, verifying messages, and so on. And we'll have to repeat these tests for every notifier object.

Having notifications logic moved into separate classes makes it easier to start the actual refactoring. Since notification channels are independent of each other and, at any point in time, we might want to add new ones, it makes sense to use a pluggable architecture or plugins (see the *Adapters versus plugins* section in *Chapter 3, More Adapters, Less Implementations*).

A sketch of a pluggable architecture for notifications

Designing a full-featured plugin system for user notifications is way beyond the scope of this book. Instead, I'd like to propose a potential API and highlight the most crucial parts of it.

Let's start with the notifier class and describe an API to plug in notification channels:

```
class Post::NotifyPublished < ApplicationNotifier
  plug :mailer, class_name: "PostMailer",
    action: "published"
  plug :sms, content: ->(post) { "Post has been published:
    #{post.title}" }
  plug :cable, event: "post.published",
    payload: ->(post) { post.slice(:id, title) }

  param :post

  def call
    post.user.subscribers.each { notify(_1, post) }
  end
end
```

The `.plug` DSL method activates a plugin specified by its ID. The options passed as keyword arguments to the `.plug` method differ for each plugin and are proxied directly to the plugin instance. The `#notify` method is the only API available to the notifier class. We call it to trigger notifications for a particular user.

Note that we no longer care about users' notifications settings—that will be the responsibility of the corresponding plugins. Let's take a look at how the `#notify` method can be implemented in the `ApplicationNotifier` class:

```
class ApplicationNotifier < ApplicationService
  def notify(user, ...)
    plugins.each { _1.notify(user, ...) }
  end
end
```

Let me skip the `#plugins` method implementation and instead demonstrate the code for one of the plugins. For example, we can imagine how the *mailer* plugin would work:

```
class MailerNotifierPlugin
  attr_reader :class_name, :action
  def initialize(class_name:, action:)
    @class_name, @action = class_name, action
  end
```

```
def notify(user, ...)
  return unless user.notifications_enabled? &&
    user.email_notifications_enabled?
  mailer = class_name.constantize.with(user:)
  mailer.public_send(action, ...).deliver_later
end
end
```

Note that now it's the plugin that's responsible for deciding whether to send a notification to the user or not. It's no longer the responsibility of a notifier object. Thus, we localized this logic in a single entity, drastically reduced code duplication, and simplified testing.

We also introduced a convention of passing a target user as a parameter to a mailer object (`.with(user:)`). Other notification arguments are passed to the mailer via the argument forwarding operator (`...`), which we use a lot to build our *notification pipeline*.

Other plugins can be implemented in a similar way. I will leave this as an exercise for the reader. Luckily, in today's Rails ecosystem, there are enough existing solutions to choose from, so building a notifications layer from scratch is quite unlikely.

Let's consider a couple of libraries.

Using third-party libraries to manage notifications

My shortlist of libraries for building a notifications layer in a Ruby on Rails application consists of two candidate gems: `active_delivery` and `noticed`. As the author of Active Delivery is yours truly, I will start with it.

Active Delivery

Active Delivery is a library heavily inspired by Action Mailer and is focused on providing a familiar, Rails-like API. It comes with a handful of abstractions to cover all your notification needs. Let's see how we can use them to refactor our original post-publication example.

For every delivery method, we must define a delivery line. A **delivery line** is an adapter that connects delivery objects with notifiers or notification backends directly.

What a gem — active_delivery

The `active_delivery` gem (`https://github.com/palkan/active_delivery`) provides abstractions to build a notifications layer in the Rails way. **Delivery objects** act as entry points for notifications encapsulating delivery mechanisms. **Notifiers** provide an Action Mailer-like API for any notification backends managed by application developers (SMS, push notifications, and so on).

Out of the box, Active Delivery provides only the *mailer* delivery line, which connects deliveries with Action Mailer classes. Let's see how we can replace `PostMailer` with the corresponding delivery class, `PostDelivery`:

```
class Post::Publish < ApplicationService
  # ...

  private
  def notify_subscribers
    post.user.subscribers.each do |user|
      PostDelivery.with(user:)
        .published(post).deliver_later
    end
  end
end
```

We just updated the class name, and that's it—the benefit of having an Action Mailer-compatible API. Also, we no longer check for `user.email_notifications_enabled?`—that becomes the responsibility of the delivery object.

Let's look at the delivery classes:

ApplicationDelivery

```
class ApplicationDelivery < ActiveDelivery::Base
  before_notify :ensure_enabled
  before_notify :ensure_mailer_enabled, on: :mailer

  def ensure_enabled = !!user&.notifications_enabled?
  def ensure_mailer_enabled
    !!user&.email_notifications_enabled?
  end
  def user = params[:user]
end
```

In the base delivery class, we use callbacks to control when to deliver notifications. (In Active Delivery, if a callback returns `false`, it halts the execution.) What's left for the `PostDelivery` class? Let's see:

PostDelivery

```
class PostDelivery < ApplicationDelivery
  delivers :published
end
```

That's it. We only specify which delivery actions are available. Active Delivery will automatically infer the mailer class (`PostMailer`) from the delivery class name and enqueue the specified message delivery. In other words, the following two expressions are equal:

```
PostDelivery.with(user:).published(post).deliver_later
# ==
PostMailer.with(user:).published(post).deliver_later if
  user.email_notifications_enabled? &&
    user.notifications_enabled?
```

With just mailers, using Active Delivery can hardly be justified. Let's continue by adding SMS notifications.

Adding an SMS notifier

We said that Active Delivery connects delivery objects to *notifiers*. For example, for emails, mailers act as notifiers. For other delivery mechanisms, we can use Abstract Notifier.

Abstract Notifier is a companion library for Active Delivery and bundled with it (since v1.0), which provides a minimal abstraction for defining mailer-like objects. Let's create a `PostSMSNotifier` class:

```
class PostSMSNotifier < ApplicationSMSNotifier
  def published(post)
    notification(
      to: user.phone_number,
      body: "Post has been published: #{post.title}"
    )
  end
end
```

It looks very similar to a mailer class; only the #mail method is replaced with the #notification method. We need to define a delivery driver to turn an abstract notifier into an SMS sender. We do that in the base SMS notifier class:

```
class ApplicationSMSNotifier < AbstractNotifier::Base
  self.driver = proc do |data|
    data => {to:, body:}
    SMSSender.new(to).send_now(body:)
  end

  private def user = params[:user]
end
```

A driver can be any callable Ruby object. In our case, we reuse the existing SMS-sending mechanism.

Finally, we need to register SMS notifiers as a delivery line in the base delivery class. To connect deliveries with SMS notifiers, we only need to specify the prefix used by notifier classes:

```
class ApplicationDelivery < ActiveDelivery::Base
  register_line :sms, notifier: true,
    prefix: "SMSNotifier"
  # …
  before_notify :ensure_sms_enabled, on: :sms

  private
  def ensure_sms_enabled
    !!user&.sms_notifications_enabled?
  end
end
```

We also define a callback to ensure SMS notifications are sent only to users who opted in to this notification method.

To add an Action Cable delivery line, you can follow the same approach as for creating custom notifiers. Alternatively, you can create a specific delivery line or even use notification callbacks to broadcast messages. I'll leave it up to you to decide and instead discuss another important topic related to defining an abstraction—testability.

Testing deliveries and notifiers

Active Delivery comes with first-class testing support. The decomposition of the notifications layer into deliveries, notifiers, and other delivery lines and drivers makes testing all components in isolation easy. Built-in deliveries help to test delivery triggering.

Here is, for example, how we can write `Post::Publish` tests with RSpec:

```
RSpec.describe Post::Publish do
  let(:post) { Post.create!(title: "Test") }
  let!(:subscriber) do
    User.create!(name: "Test", email: "a@ex.test").tap {
      post.user.subscribers << _1 }
  }
  end

  subject { described_class.call(post) }

  it "triggers delivery to subscribers" do
    expect { subject }.to have_delivered_to(
      PostDelivery, :published, post
    ).with(user: subscriber)
```

```
      end
  end
```

A similar matcher is available to test notifiers:

```
RSpec.describe PostDelivery do
  let(:user) { User.new(phone_number: "311") }
  let(:delivery) { described_class.with(user:) }

  describe "#published" do
    let(:post) { Post.new(title: "A") }
    subject { delivery.published(post).deliver_now }

    it "notifies via SMS" do
      expect { subject }.to have_sent_notification(
        via: PostSMSNotifier,
        to: "311",
        body: "Post has been published: A"
      )
    end
  end
end
```

Note that we don't need to persist Active Record objects to test notifications sent via notifiers. That makes delivery tests blazingly fast, which is essential for large test suites.

Active Delivery is flexible enough to build a notifications layer in Rails applications of any scale. However, for applications with a small number of different notifications, managing both delivery objects and notifiers can be seen as *over-abstraction*. If that's the case, you may find the abstractions provided by the Noticed library fit your needs better.

Noticed

The main conceptual difference between Noticed compared to Active Delivery or Action Mailer is the one-to-one correspondence between notifications and corresponding delivery classes (notification objects). That makes it possible to define all the logic required to deliver notifications via multiple channels in a single place.

Let's define a notification object for our post-publication use case:

```
class PostPublishedNotification < Noticed::Base
  deliver_by :email, mailer: "PostMailer",
    method: :published, if: :email?
  deliver_by :sms, class: "SMSDelivery", if: :sms?
  deliver_by :action_cable,
```

```
    channel: "NotificationsChannel",
    format: :cable_payload

  def cable_payload =
    post.slice(:id, :title).merge(
      event: "post.published"
    )

  def sms_params =
    {
      to: user.phone_number,
      body: "Post has been published: #{post.title}"
    }

  private
  alias_method :user, :recipient
  def post = params[:post]
  def email? = user.notifications_enabled? &&
    user.email_notifications_enabled?
  def sms? = user.notifications_enabled? &&
    user.sms_notifications_enabled?
end
```

The notification class defines both delivery methods and the way to generate messages (via callback methods). We can think of the notification object as a combination of both delivery objects and notifiers from Active Delivery—but all in one Ruby class!

Let's integrate it into our Post::Publish class:

```
class Post::Publish < ApplicationService
  # ...

  private
  def notify_subscribers
    PostPublishedNotification.with(post:).deliver_later(
      post.user.subscribers
    )
  end
end
```

What's *Noticed*-able here is that we pass all subscribers as an argument to the #deliver_later method without any iterations. This is one of the Noticed bonus features that improve the developer ergonomics.

> **What a gem — noticed**
>
> Noticed (`https://github.com/excid3/noticed`) is a popular Rails library providing the concept of **notification objects**. A notification object represents a single notification in the system, defines which delivery channels to use, and encapsulates notification details for each of them. Noticed supports popular delivery mechanisms out of the box and can be extended via custom plugins.

With minimal additional objects and built-in delivery adapters for popular backends, `Noticed` allows you to quickly outline the notifications layer in a Rails application. As usual, what streamlines initial development may put sticks in the application wheels as it grows.

The usage of notification class instance methods to control the behavior of different delivery methods makes it possible to put all the logic into one place. At the same time, with the growing number of delivery channels, notification classes can become hard to digest. Keeping each notification in a separate file can quickly lead to the `app/notifications` folder becoming bloated.

Either way, I'd recommend learning about both Active Delivery and Noticed design and implementation to better understand what should be taken into account during the notifications layer extraction and the possible abstractions to build it from.

In conclusion, I'd like to discuss a topic adjacent to the notifications layer—a notifications model.

Modeling user notification preferences

In the previous section's examples, we relied on the User model to answer one of the core notification system questions: should a user be notified via *channel X* or not? I intentionally used the most straightforward implementation: storing notification preferences in the `users` table as Boolean columns (`notifications_enabled`, `email_notifications_enabled`, and so on). Let's discuss the downsides of this approach.

First, we add another responsibility to the User model (it likely already has many). That takes us one step closer to creating a God object—a famous maintainability killer (see the *Seeking God objects* section in *Chapter 2, Active Models and Records*).

Second, adding a new column for every new notification type *widens* the database table. Although it's doubtful that you'll hit the limit on the number of columns (PostgreSQL, for example, allows up to 1,600 columns per table), many columns add to mental and even performance overhead. The latter is because with Active Record, most of the time, we load all tables' columns (`SELECT * FROM ...`), and even small Boolean values require deserialization backed by Ruby objects.

So, the overhead of having a few additional columns, even a dozen, would hardly be noticeable (though measurable by micro-benchmarks). However, it's still something you should keep in mind when adding yet another `add_column :user, :x` migration.

Let's consider alternative approaches to implementing the notifications part of the domain model.

Bit fields and value objects

What is the most natural way to store many Boolean values? Bit fields! A bit field is a data structure consisting of adjacent bits, where each bit acts like a state toggle, on (set) or off (not set); all bits are independent.

Bit fields provide a very compact way to store information. Unsurprisingly, 1 byte of data can represent eight different Boolean states simultaneously (imagine a binary representation of any non-negative integer less than 256, for example, $49 \rightarrow 0011\ 0001$).

Let's use a single tiny integer column, say, `notification_bits`, to store user notification preferences. To implement predicate methods used by the notifications layer, we must define them manually using bitwise operations:

```
class User < ApplicationRecord
  NOTIFICATION_BITS = {
    all: 1,
    email: 3,
    sms: 5
  }.freeze

  # …
  def notifications_enabled? =
    (notification_bits & 1 == 1)
  def email_notifications_enabled? =
    (notification_bits & 3 == 3)
  def sms_notifications_enabled? =
    (notification_bits & 5 == 5)
end
```

All predicate methods rely on the same expression with different values (by the way, note that we check for the first bit in every predicate). And we only use a single model's attribute—do you spot a pattern? Right, a value object (see the *Extracting objects from objects* section in *Chapter 3, More Adapters, Less Implementations*). We can encapsulate all the notifications-related logic into a custom model class:

```
class User::Notifications
  BITS = {
    all: 1,
    email: 3,
    sms: 5
  }.freeze

  private attr_reader :val
  def initialize(value) = @val = value
```

```
  def enabled? - (val & 1 == 1)
  def email? = (val & 3 == 3)
  def sms? = (val & 5 == 5)
end
```

In the user model, we now only need to define a method to access notifications:

```
class User < ApplicationRecord
  def notifications =
    @notifications ||=
      Notifications.new(notification_bits)
end
```

Finally, we must slightly update the code using notification predicates. Take the following example:

```
PostMailer.with(user:).published(post) if
  user.notifications.email?
```

Value objects are read-only. We can update the notification preferences by directly writing to the `notification_bits` attribute. Another option is to promote the `UserNotifications` value object to an Active Record type and make it responsible for mapping data between the application, users, and a database. This technique is out of the scope of this book.

The main downside of using bit fields is a lack of readability (when accessing raw data). Also, querying bit fields in a performant way is more complicated; you either add multiple functional indexes or deal with sequential table scans.

Moreover, notification preferences may include non-Boolean fields, too. For example, one common use case is to allow users to provide a custom email or phone number for notifications (not the one that is already present on the profile).

Notification preferences store

Another option for storing notification preferences is to use a non-structured data type, such as an array or JSON. This approach is trendy among PostgreSQL users (me included) due to enhanced support for these data types. For the rest of the chapter, let's assume that our database is PostgreSQL.

Arrays are similar to bit fields, but instead of bits, we store the identifiers of enabled notification methods. Compared to bits, arrays can be efficiently indexed, so querying for users with specified delivery channels active is not a problem. However, we still can't store plain text values this way. So, let's move on to JSON, or, more precisely, JSONB—a binary JSON format specific to PostgreSQL, which is more compact and has indexing support.

Let's assume that we have a `notifications` JSON column in the `users` table. In the *Active Model as Active Record satellite* section of *Chapter 2, Active Models and Records*, we introduced the Store

Model gem, which can be used to create a model backed by JSON attributes. Let's use it to model notification preferences.

First, let's define the `User::Notifications` model:

```
class User::Notifications
  include StoreModel::Model
  attribute :enabled, :boolean, default: true
  attribute :email_enabled, :boolean, default: true
  attribute :sms_enabled, :boolean, default: true

  attribute :email, :string
  attribute :phone_number, :string

  def email_enabled? = enabled? && super
  def sms_enabled? = enabled? && super
end
```

For every notification setting, we define an attribute. We can specify the type and a default value. Moreover, we can add validations, declare enums, modify values in place, and so on.

Now, we must attach our Settings model to the User model:

```
class User < ApplicationRecord
  attribute :notifications, Notifications.to_type
end
```

Store Model uses the Attributes API under the hood, so we declare that the `notifications` attribute should be treated as a custom Settings type.

Using stores, especially JSONB in PostgreSQL, in combination with store-backed models provides a good mix of flexibility, maintainability, and performance. However, the latter can be compromised. If JSON(B) grows big, loading it every time we query the `users` table can lead to application performance degradation. What is the solution? Right, moving notificationsin to a separate table.

A separate table for storing preferences

Database architects would suggest moving notification preferences into a separate table as the first (and probably the only) option because it follows the normalization rules (and architects like normalization). In other words, it simplifies managing the database schema and ensuring data consistency.

However, from an application development point of view, using a separate table doesn't automatically answer the question of how to model preference data. Therefore, we can still use all three approaches: many columns, bit fields, or stores. Moreover, we can mix them to best serve our needs.

Nevertheless, independently of the chosen design, the notifications-related part of the domain model must be separated from the user model.

Summary

In this chapter, you learned about abstractions to manage user notifications. You got a better understanding of Action Mailer and its place in a layered architecture. You learned about different patterns to model notifications, such as delivery and notification objects. You also familiarized yourself with the Active Delivery and Noticed libraries. Finally, you learned about multiple user notification preference models and their pros and cons.

In the next chapter, we will discuss the HTML view layer of Rails applications and how to turn HTML templates into object-oriented abstractions.

Questions

1. Where is the place of Action Mailer in the layered architecture, and why?
2. What is the difference between the Business and Services layers?
3. What is the notifications abstraction layer?
4. What's the difference between a delivery object and a notification object?
5. What are the downsides of storing notifications-related data in the User model?

Exercises

1. Finish the implementation of the pluggable delivery architecture proposed in the *A sketch of a pluggable architecture for notifications* section.
2. Implement a delivery line for Active Delivery to broadcast notifications via Action Cable for the example from the *Active Delivery* section.

11
Better Abstractions for HTML Views

This chapter will focus on classic, HTML-first Ruby on Rails applications and their data representation features, or, simply speaking, HTML views. First, we discuss built-in mechanisms for generating views in Rails, such as ERB templates and view helpers, and their drawbacks. Then, we consider an alternative approach to overcome these drawbacks and reduce the overall complexity of managing the HTML layer—**view components**.

We will cover the following topics:

- The *V* in Rails' MVC: templates and helpers
- Thinking in components

The goal of this chapter is to demonstrate how object-oriented techniques can help you to keep the view layer organized and, thus, maintainable.

Technical requirements

In this chapter and all the chapters in this book, the code given in code blocks is designed to be executed on Ruby 3.2 and Rails 7.1. Many of the code examples will work on earlier versions of the abovementioned software.

You will find the code files on GitHub at `https://github.com/PacktPublishing/Layered-Design-for-Ruby-on-Rails-Applications/tree/main/Chapter11`.

The V in Rails' MVC: templates and helpers

In a classic Rails application, we make the view layer from HTML templates. The framework introduces conventions for organizing templates that can be found if you take a look at an example project's `app/views` folder. If we generated the User resource using the Rails scaffolding system (`rails g resource user`), we would see the following files:

```
app/
  views/
    layouts/
      application.html.erb
    users/
      _form.html.erb
      _user.html.erb
      edit.html.erb
      index.html.erb
      new.html.erb
      show.html.erb
```

First, we have `layouts`—top-level templates that wrap endpoint-specific templates and contain metadata and other utility information required for all HTML pages. There are usually a few different layouts (for different parts of the application).

Then, we have resource-specific templates that can be further categorized into **action templates** and **partials**.

Action templates correspond to the controller actions, which provide HTML responses. They're named accordingly, so the Rails rendering system (Action View) can pick them up automatically without enforcing us to specify which template to render explicitly.

Templates starting with `_` are called **partials**. They represent reusable HTML fragments that can be included in other templates. The `_user.html.erb` partial name is chosen by Rails on purpose: Action View uses a naming convention to infer a partial from a model.

In this case, we can omit the template name whenever we want to render a user instance. For example, in the generated `index.html.erb` file, we can find the following snippet:

```
<div id="users">
  <%= render @users %>
</div>
```

The preceding code is similar to the following, more verbose version:

```
<div id="users">
  <%= render collection: @users, partial: "user" %>
</div>
```

Rails gives us a very intuitive way of managing HTML in applications. Conventions reduce boilerplate and the mental overhead of architecting the view layer so developers can focus solely on HTML content.

However, the simplicity of Rails templates reveals its price as the application grows. When the number of templates grows, we are likely to start struggling with their maintainability and face the pitfalls of the Rails view layer design.

Let's explore the most common problems in a bit more detail.

UI without a programming interface

Unlike most Rails entities, models, controllers, jobs, and templates do not belong to the Ruby object model. Templates are written in a markup language (such as HTML, Haml, and so on), not a programming language. Markup languages allow us to describe UIs in a human- and machine-readable text format. So, it's just a text file without any classes, methods, and so on.

Given that, we can say that templates by design do not provide any API. In other words, templates do not communicate how to use them. Let's demonstrate this with the following example—a partial that's responsible for rendering a card with a student's test result.

Here is the UI we want to build:

Figure 11.1 – A quiz result UI

The corresponding HTML partial template looks as follows (styling omitted):

```
<div>
  <header>
    <h3><%= quiz.title %></h3>
    <span class="<%= result.passed? ? "green" : "red" %>">
      <%= result.passed? ? "passed" : "failed" %>
    </span>
  </header>
  <p>
    <%- user = result.user -%>
    <i class="fa fa-user"></i>
    <%= link_to user.name, user %>
```

```
    </p>
    <div>
      <label>Score</label>
      <span><%= result.score %> / <%= quiz.score %>
      (<%= l(result.created_at) %>)</span>
    </div>
  </div>
```

Now, let's play the *Locals Game*: can you spot all the possible and required arguments we should pass to the #render method via the locals: keyword argument to render this partial? You can detect all required parameters by trying to render the partial without any arguments and looking at exceptions:

```
render partial: "quizzes/student_result", locals: {}
#=> undefined local variable or method `quiz'…
```

Here, we must pass a quiz to render this partial. If you repeat this experiment, you can find that we also need a result object. So, the final interface for this partial is as follows:

```
render partial: "quizzes/student_result", locals:
  {quiz:, result:}
```

If we had some conditions in the template, we might have other hidden, required locals. For example, we may show previous results for quizzes with multiple allowed attempts:

```
<div>
  ...
  <div>
    <label>Score</label>
    <span><%= result.score %> / <%= quiz.score %>
    (<%= l(result.created_at) %>)</span>
  </div>
  <%- if result.attempt > 1 -%>
    <div>
      <label>Previous Attempt</label>
      <span><%= prev_result.score %> / <%= quiz.score %>
      (<%= l(prev_result.created_at) %>)</span>
    </div>
  <%- end -%>
</div>
```

We may have yet another local variable inside a conditional block, but only if the condition is satisfied.

That concludes the first problem with parameterized partials—they can be hard to comprehend.

Now, imagine we use this partial in multiple places throughout the application, and we added the required conditional parameters. The chances are that we wouldn't catch all the places where we need to provide a new parameter, and a bug could sneak into production. That's the second problem that arises if you don't have a clearly defined interface.

So, partials have no signatures. That makes it hard to maintain them at scale. However, not only locals must be considered: partials may also depend on the controller's state.

Stitching controllers and templates via instance variables

Let's imagine that we want to extend our quiz `result` partial with the basic course information:

Figure 11.2 – A quiz result UI with the course information

We already have this visual in other places in the application, so it has been extracted into the `courses/side_info` partial. Let's include it in our quiz result partial:

```
<div>
  <%= render "courses/side_info", course: quiz.course %>
  <header>
    <h3><%= quiz.title %></h3>
    …
  </header>
  …
</div>
```

And now, let's try to render it again:

```
render partial: "quizzes/student_result", locals:
  {quiz:, result:}
#=> undefined method `title' for nil:NilClass…
```

We have yet another undefined method, but this time for a nil object. Let's see what's inside the course info partial:

courses/_side_info.html.erb

```
<aside>
  <label>Course</label>
  <%= link_to @course.title, @course %>
  <label>Category</label>
  <span><%= @course.category %></span>
  <label># students</label>
  <span><%= @course.students_count %></span>
</aside>
```

Do you see why we failed to render it? The reason is that the `courses/side_info` partial relies on the `@course` instance variable to be set in the controller. So, our partial has some hidden state requirements. That's a standard Rails pattern for passing some data via instance variables from controllers to templates; it's used in the code created with Rails generators.

This functionality is meant only to pass data to action templates, not any other partials. But nothing prevents developers from relying on instance variables deep down the rendering tree.

We can say that the technique of carrying forward instance variables from controllers to views is yet another Rails *anti-pattern* (in addition to those discussed in *Chapter 4, Rails Anti-Patterns?*). It makes you productive in the beginning but can become a maintenance nightmare.

Let's see the options we have to handle the partial interface problems and stay on the Rails way.

Getting strict with templates

Although markup files are mostly text files without obligations, we can bring some order to the HTML chaos and build some confidence in using partials and templates. Let's consider a couple of techniques.

Strict locals

Rails 7.1 introduced a new feature to Action View—an ability to specify which locals a partial accepts. You can add *magic comments* to the template file to list the recognized local variables as well as to specify default values.

Let's enhance our `quizzes/student_result` partial with the local schema:

```
<%# locals: (quiz:, result:, prev_result: nil) -%>
<div>
  <header>
    <h3><%= quiz.title %></h3>
    …
```

```
    </header>
    ...
</div>
```

To declare the partial's input schema, we use the same syntax as in Ruby method definitions. Now, when trying to render this partial without providing all the required arguments, we see the following exception:

```
render partial: "quizzes/student_result", locals: {}
#=> missing keywords: :quiz, :result
```

Similarly, if we tried to pass an unknown variable via locals, we would fail, too:

```
render partial: "quizzes/student_result", locals:
    {quiz:, result:, foo: "bar"}
#=> unknown local: :foo
```

This is an important difference compared to schema-less partials, which accept any Ruby hash as a bag of local variables.

Explicitly specifying the list of locals makes the partials interface more predictable and provides better control of the view layer. So, even though the magic comment seems to be more like a workaround than a final solution to the interface problem, it's better than nothing.

Let's see if we can somehow control the usage of instance variables in partials.

Linting partials with erb-lint

Detecting instance variables in partials can be done by analyzing the source code without executing it. We can do this manually: search for `/@\w+/` patterns in ERB files starting with the underscore. Luckily, we don't need to. There is a linting tool for ERB templates—`erb-lint` (`https://github.com/Shopify/erb-lint`).

`erb-lint` is a powerful linter for ERB templates with dozens of rules and plugins to integrate with other tools, such as RuboCop (`https://rubocop.org`). However, we're only interested in one particular rule—`PartialInstanceVariable`. This rule does exactly what we need: it checks whether an instance variable is used within a partial template. Let's see it in action.

First, we need to install `erb-lint`. For simplicity, we can install it globally:

```
gem install erb_lint
```

Now, we can run it with only one linting rule specified against the whole code base to find violating partials:

```
$ erblint --enable-linters partial_instance_variable \--lint-all
Linting 34 files with 1 linters...
Instance variable detected in partial.
In file: app/views/courses/_side_info.html.erb:3
1 error(s) were found in ERB files
```

Note that action templates (such as `show.html.erb`) are ignored by this rule. That gives us a great balance between the simplicity of passing date from a controller to the entry-point template without allowing instance variables to leak into nested partials.

To sum up, we can mitigate partials' implicitness and lack of interface up to some point. However, that's not the only reason to consider introducing new abstractions for the view layer.

Reusability and design systems

Partials are usually used to reuse resource-specific visuals: `quizzes/result`, `courses/info`, and so on. However, we do not use partials to extract UI building blocks, such as buttons and form inputs. Why not? It's more productive to duplicate small HTML snippets and keep their style in sync via CSS than to manage tons of partials.

Also, there are Action View helpers that help us to generate Rails-aware HTML too. So, we have two tools for maintaining the view layer, partials, and helpers. Let's see if they're enough to keep the application healthy and developers productive.

Design systems on Rails

UI elements in web applications do not live each one their life; they're connected with each other via an explicit or implicit **design system**. A design system is a collection of reusable elements and guidelines for crafting a UI. For example, colors, spacing rules, layouts (grids, tables), and fonts are all design system components.

Design systems are not static; they constantly evolve. Hence, we must reflect this evolution in the corresponding CSS and HTML code. This task can be a significant challenge if you have the same (from the design system perspective) UI element copied and pasted in multiple partials. Let's consider an example.

Imagine we have search functionality in several places throughout the application's UI:

Figure 11.3 – A search box UI element (full-size)

On some pages, the corresponding UI element may look a bit different:

Figure 11.4 – A search box UI element (compact)

There are two variations, full and short (with the icon-only button). The underlying HTML code for the full-size variant may look as follows:

```
<%= form_with(url: search_results_path, class: "searchbox")
  do |f| %>
  <%= f.text_field :q, placeholder: "Search results by quiz
    title or student name", class: "searchbox--input" %>
  <%= f.submit "Search", class: "searchbox--btn" %>
<% end %>
```

There are just a few lines of code. In addition, there are some moving parts (a submission URL and a placeholder), and sometimes we need to choose between the full and compact versions. Given that, it's hard to justify extracting this UI element into a universal partial solely from the code maintenance point of view.

Now, let's assume that our UI/UX team decided to unify the search controls interface across the application and slightly update its look and feel:

Figure 11.5 – Updated UI for a search box element

From the look, the UI changes may seem negligible. However, even though visually the difference is not that big, the underlying HTML markup has changed, not only the CSS definitions. Thus, we need to make sure we update all the templates that have a search box snippet embedded into them in order to catch up with the design system evolution. That's when you realize that the *productivity* of simple snippet duplication was just technical debt, and it's time to sign a check.

Partials and helpers for the UI kit?

To mitigate the complexity of staying up to date with ever-changing design system requirements, we should make it a part of the application's view layer. The part of the view layer responsible for implementing the design system elements is called the **UI kit**. In classic Rails, we only have two options: helpers and partials.

We covered the downsides of overusing helpers in the *Leave helpers for libraries* section in *Chapter 8*, Pulling Out the Representation Layer. In addition, we can also mention the complexity of rendering HTML content via helpers. Let's see how our search box implementation might look if defined as a view helper:

```
def search_box(url:, placeholder: "Search", variant: :full)
  form_with(url:) do |f|
    concat(content_tag(:div, "") do
      content_tag(:i, "")
    end)
    concat f.text_field :q, placeholder:
    if variant == :full
      concat f.submit "Search"
    end
  end
end
```

The preceding code requires a good knowledge of Action View helpers (for example, `#concat`) and a decent imagination to visualize the resulting UI element in your head, unlike HTML markup. (Keep in mind that we omitted all the styling in the preceding snippet; the actual code may be much more verbose.)

Using partials to put together a UI kit is a more viable option. However, the API problems and the growing complexity when including conditional logic in HTML also make partials hardly suitable for the task.

We need a better abstraction to represent UI elements in the code base, an abstraction that would make it easier to reflect the design system hierarchy in the application's view layer as well as provide better maintainability properties (isolation, reusability, testability, and so on).

Thinking in components

The problem we're trying to solve here—increasing the maintainability of the view layer—is not new. In the last decade, one design paradigm became prevalent: breaking down views into isolated, self-contained components. Every logical piece of UI must be backed by a component in your code base. Think in components, not templates.

This approach proved to be efficient in the world of frontend development. Modern libraries such as React, Vue, and Svelte all drive the component-based architecture.

How can we use this idea in Rails? Let's try to build some view components!

Turning partials and helpers into components

Let's consider what we need to turn partials and helpers into components. Components are isolated and self-contained. Thus, we need to keep all the logic related to a UI element in a single place. Isolation also means that we shouldn't have access to a global state (for example, a controller's instance variables) and have explicit dependencies.

Also, having an explicit interface would make components self-descriptive and, thus, predictable. Given all that, the best way to represent view components in the code base is to use Ruby classes. This way, we can turn our views into objects and leverage all the power of object-oriented programming.

Components as Ruby objects

Let's continue using our search box example and try to turn it into a component.

First, we need to define a Ruby class representing the state of the component and implementing its logic rules:

```ruby
class SearchBox::Component
  attr_reader :action, :placeholder
  def initialize(
    action:, placeholder: "Search", variant: :full
  )
    @action = action
    @placeholder = placeholder
    @variant = variant
  end
  def button? = @variant == :full
end
```

In this Ruby class, we defined an explicit interface for our component via keyword arguments. We also added the #button? helper method that we will use in the component's HTML template to toggle the submit button visibility.

This way, we separate the component's logic from its display—the template shouldn't know about variants; it only needs to know whether to render a button. We can think of component methods as internal view helpers.

We also define the Component class in the SearchBox namespace. We will reveal the purpose of this decision later. Let's move on to the next part of componentizing views: where should we put HTML templates?

HTML for components

Even though the logic of our component now lives in a Ruby class, we still need a good location to define the markup. A straightforward option is to keep it in an HTML template next to the component class definition. So, let's start with this.

First, we define the template:

```
<%= form_with(url: c.action) do |f| %>
  <div>
    <i class="fa fa-search"></i>
  </div>
  <%= f.search_field :q, placeholder: c.placeholder %>
<%- if c.button? -%>
  <%= f.submit "Search" %>
<%- end -%>
<% end %>
```

We refer to the component instance via the c local variable in the template. Let's see how we invoke our template from the Component class:

```
class SearchBox::Component
  # ...
  def render_in(view_context)
    view_context.render(
      partial: "components/search_box/component",
      locals: {c: self}
    )
  end
end
```

The #render_in method is a part of the Action View API. Whenever we pass an object that responds to #render_in to the #render helper in a Rails view, Action View assumes that this is a *renderable* object and delegates the rendering to it by passing a view context. This makes it possible to use our component in other templates as follows:

```
<%= render SearchBox::Component.new(action: "#") %>
```

It's possible to keep the template contents in the Ruby class and call render(inline: "<HTML template>", locals: { ... }) in the #render_in method instead. However, by storing the HTML template as text in a Ruby source file, we are likely to lose many **developer experience (DX)** benefits (IDE support, linting tools integration, and so on). Thus, we will keep the HTML and Ruby parts of the component in two separate files. How should we organize component source files then?

Organizing component source files

You probably noticed that we put the search box component's partial into the `components` folder. Now, let's put the Ruby class next to the template to have the following folder structure:

```
app/
  views/
    components/
      search_box/
        component.rb
        _component.html.rb
```

To make Rails pick up component classes from the `app/views/components` folder, we need to configure the autoload paths:

config/application.rb

```
config.autoload_paths << Rails.root.join("app", "views",
  "components")
```

By keeping all the component's source files in the same folder, we physically localize it. There can be more than just two files, Ruby and HTML. We can also put corresponding JavaScript and CSS files or other assets into this folder. Everything the component needs to work in a single folder—a huge maintainability level-up.

The folder structure is not the primary benefit of splitting views into components. What's more important is that we introduced a much higher level of isolation. Templates and helpers are internal implementation details of a component. The outside world only needs to know about the component's explicit API.

Let's see how we can make view components even more helpful.

View components as an abstraction layer

The ad hoc view components implementation from the previous section gives us a sense of what it means to think in components. Now, it's time to take the next step and design a proper abstraction layer out of view components. And for that, we will use the library that has the same name as the pattern—View Component.

> **What a gem – view_component**
>
> ViewComponent (`https://viewcomponent.org`) is a framework for building component-based views in Ruby on Rails. The library was developed at GitHub and originally was meant to be a part of the Rails framework. Thus, it perfectly fits the Rails way and can be seen as a natural extension of Action View.

View Component uses a similar approach to the one we developed ourselves. A view component is a combination of a Ruby object and a template. The framework takes care of gluing components with the Rails' rendering system and provides additional features:

- Components composition (Slots API)

- Life cycle events (`before_render`)

- Utilities to test components in isolation

- Built-in instrumentation (via `ActiveSupport::Notifications`)

- Internationalization (I18n) support

- Component previews (similar to mailer previews)

Thus, View Component solves the most common problems related to maintaining view components in Rails applications and in a Rails way. It's a perfect candidate for introducing a new abstraction layer to an application that needs to manage complex HTML-based UIs.

Let's see some of these features by refactoring our custom component to use the View Component library.

View Component by example

As the first step, we can inherit our component class from the View Component base class and drop the #render_in method—it's part of the library; we don't need to worry about such low-level things anymore. Thus, we have the following Ruby class:

```ruby
class SearchBox::Component < ViewComponent::Base
  attr_reader :url, :placeholder

  def initialize(
    url:, placeholder: "Search", variant: :full
  )
    @url = url
    @placeholder = placeholder
    @variant = variant
  end

  private def button? = @variant == :full
end
```

We also renamed `action` to `url` and made the #button? method private. Why? Let's see what the updated HTML template for the component looks like:

```erb
<%= form_with(url:) do |f| %>
  <div>
    <i class="fa fa-search"></i>
```

```
    </div>
    <%= f.search_field :q, placeholder: %>
    <% if button? %>
      <%= f.submit "Search" %>
    <% end %>
  <% end %>
```

The template is rendered within the component context; there's no need to pass any magic variables (like we did before with the c variable). The Ruby object and the HTML partial are now inseparable.

This is an elementary example of using the View Component library. So far, it's not that different from the hand-crafted componentization we built in the previous section. Let's explore what else View Component gives us.

Testing view components

One of the requirements of a *good abstraction* is to improve the code base's testability, that is, to make it easier to add new tests and maintain the existing ones. Since view components are self-contained by design, we can test them in isolation. We don't have to write many integration tests to cover all the UI-related edge cases and increase the coverage and confidence of the test suite by adding more unit tests for components.

However, since our components are integrated into the Action View rendering pipeline, testing them requires some effort. Luckily, View Component provides test helpers to hide the internal complexity of the rendering engine and let us focus on the actual test scenarios.

Let's write a test for our search box component:

```
class SearchBox::ComponentTest < ViewComponent::TestCase
  def test_render_default_full
    render_inline(
      SearchBox::Component.new(
        url: "#", placeholder: "Search things"))

    assert_selector "input[type='submit']"
    assert_selector(
      "input[type='search'][placeholder='Search things']"
    )
  end

  def test_render_compact
    render_inline(
      SearchBox::Component.new(
        url: "#", variant: :compact))
```

```
    assert_no_selector "input[type='submit']"
  end
end
```

In the test, we use the `#render_inline` helper provided by View Component to render the component with the provided configuration and then assess the rendered HTML contents using assertion methods provided by Capybara (`https://github.com/teamcapybara/capybara`).

The best thing about view component tests is that we don't need any setup or context. Thus, there is less conceptual overhead for writing such tests, and they are faster to run than integration tests.

View Component goes even further and supports writing browser (system) tests for interactive components in isolation. I invite the reader to learn about this feature on their own.

Let's see how we can make our component classes less verbose and more robust.

Dry initializers, I18n, and callbacks

In the `SearchBox::Component` class we defined earlier, most of the code is the component initialization. We can reduce this boilerplate by migrating from the imperative way of declaring the initial state (via `#initialize`) to the declarative one, or DSL. For that, we can use the dry-initializer gem (`https://dry-rb.org/gems/dry-initializer`), which we used in the *From fat models to services* section of *Chapter 5, When Rails Abstractions Are Not Enough*.

Let's start by defining a base class for all view components:

```
class ApplicationViewComponent < ViewComponent::Base
  extend Dry::Initializer[undefined: false]
end
```

In general, it's a good practice to use application-specific base classes for all objects. This way, we can hide the implementation details related to a particular dependency used as a core for the abstraction. In our case, we enhance components with the dry-initialize DSL to declare parameters. This is how our refactored Ruby class for the search box component would look with a *dry* DSL:

```
class SearchBox::Component < ApplicationViewComponent
  option :url
  option :placeholder, optional: true
  option :variant, default: proc { :full }

  private def button? = variant == :full
end
```

Note that we marked the `placeholder` option as `option` but didn't provide a default value (we had `Search` in the original version). That's because we want to keep string literals used in UI in translation files to make a part of localization, not code.

View Component integrates with the Rails internationalization system and allows you to store translation files in the same folder as other components' source files, thus keeping the component self-contained.

Let's create a `component.yml` file with the following contents in the `app/views/components/search_box` folder:

```
en:
  placeholder: "Search"
```

Now, we can refer to the localized placeholder in the component's class as follows:

```
class SearchBox::Component < ApplicationViewComponent
  # ...

  def before_render
    @placeholder ||= t(".placeholder")
  end
end
```

Due to current technical limitations, it's only possible to access relative translations at render time. That's why we use the `#before_render` hook to populate the placeholder if it hasn't been defined by a user. We can also use this hook to perform parameter validation. Here's an example:

```
def before_render
  raise ArgumentError, "Unknown variant: #{variant}" unless
    %i[full compact].include?(variant)
  @placeholder ||= t(".placeholder")
end
```

This is how we can make our components stricter. It's possible to add a proper validation system for view components if the validation use case becomes common in the application's code base. You can even use Active Model validations for that or any other library—view components are just Ruby objects; you can enhance them in any way you want.

However, we should never forget about the cost of adding new features to the abstraction. Both conceptual and performance overhead must be considered.

In the case of performance, View Component can be up to 10x faster than Rails partials due to the optimized rendering pipeline. Helpers are the slowest because they cannot be precompiled, unlike HTML templates. Thus, the more you use helpers in components, the smaller the difference between partials and view components is in terms of rendering speed.

View components for mixed teams

Bringing UI components to Rails has one important positive side-effect for dual-stack teams and hybrid applications (with HTML and JavaScript frontends). Both frontend and backend teams start using the same concepts and speaking the same language regarding UI. This parity increases the overall team productivity and encourages knowledge sharing between sub-teams.

To sum up, view components help deal with the view layer complexity but also help to improve communication between different teams responsible for shipping software projects: backend/frontend engineers and UI/UX designers.

Summary

In this chapter, you've learned about the shortcomings of the classic Rails HTML layer, templates, and partials. You've learned how to make the partials interface explicit using template annotations (*magic comments*). You've familiarized yourself with linting tools for Rails templates and learned how to use them to reduce coupling between controllers and views.

You've learned about design systems and why they must be taken into account when designing a view layer of a Rails application. You've learned about the component-driven approach to building Rails views. You've familiarized yourself with the View Component library and learned how it can help to build a Rails view layer from self-contained components.

In the next chapter, we will go down to the Infrastructure layer and discuss the techniques to keep application configuration under control.

Questions

1. What are the three types of HTML templates in Rails?
2. What are the two significant weak points of Rails partials? How can we overcome them without introducing any new abstractions?
3. What is a design system? How is it reflected in the code base?
4. What are the primary characteristics of view components?
5. What's the difference between a helper, a partial, and a view component?

Further reading

View Component in the Wild (Evil Martians Chronicles): `https://evilmartians.com/chronicles/viewcomponent-in-the-wild-building-modern-rails-frontends`

12

Configuration as a First-Class Application Citizen

In this chapter, we go down the layered architecture and reach the Infrastructure layer; or, more precisely, the part of it responsible for application configuration. We'll start by discussing the various ways we have, in Ruby on Rails applications, to provide configuration values and how this variety affects the code base's maintainability.

After that, we'll talk about different types of configuration parameters, such as settings and secrets, and why it's important to distinguish them. Finally, we'll demonstrate a technique for moving configuration up the architecture stack and separating the configuration model from data sources via configuration objects.

We will cover the following topics:

- Configuration sources and types
- Using domain objects to tame configuration complexity

This chapter aims to demonstrate how the object-oriented approach can help to keep application configuration under control as the code base grows to improve its maintainability.

Technical requirements

In this chapter, and all chapters of this book, the code given in code blocks is designed to be executed on Ruby 3.2 and Rails 7. Many of the code examples will work on earlier versions of the previously mentioned software.

You will find the code files on GitHub at `https://github.com/PacktPublishing/Layered-Design-for-Ruby-on-Rails-Applications/tree/main/Chapter12`.

Configuration sources and types

Modern web applications rely on dozens of configuration parameters. The more your application grows and matures, the harder it is to deal with API keys, encryption secrets, and other settings. Instead, you need to think about where to store them securely, how to share them with the team, how to rotate values, and last but not least, how to *inject* them into the application and access them throughout the code base. The code aspects of managing configuration are what we talk about in this chapter.

Let's start with an overview of the configuration providers available in Ruby on Rails.

Files, secrets, credentials, and more

Every Rails application comes with a `config/` folder. What can you find there? The actual contents depend on the chosen Rails components and third-party libraries, but the following three are likely to present:

- Ruby configuration files (`application.rb` and `environment/*.rb`)
- A database configuration file (`database.yml`)
- Encrypted credentials (`credentials.yml.enc`)

In Ruby config files, we usually configure the framework itself, for example, choose adapters for Active Job or Action Mailer or configure the Rack middleware stack.

Credentials are used to store arbitrary, application-specific configuration values. They're meant for storing sensitive information, such as API keys, though developers are not restricted from using them as a single source of configuration truth. Credentials are stored in an encrypted YAML file, so committing them to a source control system is safe.

That makes delivering production settings and sharing required development configuration information across the team much easier—just share a master key! You can access the values in the application code via the application's singleton object: `Rails.application.credentials.my_api_token`.

Rails also uses plain YAML files to configure framework components, for example, Active Record (`database.yml`) and Action Cable (`cable.yml`). Why spread configuration between Ruby and YAML files? Becauase the configuration aspect of the application should be closer to humans than to machines. We want the configuration to be easily accessible and readable by developers as well as easily editable (even by less experienced users). We also want to localize the values related to a particular application component. YAML is a perfect markup language for declaring configuration values. It has basic data structures and types of support and aliases to share common data, and is extremely human-friendly.

If you look inside the database.yml file, for example, you can also spot some ENV references there:

```
default: &default
  pool: <%= ENV.fetch("RAILS_MAX_THREADS") { 5 } %>
  timeout: 5000
```

Thus, Rails also uses environment variables. This adds yet another (and, going forward, the most popular) way of providing configuration information for Rails applications.

To summarize, we have at least four configuration providers in Rails applications: Ruby code, YAML files, credentials, and environment variables. So, where should you put your application configuration? Statistically, in the Rails world, most teams bet on environment variables. Let's discuss the pros and cons of this approach.

Environment variables as a primary configuration source

We can say for sure that, as of the time of writing, environment variables are way ahead of all other configuration sources. Why did this happen and where that can take you? Let's see.

The Twelve Factors

Since the appearance of container-based and alike deployment environments (such as Heroku and Docker), most web applications have adopted the Twelve-Factor App methodology (https://12factor.net) for developing and deploying software. The methodology describes the best practices for building software services in the cloud era. For example, one of the rules states the configuration must be stored in environment variables.

The motivation is simple: *keep code independent of configuration values*. In other words, do not hardcode configuration in your source files. That makes running the same distribution (a Docker image or Heroku slug) possible in different deployment environments (production, staging, and so on).

The separation idea follows the separation of concerns principle—one of the pillars of maintainable code. However, in practice, going all in with environment variables can quickly lead to a maintainability disaster—the ENV (or .env) hell.

The ENV hell

Environment variables suit production environments very well. However, we do not manually configure a Ruby process environment for development and testing. Instead, we use tools to populate the ENV with the values stored in a file. Thus, to test or run the application locally depending on environment variables, we must do the following:

- Add a library to load environment variables from files, for example, the dotenv gem (https://github.com/bkeepers/dotenv).

- Keep the `.env` file or separate `.env.development` and `.env.test` files with the configuration required for development and testing. Usually, the development configuration is not stored in source control and is shared between teammates using some external secrets manager or by word of mouth.

This doesn't sound like a big deal, right? Now, imagine that over time the number of entries in the `.env` file reached a few dozen and no longer fits a single screen on your display. This is the first sign of approaching the ENV hell—the situation when application configuration becomes barely comprehendible and negatively affects the development process. The typical symptoms of the ENV hell besides the ever-growing `.env` file are as follows:

- Local `.env` file copies frequently go out of sync across the team, causing hard-to-debug failures and time wasted to find newly added or updated values

- Relying on ENV in the code base introduces a global state controlled by the outer world that makes debugging and testing harder (see the *Global and current state* section in *Chapter 4, Rails Anti-Patterns?*)

- Using a schema-less object (ENV) is more error-prone; a typo in the key name may stay unnoticed (since `ENV["UNKNOWN_KEY"]` returns `nil`, which may be an expected behavior)

Another problem with the ENV approach is that we tend to mix configuration values of different kinds and for various application components. As a result, we lose semantic meanings of parameters; they all just become strings.

Treating different kinds of configuration parameters differently can help us to reason about where to keep them. Let's learn more about these kinds.

Settings and secrets

Putting all the configuration into a single, flat structure hides the nature of the values. We have a melting pot of sensitive and non-sensitive business logic- and framework-specific parameters in one place.

Let's look at configuration from a different perspective and split all the parameters into two groups: *settings* and *secrets*.

Settings and sensible defaults

Settings define the technical characteristics of the application and the Rails framework.

For example, we have the `WEB_CONCURRENCY`, `RAILS_MAX_THREADS`, and `RAILS_SERVE_STATIC_FILES` environment variables to define the web server configuration—these are the framework settings. They are used by Rails itself as well as third-party libraries following the Rails conventions.

Other examples of framework parameters are adapter settings for Active Job or Action Mailer.

Application settings may control the availability of some components (usually development tools). For example, when we use **Lookbook** (`https://github.com/ViewComponent/lookbook`) to preview view components (see *Chapter 11*, *Better Abstractions for HTML Views*), we toggle it on and off based on the environment variable in addition to having it always on in development:

```
config.lookbook_enabled =
  ENV["LOOKBOOK_ENABLED"] == "true" ||
  Rails.env.development?
```

This way, we make it possible to enable component preview functionality in any environment without touching the code.

All settings carry one important common property—they have sensible defaults. Even though we use environment variables, we don't always have to provide them; the default configuration must be good enough for most use cases, especially for development and test environments, so we can start hacking around with the application source code without worrying about where to obtain the required configuration values.

Sensible defaults are usually hardcoded in the application code (for example, `ENV.fetch("RAILS_MAX_THREADS", 5)`) and are rarely changed. In most cases, we define the defaults in the environment-specific configuration files (for example, `config/environment/test.rb`). At the same time, we can tweak the configuration via environment variables if we need to tune the configuration.

To sum up, application settings are non-sensitive, technical parameters for which we must provide sensible defaults and allow overriding them on the fly (for example, via environment variables). Ruby configuration files and ENV are good candidates to store this kind of configuration parameter.

Let's move on and talk about the second group—secrets.

Secrets and sensitive information

Secrets store the configuration required to interact with other systems and services as well as sensitive data, such as encryption keys.

Secrets can be essential or secondary. For example, a database is vital to the application's infrastructure; thus, the database credentials belong to the essential secrets. Secondary secrets include, for example, API keys for third-party services, which are optional for the application to serve its primary purpose—for example, analytics tools, instrumentation agents, and similar.

We must design the application in a way that if a secondary secret is missing, we disable the corresponding service integration and continue operating without it. In contrast, if an essential secret is missing, the application must not pass the *Boot Test*—running `rails s` or `rails c` must fail. The earlier developers discover the environment is misconfigured, the quicker they can fix it. The simplest way to implement a boot test is to add a check to an initializer file. For example, if your application depends on **Amazon Web Services** (**AWS**), you can add the following line to the `config/initializers/aws.rb` file:

```
raise "AWS credentials are missing!" unless ENV["AWS_ACCESS_KEY_ID"].
present?
```

Now, whenever you run your application (either Rails console or server) without the corresponding environment variable configured, it would fail to boot and tell you why.

By distinguishing between essential and secondary secrets, we can drastically decrease the amount of configuration required for a minimal application setup and reduce the conceptual overhead for new engineers on the project.

Finally, although the word *secret* implies that we store some sensitive information, we also count as secrets non-sensitive, supporting configuration parameters, such as API hostnames, versions, and limits. So, where do we keep secrets in a Rails application? Credentials seem like a natural choice for sensitive information, but storing non-sensitive secrets in an encrypted file is overkill. A service-specific YAML file fits well to store non-sensitive configuration that is not updated frequently.

So, different configuration types must be treated differently in terms of default values and application requirements. We also must take into account different runtime environments when designing a robust configuration system.

Production, development, and local configurations versus data providers

Ruby on Rails applications come with three preconfigured runtime environments by default: production, development, and test. The difference is in the framework settings (stored in the respective files in the `config/environments` folder) and the application settings in YAML files (each YAML file has a section for each environment).

For different environments, it makes sense to manage configuration values differently. For example, tests must not require any configuration to run besides what's present in the project's source code. That simplifies both local development and **continuous integration** (**CI**)—the fewer places there are to synchronize configuration between, the better.

In development, we need a way to share common secrets across the team and, at the same time, provide an ability to override them locally.

The way we maintain production configuration highly depends on the deployment platform and the number of different production environments (yes, there can be many).

Thus, every runtime environment has its own preferences regarding how to maintain configuration. Combining this with multiple configuration parameter types justifies using different configuration providers across the application code base: ENV, YAML files (via `Rails.application.config_for`), and credentials (via `Rails.application.credentials`).

However, referring to multiple configuration providers in the application's code can be confusing: why do we use credentials over environmental variables and YAML files over hardcoded values in Ruby files for X feature configuration? We can avoid this confusion if we add the layered architecture to the equation.

Layered architecture versus configuration

Every configuration provider is an implementation detail; a provider is a part of the Infrastructure layer. According to the layered architecture principles, we don't want entities from the top layers (for example, the Presentation layer) to rely on the infrastructure directly (see the *On layered architecture and abstraction layers* section in *Chapter 5, When Rails Abstractions Are Not Enough*).

Thus, we either need to introduce intermediate objects and build an *access chain* or we can promote configuration to the Domain layer by separating data sources from the *configuration schema*. The latter means introducing the *configuration abstraction layer* as a part of our domain model—let's do that!

Using domain objects to tame configuration complexity

Application configuration complexity arises from the number of configuration parameters, different data sources, and runtime environments. If we do not take measures, this complexity can quickly spread like a virus all over the code base and, though hardly noticeable in a particular class or object, can have a negative cumulative effect on the project's maintainability.

Thus, the first step toward maintainable configuration is to prevent the spread and localize the complexity in a single place. We can start with the built-in Rails configuration files.

Separating application code from configuration sources

Let's consider an example of configuring an imaginary third-party service named *Layerize.cake*, which provides an API to generate a layered cake recipe based on given ingredients and specifications using some AI model under the hood. To use the API, we need to provide a model ID, an API key, and a callback URL to asynchronously receive results via a webhook (since generation can take a long time). Let's decide where to store this information.

In tests, we do not perform real HTTP requests (tests must be isolated from the outer world). Instead, we can use an HTTP mocking tool, for example, the Webmock gem (`https://github.com/`

bblimke/webmock), to interrupt HTTP requests and return pre-recorded responses. Thus, we can hardcode made-up configuration parameters for this service and use them in HTTP stubs in tests.

In development, all the team members may share the same API key and use a shared request bin service to collect webhooks. Since both the dev API key and the request bin URL are sensitive values, we can store them in the development credentials. Rails supports per-environment credentials since v6.0. It's a perfect way to manage, share and sync team-wide secrets—all you need to share beyond the source code is the encryption key.

Sometimes, a developer may need to test webhooks locally. For that, they can set up an HTTP tunnel to consume webhooks on their local machine. That would require providing a custom callback URL, specific to this local installation. Thus, we need a way to dynamically override the corresponding configuration parameter. We can use an environment variable for that.

Finally, for production, we must store the API key in a secure place, such as production credentials. The callback URL and the AI model ID may be stored as plain text.

Given all the preceding, we can use the following configuration sources.

Let's use a service-specific YAML configuration file to keep all non-sensitive information:

```
default: &default
  model: "CakeGPT-1.0"

development:
  <<: *default

test:
  <<: *default
  api_key: secret_cake
  callback_url: "http://localhost:3000/callbacks/test"

production:
  <<: *default
  # We use a newer, more expensive, and slower model in
    production
  model: "CakeGPT-2.0"
  callback_url: "https://callbacks.myapp.io/cakes"
```

We use the aliasing feature of YAML to share common configuration parameters between environments. Production and development API keys go to the corresponding credential files.

Let's see how we can access the configuration in the API client code:

```
class LayerizeClient
  def initialize
```

```ruby
    @api_key = credentials&.api_key || yml_config[:api_key]
    @model = yml_config[:model]
    @callback_url = ENV["LAYERIZE_CALLBACK_URL"] ||
       credentials&.callback_url ||
       yml_config[:callback_url]
  end

  private
  def credentials = Rails.application.credentials.layerize
  def yml_config =
     @yml_config ||= Rails.application.config_for(:layerize)
end
```

The preceding code is a configuration nightmare. It takes quite some time to understand how we build the final configuration. What about testing? Every | | operator is a logical branching—a separate test example. This is an example of how configuration complexity affects the code base.

A reasonable question to ask is: *How is this better than putting everything into the .env file?* We sacrificed code readability for configuration management, or code quality for developer experience. Luckily, we don't have to compromise; we can make both the configuration and the code using it maintainable.

Moving all data sources to YAML

Let's note that Rails' #config_for method supports injecting dynamic values via ERB interpolation. We can use this feature to hide the complexity within the YAML file as follows:

```yaml
default: &default
   model: "CakeGPT-1.0"
   api_key: <%= Rails.application.credentials.
     layerize&.api_key %>

development:
  <<: *default
  callback_url: <%= ENV.fetch("LAYERIZE_CALLBACK_URL") {
  Rails.application.credentials.layerize&.callback_url } %>

test:
  <<: *default
  api_key: secret_cake
  callback_url: "http://localhost:3000/callbacks/test"

production:
  <<: *default
  # We use a newer, more expensive, and slower model in
```

```
    production
  model: "CakeGPT-2.0"
  callback_url: "https://callbacks.myapp.io/cakes"
```

Now the client code looks more readable because it uses a single source of configuration truth—a YAML file:

```ruby
class LayerizeClient
  def initialize
    @api_key = config[:api_key]
    @model = config[:model]
    @callback_url = config[:callback_url]
  end
  private
  def config =
    @config ||= Rails.application.config_for(:layerize)
end
```

The client code now only knows about the YAML configuration. Can we *erase* this knowledge? Yes. Let's see how.

Using a singleton configuration object

We can go further and move the #config_for call to the application configuration phase and call it just once. For that, we can extend the Rails application configuration object. In config/ application.rb, we can write the following:

```ruby
config.layerize = Rails.application.config_for(:layerize)
```

Now, we can reuse the configuration object (which is just a hash) and avoid double-loading:

```ruby
class LayerizeClient
  # ...
  private
  def config = Rails.application.config.layerize
end
```

The configuration object we use in the client source code is no longer coupled with data sources. This is great—we achieved the separation! However, the readability of our human-friendly YAML configuration file has suffered. We will learn how to bring back its readability soon.

Now, let's discuss one special case of the configuration virus spreading not related to data sources and how to contain it.

Making the code base environment-free

Accessing configuration sources directly is not how the application code may become coupled with configuration. In Rails, it's a common pattern to check for the current runtime environment type (`Rails.application.production?` or `Rails.application.test?`) to tweak the application's behavior. In Rails 7.1, a new helper, `Rails.application.local?`, was added to indicate one of the two local environments, development or test.

These helpers are typical examples of Rails productivity hacks: helpful at the beginning but costly to deal with in the long haul. They introduce imparity to the application code and, thus, can result in production bugs (since some code paths are only executed in specific environments). From this perspective, the most dangerous helper is the `Rails.application.production?` one.

Adding a new environment, say, staging, also becomes more complicated since we need to take it into account in every place in the code base we checked for production and development (staging usually combines the features of these two).

To avoid such problems, we can replace environment checks with custom configuration options. Let's recall our Lookbook example from the *Settings and sensible defaults* section:

```
config.lookbook_enabled =
  ENV["LOOKBOOK_ENABLED"] == "true" ||
  Rails.env.development?
```

The new `lookbook_enabled` option can be used in the code base to detect whether we use the tool. The name of the variable clearly communicates its purpose; we also have a sensible default—enable it in the development environment.

Thus, it's a good idea to replace environment checks with custom configuration options and only use the checks to provide sensible defaults.

Enforcing environment-free code with linters

We can turn a strict mode on and programmatically prevent the appearance of environment checks in the application code by writing a linter. For example, we can write a custom RuboCop (https://rubocop.org) rule to warn about the `Rails.env` usage:

```
module RuboCop
  module Cop
    module Lint
      class RailsEnv < RuboCop::Cop::Cop
        MSG = "Avoid Rails.env in application code, " \
              "use configuration parameters instead"

        def_node_matcher :rails_env?, <<~PATTERN
          (send {(const nil? :Rails) (const (cbase)
```

```
                  :Rails)} :env)
          PATTERN

          def on_send(node)
            return unless rails_env?(node)
            add_offense(
              node.parent.type == :send ? node.parent : node,
              location: :selector, message: MSG)
          end
        end
      end
    end
end
```

Add the cop to the `.rubocop.yml` file and configure it to ignore files from the `config/` directory:

```
require:
  - ./lib/rubocop/cop/lint_rails_env

Lint/RailsEnv:
  Enabled: true
  Exclude:
    - 'config/**/*.rb'
```

Now, when you run the `rubocop` command, you can catch the violating code. Say we have the following code snippet:

```
client = LayerizeClient.new
client.test_mode = Rails.env.local?
```

We will see the following output:

```
$ bundle exec rubocop
Offenses:
W: Lint/RailsEnv: Avoid Rails.env in application code, use
configuration parameters instead
client.test_mode = Rails.env.local?
                          ^^^^^^^
```

In a similar fashion, we can create linting rules to *catch* other configuration leakages into the source code and enforce the separation.

So far, we have figured out how to make the source code free of environment knowledge and configuration data sources. However, we just swept the complexity under the YAML rug. It's still in the code base. Let's take a step beyond the RailsWay and introduce smart configuration objects to truly eliminate the configuration complexity.

Using specialized configuration classes

The configuration separation technique described in the previous section has two major downsides:

- We still have the complexity of dealing with multiple data sources in YAML files.

- Configuration information is represented as a Ruby hash and accessed via the global application configuration object. Thus, the global configuration object (`Rails.application.config`) knows about all the services and systems we interact with and is responsible for preparing the configuration parameters for them.

To overcome these downsides, we can introduce **configuration objects**—objects providing configuration information for different services and encapsulating the underlying configuration providers or data sources.

In Ruby on Rails, we can introduce configuration objects via the Anyway Config library.

> **What a gem — anyway_config**
>
> Anyway Config (`https://github.com/palkan/anyway_config`) is a configuration library for Ruby applications that aims to reduce the complexity of dealing with different data sources and advocates for using named, specialized configuration objects instead of a global configuration store.

Originally, it was designed to abstract configuration aspects in Ruby gems so users are able to choose their favorite method of keeping settings (such as files, environments, and external providers). Over time, it proved to be useful to manage configuration in larger Rails applications, too, since it helps to manage configuration for different components independently.

Keeping configuration with Anyway Config

With Anyway Config, we treat configuration parameters as part of the domain they belong to. That is, if we need to manage configuration for feature X, we create a dedicated config object responsible solely for providing information for this feature.

Example configuration class

Let's refactor our Layerize service configuration to be backed by a Ruby class:

```ruby
class LayerizeConfig < ApplicationConfig
  attr_config :api_key, :callback_url,
      model: "CakeGPT 1.0", enabled: true

  required :api_key
end
```

The `LayerizeConfig` class defines the configuration schema via the `.attr_config` method. Having an explicitly defined configuration interface is a major benefit compared to plain Ruby hashes.

Whenever we need a configuration for the service, we can create a new configuration object as follows:

```ruby
config = LayerizeConfig.new
pp config
#=>
#<LayerizeConfig
  config_name="layerize"
  env_prefix="LAYERIZE"
values:
  model => "CakeGPT 1.0" (type=defaults),
  enabled => true (type=defaults),
  api_key => "super-secret"
    (type=credentials store=config/credentials.yml.enc),
  callback_url => "https://team.request-bin.dev/layerize"
    (type=credentials store=config/credentials.yml.enc)>
```

Note that we don't pass any arguments to the constructor: the config automatically loads from the known sources using the configuration name. By default, Anyway Config supports loading data from YAML files, Rails credentials and secrets, and environment variables—and you don't need to pollute YAML files with manual values retrieval, so you are able to keep it clear. The config instance provides introspection into where each value came from (see the pretty print output).

In the configuration class, we can also declare the default values and list the required parameters. If a required parameter is missing or empty, initializing a configuration object fails:

```ruby
LayerizeConfig.new(api_key: "")
#=> Anyway::Config::ValidationError: The following config parameters
for `LayerizeConfig(config_name: layerize)` are missing or empty: api_
key
```

The base configuration class contains code to access a singleton configuration instance via the class interface:

```
class ApplicationConfig < Anyway::Config
  class << self
    delegate_missing_to :instance

    def instance
      @instance ||= new
    end
  end
end
```

Now we can access the default instance values via class accessors:

```
LayerizeConfig.api_key #=> "super-secret"
```

Using configuration objects in code

Given that, we can rewrite our `LayerizeClient` class as follows:

```
class LayerizeClient
  def initialize(config: LayerizeConfig)
    @api_key = config.api_key
    @model = config.model
    @callback_url = config.callback_url
  end
end
```

Note that we pass the configuration object as a constructor argument and use a singleton by default. That makes it possible to easily create a client with different credentials:

```
config = LayerizeConfig.new(api_key: "another-key")
LayerizeClient.new(config:)
```

In the preceding example, we create a new configuration object and override the API key; all other parameters stay the same (they're loaded from the sources).

Configuration objects as an abstraction layer

Since configuration objects are just Ruby classes, we can make them be much more than configuration data containers. For example, we can add custom helper methods, validate parameters, or perform type casting. Here is how we can do all of these with Anyway Config classes:

```
class LayerizeConfig < ApplicationConfig
  attr_config :api_key, :callback_url, :enabled,
```

```ruby
      model: "CakeGPT 1.0"

  required :api_key

  coerce_types enabled: :boolean

  on_load :validate_model

  def model_version = model.match(/(\d+\.\d+)/)[1]

  private
  def validate_model
    return if model&.match?(/^CakeGPT \d+\.\d+$/)
    raise ArgumentError, "Unknown model: #{model}"
  end
end

LayerizeConfig.new(model: "CakeGPT 1.5").model_version
#=> 1.5

LayerizeConfig.new(model: "CandyLLM 1.0")
#=> ArgumentError: Unknown model: "CandyLLM 1.0"

ENV["LAYERIZE_ENABLED"] = "0"
LayerizeConfig.new.enabled? #=> false
```

All the features demonstrated previously (validations, type casting, and so on) make the configuration more powerful. This way, we turn configuration objects into a proper abstraction providing solutions to many common tasks and encapsulating the implementation details.

Let's see how this abstraction helps us to reason about where to keep configuration data.

The configuration way with Anyway Config objects

Anyway Config provides you with a common abstraction that suits all cases—now you are free to mix, match, and override pieces of configuration coming from different sources without additional conceptual overhead.

Thus, you can keep configuration data in a place where it better fits from a developer experience point of view. Here is an example convention for storing configuration:

- Store sensitive information in Rails credentials. Teamwide development secrets go into `credentials/development.yml.enc`—this is how we simplify onboarding and secrets synchronization across the team.

- Keep non-sensitive information and test configuration in named YAML configs.

- Use environment variables if you need to override some parameters.

- Store personal development secrets and settings in `*.local.yml` and `credentials/local.yml.enc` files. Anyway Config loads configuration from these files with a higher priority.

- If you have multiple different production environments (for example, for each regional deployment), consider using an external configuration provider, such as Doppler (`https://www.doppler.com`). No worries, Anyway Config has you covered here, too, via custom loaders support.

This is the (configuration) way.

Summary

Configuration is one of the critical markers of code base health. In this chapter, you've learned how managing configuration can become a maintainability problem and a productivity bottleneck. You've learned about the built-in Rails mechanisms to provide configuration information. You've become familiar with the Twelve-Factor methodology and how it has made environment variables the most popular way for storing configuration.

You've learned about the problems related to the heavy usage of ENV in the code base. You've learned how to classify configuration parameters into different kinds (settings and secrets) and how it affects decisions about where to store them. You've learned how to separate application code and configuration sources the Rails way. You've also learned how introducing configuration objects helps to keep configuration under control and provides a better developer experience.

In the next chapter, we will continue exploring the Infrastructure layer and discuss how abstractions can help with logging, instrumentation, and other technical aspects of the application.

Questions

1. Where can we store configuration information in a Rails application?
2. What are the pros and cons of using only environment variables for configuration?
3. What are the two types of configuration parameters?
4. Why is it important to separate application code from configuration sources? How can we achieve this in Rails?
5. What is a configuration object?

Exercises

Write a RuboCop rule to detect and warn against the direct usage of `Rails.application.credentials` in the application's code base (the `app/` folder). Use the `Lint/RailsEnv` cop from the *Enforcing environment-free code with linters* section as an example.

13
Cross-Layers and Off-Layers

In this closing chapter, we will provide an overview of various infrastructure concepts in Rails applications, including logging, monitoring, and exception tracking. We will discuss the benefits of having conventions and *cross-layer* abstractions to standardize infrastructure management in Rails code bases. Finally, we will talk about how a proper level of abstraction can help to extract low-level implementation from the application to a standalone service.

We will cover the following topics:

- The Rails infrastructure layer and its diversity
- Across the layers – logging and monitoring
- Extracting implementations into services

The goal of this chapter is to get familiarized with the Rails infrastructure layer, learning how adding mediator abstractions on top of low-level implementations can help to improve an application's maintainability and performance.

Technical requirements

In this chapter, and all chapters of this book, the code given in code blocks is designed to be executed on Ruby 3.2 and Rails 7. Many of the code examples will work on earlier versions of the aforementioned software.

You will find the code files on GitHub at `https://github.com/PacktPublishing/Layered-Design-for-Ruby-on-Rails-Applications/tree/main/Chapter13`.

The Rails infrastructure layer and its diversity

When we talk about the infrastructure layer of a Rails application, we mean all the tools and services that the application relies on and are not part of the business or presentation logic. Infrastructure components act as a low-level base upon which we build an application. What does this base consist of? The following list is not exhaustive but should be enough to give you an idea of what belongs to the infrastructure layer:

- Database adapters

- Third-party API clients

- Caching and storage systems (that is, Active Storage backends)

- Configuration providers (credentials, secrets, and so on)

- Background processing engines (for example, Sidekiq and GoodJob)

- Web servers (for example, Puma and Unicorn) and Rack middleware

- Logging and monitoring tools

As you can see, infrastructure spans the whole application and has different forms and factors. However, if we take a closer look at how Rails designs infrastructure concepts, we can spot a pattern – there is usually a framework-level abstraction on top of the actual implementation.

Infrastructure abstractions and implementations

Rails provides powerful APIs and abstractions for us to use to craft web applications. For example, Active Record and Active Model help to design an application's domain logic without thinking about the underlying database management; Active Storage encapsulates everything related to handling and serving file uploads, with just a single declaration in a model (for example, `has_one_attached :file`).

At the same time, these high-level APIs are built on top of lower, framework-level abstractions (or maybe multiple levels of them). If we dig deeper, we will eventually reach low-level, implementation-specific components (usually provided by third-party dependencies). For example, for Active Record, the lowest level would be a database driver. For Active Storage, it would be an image transformation tool or a cloud storage API client.

The **abstraction distance** (the number of in-between abstractions before we reach the actual implementation) can be big in Rails. It's highly unlikely that we ever need to go in too deep and reach for implementations. There is always a framework-level interface on the way down that should meet our needs.

In Active Record, for example, we can use an `ActiveRecord::Base.connection` object to perform arbitrary database operations. It's still not the actual database connection wrapper (which is database-specific) but, instead, an *infrastructure abstraction* provided by the framework.

And here lies the most significant difference – implementations are not owned by our application or the framework, while infrastructure abstractions are. Why is this important? Having more control over the components we rely upon and having in-between abstractions on top of implementations makes our code base more robust to low-level interface changes.

In *Chapter 3, More Adapters, Less Implementations*, we discussed design patterns in detail, such as adapters and wrappers, which Rails use to define infrastructure abstractions for Active Job and Active Storage. We didn't use the term *infrastructure* there because it is introduced further in the book, but that's exactly what we are talking about – how to introduce an infrastructure abstraction to draw a line between the code base/framework and an implementation.

In the rest of this chapter, we will talk about other use cases and the implications of bringing abstractions to the infrastructure layer. Let's start with cross-layer infrastructure components.

Across the layers – logging and monitoring

Infrastructure components can be divided into ones that power the application features and the ones that serve the production team's needs. The latter group includes visibility and observability functionality, such as **logging and monitoring**.

Logging and monitoring can be attached to any architecture layer of an application. That's why we call the corresponding abstraction layers the **cross-layers**. What abstractions can they have? Let's start with the logging layer.

Logging

Logging is essential for any software, since it provides visibility to the events that happen within the application. We scan logs to look for errors, warnings, and events preceding them, to learn about the current application state (configuration) and system-wide events, or even to figure out how users interact with the application.

Rails comes with the essential log support out of the box. Depending on the log level, you may see the following events in the log stream – HTTP request information, the database queries performed, the Action Cable broadcasts made, and so on.

However, for your custom logic, it's up to you how and where to introduce logging. Let's see what options we have.

All you need is Logger

The simplest way to add logging to your code, especially in a development environment, is to drop a `puts "smth"` statement. Let's consider an example – a simple service object to fetch the number of GitHub stars for a given repository.

Let's also assume that we want to provide visibility of the requests made and their statuses. Then, the code will look like this:

```ruby
class GitStarsFetcher
  URL_TEMPLATE = https://api.github.com/repos/%s/%s

  def stars_for(org, repo)
    puts "Fetching stars for: #{org}/#{repo}"
    uri = URI(URL_TEMPLATE % [org, repo])
    res = Net::HTTP.get_response(uri)
    stars = JSON.parse(res.body).fetch("stargazers_count")
    puts "Stars fetched successfully: #{stars}"
    stars
  rescue Net::HTTPError, JSON::ParserError => error
    puts "Failed to fetch stars: #{error.message}"
  end
end
```

Now, whenever we use the service, we see the logs printed in a standard output like this:

```ruby
GitStarsFetcher.new.stars_for("rails", "rails")
#=> Fetching stars for: rails/rails
#=> Stars fetched successfully: 52998
```

Can we say that we increased the visibility? Sure. What about the quality of this solution? It's far from perfect – no context information (such as timestamps), no control over the logging device (where to print logs), no way to turn logs off for a particular environment, and so on. Logging is a bit more sophisticated than just printing information on a screen.

Also, by using `puts`, we make our code dependent on the actual logging implementation; there is no intermediate abstraction. Thus, the service object becomes responsible for all logging aspects.

Luckily, we don't need to reinvent the wheel and can use an abstraction that is a part of the Ruby standard library – a **logger object**. That's what Rails uses under the hood and exposes via the `Rails.logger` method, so you can use it in your code.

Let's rewrite our `GitStarsFetcher` class to use a logger:

```ruby
class GitStarsFetcher
  def stars_for(org, repo)
```

```
    Rails.logger.debug "Fetching stars for: #{org}/#{repo}"
    # ...
    Rails.logger.debug "Stars fetched successfully:
      #{stars}"
    stars
  rescue Net::HTTPError, JSON::ParserError => error
    Rails.logger.debug "Failed to fetch stars:
      #{error.message}"
  end
end
```

Executing the updated version will result in the following logs being printed:

```
GitStarsFetcher.new.stars_for("anycable", "anycable")
#=> D, [2023-06-16T17:17:59] DEBUG -- : Fetching stars for:
  anycable/anycable
#=> D, [2023-06-16T17:18:00] DEBUG -- : Stars fetched
  successfully: 1760
```

Now, our log messages have timestamps attached and a logging level defined (so we can control the program's output verbosity). Our service object no longer cares about where logs should go either – Rails.logger is set up once in the application configuration. Besides levels and outputs, we can also configure a *log formatter* (for example, to implement structured logging), although this topic is out of the scope of this book.

Ruby's Logger class is the perfect abstraction for dealing with logs. Rails makes it even better by enhancing its functionality. Let's look at one of the extensions – **tagged logging**.

Tags for logs

By default, Rails.logger has the ActiveSupport::TaggedLogging module mixed in. This module allows you to define log tags (arbitrary strings), which are prepended to every message logged. Tags help you to filter logs related to a particular execution context.

Rails allows you to define global tags via configuration. For example, you can (and should in production) add request identifiers as tags by adding the following to your configuration:

```
config.log_tags = [:request_id]
```

We can also add a proc object to the list of tags. It will be used to extract tags from requests:

```
config.log_tags = [
  :request_id,
  proc { |request| request.headers["X-USER-ID"] }
]
```

We can see log tags in action by performing an HTTP request with the corresponding headers provided (a request identifier can be provided via the `"X-Request-ID"` header):

```
Get "/", headers: {"X-Request-ID" => "req-1",
  "X-User-ID" => "42"}
#=> INFO -- : [req-1] [42] Started GET "/" at 2023-06-16
#=> INFO -- : [req-1] [42] Completed 200 OK in 7ms
```

> **Note**
> The log timestamps are omitted from the preceding example output.

Any *callable* Ruby object can be used as a *tag extractor*, not only a proc instance. Hence, we can say that a log tag extractor is yet another abstraction that helps us to provide a better logging experience.

You can also tag logs from code, either by creating a logger instance copy or by wrapping some execution with the `logger.tagged(tags) { ... }` block. Let's refactor our `GitStarsClient` class to use a tagged logger:

```ruby
class GitStarsFetcher
  private attr_reader :logger

  def initialize
    @logger = Rails.logger.tagged("☆")
  end

  def stars_for(org, repo)
    logger.debug "Fetching stars for: #{org}/#{repo}"
    stars = # ...
    logger.debug "Stars fetched successfully: #{stars}"
    stars
  end
end
```

We created a custom logger object with the "☆" tag attached to be used within the service object. That makes our logs more beautiful (don't repeat this in production, though):

```
GitStarsFetcher.new.stars_for("test-prof", "test-prof")
#=> DEBUG -- : [☆] Fetching stars for: test-prof/test-prof
#=> DEBUG -- : [☆] Stars fetched successfully: 1668
```

To sum up, Rails comes with a comprehensive logging system with many abstractions involved to help you better utilize an application's logs. However, some events require a different level of attention from developers and, thus, must be captured differently from other log events. Let's talk a bit about exceptions.

Exception tracking

Exceptions are inevitable. No matter how hard you try to keep your code 100% correct, there are still many other factors you cannot control, such as user input, external APIs and services, and the operating system you run your application within.

Your goal is not to write software that makes exceptions impossible but to write software that knows how to make developers and users aware of unexpected situations. Awareness is the key to stability. That's why exceptions must be treated with special care.

First, we need a way to notify about exceptions in real or near-real time. The quicker we react to a problem, the fewer users will be affected by it. Secondly, failure reports must provide as much context as possible to help us narrow down potential root causes. Such context may include call stacks, execution environment metadata, and system information.

Similar to logging, Rails and its ecosystem has us covered with regard to exception tracking. All we need to do is choose an exception monitoring tool (Sentry or Honeybadger, to name a few) and install the corresponding Rails plugin (a Ruby gem). All the exceptions that occur in our application and are not *rescued* by us will be captured and reported to the monitoring system. What if we need to report an exception manually (for example, when we want to stop propagation and be rescued from it)?

Since Rails 7.0, we no longer need to pollute our code with implementation-specific exception tracking code (for example, `Sentry.capture` or `Honeybadger.report`). Now, we can use a **universal error-reporting interface**, accessible via the `Rails.error` object.

Let's demonstrate how Rails' error reporter works by adding the corresponding functionality to our `GitStarsFetcher` class:

```
class GitStarsFetcher
  # ...
  def stars_for(org, repo)
    logger.debug "Fetching stars for: #{org}/#{repo}"
    stars = # ...
    logger.debug "Stars fetched successfully: #{stars}"
    stars
  rescue Net::HTTPError, JSON::ParserError => error
    Rails.error.report(error, handled: true)
    logger.error "Failed to fetch stars: #{error.message}"
  end
end
```

We only added a single line to report an exception. The code stays implementation-agnostic – it doesn't matter which monitoring tool we use; the code stays the same.

If this book targeted Rails <7, we would dedicate this section to implementing such universal error-reporting abstraction ourselves. In modern Rails, it's no longer needed. Therefore, we can jump right to the next topic – **instrumentation**.

Instrumentation

Instrumentation implies collecting and exposing (in a machine-readable format) vital characteristics or metrics of the software under consideration. Instrumenting a code base means adding specific code to track such metrics.

What characteristics are vital for a Rails web application? There are universal metrics for all Rails applications, such as request latencies and queueing times, database query times, background processing queue sizes, and Ruby VM statistics (object allocations and garbage collection information). There are also underlying system metrics, such as RAM and CPU usage. Finally, you can add your custom metrics to monitor characteristics specific to your application.

As with logging and exception tracking, existing Rails plugins allow you to instrument framework-level functionality (HTTP requests and background jobs) without a single line of code. And again, as in previous sections, our work begins as soon as we need to instrument our application code.

Let's see how we can instrument our code by following Rails' design patterns.

Active Support Notifications

Rails comes with a built-in instrumentation framework – Active Support Notifications. This framework provides an API to publish and subscribe to events happening in an application while it's running (for example, Rails instrument database queries and HTML template rendering), so you can *listen* to these events and perform some side effects, such as the following:

```
ActiveSupport::Notifications.subscribe("sql.active_record")
  do |event|
  puts "SQL: #{event.payload[:sql]}"
end

User.first
#=> SQL: SELECT * FROM users ORDER BY id ASC LIMIT ?
```

We can use Active Support Notifications to instrument our code, too. Let's continue using our previous example and instrument HTTP calls within the `GitStarFetcher` class:

```
class GitStarsFetcher
  # ...
  def stars_for(org, repo)
    uri = URI(URL_TEMPLATE % [org, repo])
    payload = {repo: "#{org}/#{repo}"}
```

```
    ActiveSupport::Notifications.instrument(
      "fetch_stars.gh", payload) do
        response = Net::HTTP.get_response(uri)
        stars = JSON.parse(response.body)
                   .fetch("stargazers_count")
        payload["stars"] = stars
      end
    rescue Net::HTTPError, JSON::ParserError => error
      Rails.error.report(error, handled: true)
    end
  end
```

We wrapped an HTTP request execution into the `Notification.instrument` block and passed the event name (`"http.git_stars"`) and an additional context (the repository name). Now, we can subscribe to this event anywhere in our code base and process the instrumentation information:

```
ActiveSupport::Notifications.subscribe("fetch_stars.gh") do
  puts("repo=#{_1.payload[:repo]} " \
     "stars=#{_1.payload[:stars]} duration=#{_1.duration}")
end

GitStarsFetcher.new.stars_for("rails", "rails")
#=> repo=rails/rails stars=53001 duration=0.63
```

As you can see, Active Support Notifications automatically measure the duration of the instrumented block execution, which can be a useful piece of information for us – our vital characteristic.

But where have our log statements gone? Adding instrumentation doesn't mean we no longer need logs; however, instrumentation can also be used to record logs. We even have a dedicated abstraction in Rails – **log subscribers**.

Log subscribers

A log subscriber is an object that listens for events from a particular *source* via Active Support Notifications. What is a source? It's the second part (after the dot) of the event name. It's a Rails convention to define event sources this way. Having an event type as a prefix of the full event name makes it possible to subscribe to similar events from different sources using a wildcard (for example, `"sql.*"`).

Let's define a log subscriber for GitHub-related events:

```
class GHLogSubscriber < ActiveSupport::LogSubscriber
  def fetch_stars(event)
    repo = event.payload[:repo]
    ex = event.payload[:exception_object]
    if ex
```

```
        error do
          "Failed to fetch stars for #{repo}: #{ex.message}"
        end
      else
        debug do
          "Fetched stars for #{repo}: #{event.payload[:stars]} (#{event.
duration.round(2)}ms)"
        end
      end
    end
end
```

For every event type we want to log, we define a public method with the corresponding name (#fetch_stars). The method accepts an *event* object, which we can use to generate a log message. Active Support Notifications dispatches events even if an exception occurred during the instrumented code execution. In this case, the :exception_object and :exception keys are added to the event's payload. We can use them to distinguish successful events from failures and log them differently.

To activate our subscriber, we must attach it to the source:

```
GHLogSubscriber.attach_to :gh
```

After the log subscriber has been attached, it will produce logs every time the event is triggered:

```
GitStarsFetcher.new.stars_for("rails", "rails")

#=> DEBUG -- : Fetched stars for rails/rails: 53009 (48ms)
```

Now, let's go back to our initial monitoring task – we need a way to expose the collected instrumentation data to a monitoring service.

Abstracting monitoring services from instrumentation data

Simply logging instrumentation events doesn't give us observability. We need to put the collected data into a system that will help us to analyze the information and give us insights into the system's state as a whole.

Most monitoring tools provide APIs to ingest metrics manually. So, we could put an implementation-specific code into a subscriber block to do that. Doing so will have the following drawbacks. Performing ingestion right from the subscriber can result in performance degradation since subscribers are executed synchronously right after an event has occurred.

Also, some instrumentation data requires aggregation before it can be pushed into a collecting system (for example, histogram calculation). Finally, putting implementation-specific code to every subscriber (if we have many custom metrics) makes the code base coupled with this implementation.

We need a universal way to define metrics and their types, with the ability to ingest collected information into any monitoring data store. In the Ruby world, we have a tool for that called Yabeda.

What a gem – yabeda

Yabeda (`https://github.com/yabeda-rb/yabeda`) is an instrumentation framework for Ruby applications that provides both metrics collection plugins for popular libraries (Rails, Sidekiq, AnyCable, and so on) as well as different metrics-exporting adapters (Prometheus, DataDog, and so on). With Yabeda, you declare and update metrics via a standard API not coupled with any monitoring system.

Let's finish our `GitStarFetcher` example by introducing Yabeda-managed metrics.

First, we need to declare the metrics somewhere in the application initialization code (say, `config/initializers/metrics.rb`):

```
Yabeda.configure do
  counter :gh_stars_call_total
  counter :gh_stars_call_failed_total
  histogram :gh_stars_call_duration, unit: :millisecond
end
```

We defined two counters and a histogram. Yabeda follows Prometheus (`https://prometheus.io`) conventions for metrics data types, since they cover the most common use cases and are compatible with many monitoring systems.

After we configure metrics, we can update them from a notifications subscriber as follows:

```
ActiveSupport::Notifications.subscribe("fetch_stars.gh") do
  Yabeda.gh_stars_call_total.increment({})
  if _1.payload[:exception]
    Yabeda.gh_stars_call_failed_total.increment({})
  else
    Yabeda.gh_stars_call_duration.measure({}, _1.duration)
  end
end
```

Finally, you will need to install a Yabeda exporter plugin for your monitoring system. And that's it! You now have an implementation-agnostic instrumentation system in your application.

Note that even though Yabeda provides an abstract way of collecting instrumentation data, we still don't use it directly in our code but through Active Support Notifications. This way, we separate generic instrumentation from updating specific metrics. We already saw how it can be used for logging, for instance. Finally, making the application code dependent only on Rails makes our code closer to the Rails Way with all its benefits.

Extracting implementations into services

Having low-level implementation separated from the application-level interface via intermediate abstractions has one more interesting positive effect worth mentioning in this book.

When the abstraction distance is *high*, it can be possible not only to switch from one implementation library to another in a Ruby application but also to *move* the implementation, and even some infrastructure abstractions, to a separate service without affecting the rest of the application's code base.

What could the motivation for splitting a majestically monolithic Rails application into multiple services be? Performance. There are some load scenarios in which Rails and Ruby do not act as the best performers. Extracting low-level, logic-less functionality into a heavily optimized service away from Rails can drastically increase the scalability of your application, and proper abstractions can make performing such a migration transparent

Let's take a quick look at a couple of examples of such services.

Separating WebSockets from Action Cable with AnyCable

AnyCable (`https://anycable.io`) can be used as an alternative WebSocket server for Action Cable. Being written in Go and optimized for concurrency, it can handle many times more simultaneous clients and provide a better real-time experience (for example, latency) while using fewer system resources than Action Cable.

However, the most important (for Rails applications) feature of AnyCable is being a drop-in replacement for the Action Cable – that is, your application code (channel classes) stays the same when you switch from Action Cable to AnyCable.

Such interoperability is possible due to the design of Action Cable. The *distance* between your business logic defined in channel classes and low-level WebSocket handling is high enough to make it possible to replace internal Action Cable infrastructure abstractions (a server, an event loop, and so on) with an external service.

Finally, having the broadcasting logic *adapterized* helps you to easily integrate any third-party publish-subscribe implementation to deliver messages from Rails to WebSocket clients.

The following diagram shows the difference between the Action Cable and AnyCable underlying infrastructures:

Figure 13.1 – Action Cable versus AnyCable infrastructure components

As you can see, the channel abstraction stays as the invariant. If it had an explicit dependency on any of the components from the upper branch (for example, a server), it wouldn't be so simple to extract WebSocket connection handling from Rails.

Let's move on to another example of leveraging well-designed abstractions for service extraction.

Processing images on the fly and off Rails

Active Storage comes with everything you need to work with user-uploaded files. When it comes to images, Active Storage allows you to easily generate variants (or *representations*). All you need is to define the required transformations when providing an URL to fetch an image. The actual transformation happens on the fly – the first time the image is requested.

Let's see which URLs Rails generates for Active Storage blobs and representations. Assuming that we have the User class with has_one_attached :avatar, the following URLs will be constructed for accessing a user's avatar:

```
url_for user.avatar
#=> http://example.com/rails/active_storage/blobs/redirect
    /eyJfcmFpbHMiOnsibW...--76325a8eb0da9d85/me.png
url_for user.avatar.variant(resize: "200x150")
#=> http://example.com/rails/active_storage/representations
    /redirect/eyJfcmFpbHMiO...--85e1c8f4fe/me.png
```

We can see that both URLs start with "/rails/active_storage". Routes with the "/rails" prefix are internal Rails routes – that is, they're served by the framework controllers. By default, Rails doesn't provide a direct access link to files stored with Active Storage. Instead, it *serves* files via the application. Why? First, this is how on-the-fly image transformation is implemented. Second, it's a security concern – we need to verify access (the Base64-encoded part of the URL is a signed attachment identifier).

The URLs also contain the "/redirect" part. It instructs Active Storage to respond with a redirect response with the actual attachment URL after performing transformation (if needed) and authorization. Redirecting is not the only available mode; Active Storage also supports proxying files (useful when working with **Content Delivery Networks** (**CDNs**)). The behavior is controlled via the config. active_storage.resolve_model_to_route option.

Why did we dig so deep into the Active Storage internals? We need to find a level of abstraction at which we can inject our custom logic of serving Active Storage-backed files.

We're interested in optimizing image transformation. Even though Rails performs conversion on the fly and allows you to use modern image manipulation libraries (such as libvips), requests are still served by a Rails web server, typically Puma, which has limited throughput. For applications with a high rate of image uploads, serving them via Active Storage may negatively affect the overall application performance (since the web server resources are shared by all kinds of requests).

In this case, we can benefit from moving image transformation to a separate service, such as **imgproxy** (https://imgproxy.net). And, thanks to Active Storage design, we can do this transparently by implementing a custom `resolve_model_to_route` logic.

The value we provide with `resolve_model_to_route` is the name of a route helper used to resolve URLs from objects. We must define it in the `routes.rb` file:

```ruby
Rails.applications.routes.draw do
  direct :imgproxy_active_storage do |model, options|
    expires = options.delete(:expires_in) do
      ActiveStorage.urls_expire_in
    end

    # Serve originals via the built-in Rails proxy
    if model.respond_to?(:signed_id)
      route_for(
        :rails_service_blob_proxy,
        model.signed_id(expires_in: expires),
        model.filename,
        options
      )
    else
      options = {expires:, filename: model.filename}
      # TODO: options.merge!(variation_to_imgproxy)
      model.blob.imgproxy_url(**options)
    end
  end
end
```

The route helper defined previously looks very similar to the ones implemented by Active Storage (you can find them in the Rails source code). The only difference is that when the passed object is a variant, we return an `imgproxy` URL. Note that the previous implementation is just a proof of concept.

We still need to figure out how to convert the variation's transformations into *imgproxy* parameters and filter out non-image files. However, that is the only change we need to introduce into our code base to switch image transformation from Rails to an external proxy.

Now, you can, for example, enable *imgproxy* integration by simply changing the configuration:

```ruby
config.active_storage.resolve_model_to_route =
  :imgproxy_active_storage

url_for user.avatar
#=> http://example.com/rails/active_storage/
 blobs/proxy/eyJfcmFpbHMiOnsibW...--76325a8eb0da9d85/me.png
```

```
url_for user.avatar.variant(resize: "200x150")
#=> https://imgproxy.example.com/
    wluZbsrqmY4/fn:me.png/aHR.../ZWIwZGE5ZDg1L211/LnBuZw
```

The extraction examples we explored demonstrate how having proper abstraction levels helps to scale Rails applications beyond Ruby and Rails capabilities. Although we only covered use cases of replacing Rails parts with external services, the idea can be extrapolated to your code base – just keep this in mind when you design your abstraction layers.

Summary

In this chapter, you familiarized yourself with the infrastructure layer of a Rails application and its diversity. You learned how Rails uses abstractions to keep the framework and applications built with it less dependent on implementations.

You learned about different visibility concepts, such as logging, exception tracking, and monitoring, and how to implement them in Rails without making the code base highly coupled with the implementation of the corresponding service. You learned through examples when it's worth extracting low-level functionality into separate services and how well-designed abstractions make the process of extraction smooth.

This chapter finishes our journey through abstraction layers in a Rails application. We started by learning about the framework itself, the ideas, and the design techniques behind it. Then, we spiced up this knowledge with the layered architecture concept to come up with the final recipe – introducing abstraction layers into a Rails application, or the *Extended Rails Way* recipe (as we called it at the very beginning of the book).

The recipe's ingredients are as follows:

- Stay on the Rails Way. Learn how the framework works and reuse its patterns and building blocks.

- Use layered architecture ideas. Architecture layers help to separate abstraction layers and define boundaries.

- Perform complexity analysis, identify abstractions in your code, and gradually extract them into full-featured layers. Avoid premature abstraction and over-abstraction.

Feel free to use this topic, and don't hesitate to experiment with the ingredients. Remember – there is no single correct way of designing software.

Questions

1. What is the primary difference between the infrastructure layer and other architecture layers?

2. What infrastructure components are present in all Rails applications?

3. What is the abstraction distance?

4. What's the purpose of logging?

5. What is the difference between logging and exception tracking?

6. What is instrumentation?

7. What is the main reason to extract some infrastructure concepts from a Rails application into a standalone service?

Index

Lookbook
reference link 235

M

mailers 194
middleware 10
model-less forms 139, 140
models
decoupling from views, with presenters 150
extracting, from models 74
query objects, used for extracting
queries from 104-06
value objects, extracting from 74, 75
versus UI forms 122
monitoring services
abstracting, from instrumentation
data 258, 259
multi-model forms 137-139
multi-model presenters 155
example 155, 156, 157
MVC framework 12

N

N+1 authorization problem
in representation layer 187-189
normalization callback 65
notification objects 208
notifications layer
ad hoc abstraction 199
extracting 198
responsibilities 198
third-party libraries, using to
manage notifications 202
notifiers 202

O

object-oriented (OO) approach 94
object-relational mapping (ORM) 23, 94
objects
extracting, from objects 73
omakase 42
open/closed presenter 154
over-abstraction 206

P

page objects 157
parameterized module approach 114
params filtering 136
partials 214
policy-based access control (PBAC) 178
policy classes
conventions 181, 182
policy objects 178, 179
extracting 179, 180
PostgreSQL database
URL 34
Prometheus
URL 259

Q

queues 14
adapterizing 43-45

Gems and Patterns

www.packtpub.com

Subscribe to our online digital library for full access to over 7,000 books and videos, as well as industry leading tools to help you plan your personal development and advance your career. For more information, please visit our website.

Why subscribe?

- Spend less time learning and more time coding with practical eBooks and Videos from over 4,000 industry professionals

- Improve your learning with Skill Plans built especially for you

- Get a free eBook or video every month

- Fully searchable for easy access to vital information

- Copy and paste, print, and bookmark content

Did you know that Packt offers eBook versions of every book published, with PDF and ePub files available? You can upgrade to the eBook version at www.packtpub.com and as a print book customer, you are entitled to a discount on the eBook copy. Get in touch with us at customercare@packtpub.com for more details.

At www.packtpub.com, you can also read a collection of free technical articles, sign up for a range of free newsletters, and receive exclusive discounts and offers on Packt books and eBooks.

Other Books You May Enjoy

If you enjoyed this book, you may be interested in these other books by Packt:

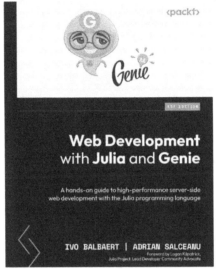

Web Development with Julia and Genie

Ivo Balbaert | Adrian Salceanu

ISBN: 9781801811132

Understand how to make a web server with HTTP.jl and work with JSON data over the web.

Discover how to build a static website with the Franklin framework.

Explore Julia web development frameworks and work with them.

Develop an MVC web app with the Genie framework.

Understand how to add a REST API to a web app.

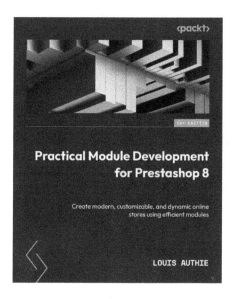

Practical Module development for Prestashop 8

Louis AUTHIE

ISBN: 9781837635962

- Understand the structure of PrestaShop's core.

- Explore hooks and their functions.

- Create a hello world module.

- Build modules to display blocks in the front office with different styles.

- Design a module to add fields to the category pages and manage them.

- Fashion a blogging module with front and modern back-office controllers.

Packt is searching for authors like you

If you're interested in becoming an author for Packt, please visit `authors.packtpub.com` and apply today. We have worked with thousands of developers and tech professionals, just like you, to help them share their insight with the global tech community. You can make a general application, apply for a specific hot topic that we are recruiting an author for, or submit your own idea.

Share your thoughts

Now you've finished *Layered Design for Ruby on Rails Applications*, we'd love to hear your thoughts! Scan the QR code below to go straight to the Amazon review page for this book and share your feedback or leave a review on the site that you purchased it from.

`https://www.amazon.in/review/create-review/error?asin=1801813787`

Your review is important to us and the tech community and will help us make sure we're delivering excellent quality content.

Download a free PDF copy of this book

Thanks for purchasing this book!

Do you like to read on the go but are unable to carry your print books everywhere?

Is your eBook purchase not compatible with the device of your choice?

Don't worry, now with every Packt book you get a DRM-free PDF version of that book at no cost.

Read anywhere, any place, on any device. Search, copy, and paste code from your favorite technical books directly into your application.

The perks don't stop there, you can get exclusive access to discounts, newsletters, and great free content in your inbox daily

Follow these simple steps to get the benefits:

1. Scan the QR code or visit the link below

https://packt.link/free-ebook/9781801813785

2. Submit your proof of purchase

3. That's it! We'll send your free PDF and other benefits to your email directly